Ethnicity and the State in Eastern Africa

Edited by

M.A. Mohamed Salih and John Markakis

Nordiska Afrikainstitutet, Uppsala 1998

Indexing terms

Ethnicity
State
Political aspects
Dispute settlement

East Africa

This book is published with support from Sida, Swedish International
Development Cooperation Agency, Stockholm, Sweden.

*The opinions expressed in this volume are those of the authors and do not
necessarily reflect the views of Nordiska Afrikainstitutet.*

Cover: Per Elfström

Language checking: Peter Colenbrander

ISBN 91-7106-418-4

Printed in Sweden by Elanders Gotab, Stockholm 1998

Contents

PART I: NARRATIVES OF ETHNICITY

PART II: CASE STUDIES

Preface

This collection of essays is the outcome of a workshop on Ethnicity and the State in Eastern Africa, organized jointly by the Nordic Africa Institute and the Organization for Social Science Research in Eastern and Southern Africa (OSSREA). The workshop was held in Addis Ababa from 3 to 5 June 1996. At that time, the Ethiopian political experiment, which relies on ethnicity as the basic principle of decentralization, was five years old, an appropriate milestone for an initial assessment of its progress. The workshop was originally planned to present the research carried out by Ethiopian scholars among Ethiopian ethnic groups or "nationalities". The Ethiopian research papers and the workshop were both sponsored by the Swedish International Development Cooperation Agency (Sida). The remaining contributors joined at different stages of the process which led to the production of this volume.

The question that inspired the Ethiopian research was how ethnic identification has itself been affected by the profound institutional changes within which ethnicity is intended to play a leading political role in Ethiopia. If ethnicity is socially constructed, what are the significant political repercussions it has had on the making of the contemporary Ethiopian polity. The main objective was to explore the impact of recent constitutional development on ethnicity in Ethiopia, and nearly half the workshop contributions were devoted to this issue. A second objective was to depict the increasing prominence of ethnicity in the political transformation now under way in the states of Eastern Africa. This was made possible by comparing the relevant experiences of some of these states. The third objective was to compare state policies designed to deal with ethnicity: in the case of Ethiopia and Uganda, these offer a sharp contrast.

In addition to the contributors to this volume, the workshop was attended by a number of scholars, researchers and policymakers. Their participation greatly enriched the debate and gave it a sense of immediacy, because some of these participants were involved in research and policymaking in the area of immediate concern to the workshop.

We are grateful to Lennart Wohlgemuth, director of the Nordic Africa Institute, who promoted the research and the workshop, and Sida, which sponsored it. We are thankful to Dr. Tegegne Teka of OSSREA, who coordinated the research and organized the workshop in Addis Ababa, and to Professor Abdel Ghaffar Mohamed Ahmed, Executive Secretary of OSSREA. Finally, we thank Ms. Kara Maria Johnson Molina for her assistance in editing the manuscript.

The Hague, February 1998

M.A. Mohamed Salih and John Markakis

Eastern Africa and ethnic groups studied in this book

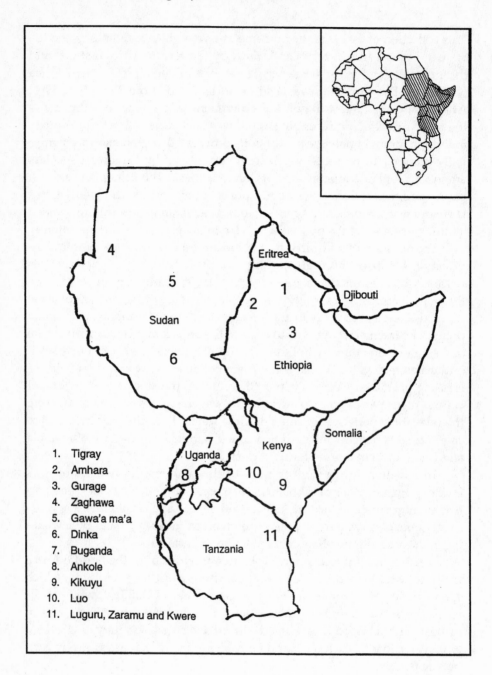

1. Tigray
2. Amhara
3. Gurage
4. Zaghawa
5. Gawa'a ma'a
6. Dinka
7. Buganda
8. Ankole
9. Kikuyu
10. Luo
11. Luguru, Zaramu and Kwere

Introduction

M.A. Mohamed Salih and John Markakis

The first chapter in the modern political history of Africa opened with the rise of nationalism in the middle of the century. With independence soon afterwards, a pattern of power distribution was established in the post-colonial state that determined access to social and material resources. Since power was unevenly distributed, access to resources proved inequitable. Because the state controlled the production and distribution of resources, competition for them was waged in the political realm, making the state the focus of social conflict. The failure of the state to satisfy the expectations fostered by nationalism of development and democracy, discredited the ideology and undermined postcolonial regimes. At the close of the century, a struggle is being waged throughout the continent to create a new pattern of power distribution and access to resources, thus marking the opening of the second chapter in Africa's modern political history. The struggle is carried on under many banners, democratization being one, religion another. Ethnicity, however, has proved the most potent force for political mobilization by far throughout black Africa. Anathematized and outlawed by nationalism early in the postcolonial period, it has now eclipsed its rival in the continent.

Eastern Africa is no exception. The studies included in this volume provide ample evidence of the potency of ethnicity as the basis for political mobilization within this region. By and large, the authors avoid the inconclusive theoretical debate on the nature of ethnicity often waged in scholarly circles. Instead, they focus on its relationship to the state, a manifestly political matter, and try to account for the twists and turns that mark the history of this relationship in the postcolonial era. In other words, the studies address the politicization of ethnicity and its impact on the state. Contrary to the familiar depiction of it as an atavistic remnant, ethnicity is shown here to be a modern phenomenon demanding accommodation within the political life of Africa.

Such accommodation is currently being tested in Ethiopia, a state brought to the brink of disintegration by conflict in which ethnicity featured prominently. Nearly half the contributions to this volume are devoted to

Ethiopia. They depict a variety of factors that account for the politicization of ethnicity and the volatility of its relationship with the state. The authors analyze the role of culture in the formation of ethnic identities and its involvement in the power struggles that ethnicity wages. More interestingly, they describe attempts in Ethiopia to use ethnicity as a medium of conflict regulation. This involves the political accommodation of ethnicity in a reconstructed state whose most prominent feature is decentralization. Decentralization in Ethiopia is not seen merely as a device for the satisfaction of ethnic political demands, but also as the path leading to democratization, through the devolution of decisionmaking in a manner that enables more people to influence the political process. Furthermore, since decentralization and democratization are regarded as requisite to development, the empowerment of ethnicity is intended to harness ethnicity to the purposes of development. In the interests of clarity, it should be noted that "nation", "nationality" and "nationalism" are the preferred terms used in Ethiopia instead of "ethnic group" and "ethnicity". This usage is adopted by some of the contributors to this volume.

The Ethiopian experiment is far from finished, and its success is far from assured. Success or failure will depend on whether the formal, i.e., constitutional, provisions for decentralization and democratization are realized in practice. Even more important is the question of whether greater access to power will bring greater access to resources for those who fought for it. Of course, resources must be produced before they can be distributed. In the final analysis, therefore, the fate of the experiment hangs on the degree of material improvement it will bring to the lives of the people.

Five themes drawn from the Ethiopian experience tie together the studies of this volume. They are ethnicity as, 1) the mediation of culture in the struggle for state power; 2) a medium in conflict regulation; 3) a basis for decentralization; 4) a dimension of democratization; and 5) a factor in development. The studies are in two parts. The first comprises Narratives of Ethnicity which analyze these themes separately and also link them to one another.

Doornbos sketches a broad analytical framework within which ethnicity is seen to function in conjunction with various other factors. He underlines the fact that ethnicity as such does not explain anything: it, itself, needs to be explained, and that can only be done contextually. The context he focuses on is the struggle for liberalization-cum-democratization being waged throughout Africa as the twentieth century draws to a close, and he speculates on ethnicity's possible role in that struggle. He identifies a positive "liberatory" contribution that ethnicity has made to mobilizing resistance against the excesses of the postcolonial state, while also recognizing that ethnicity also has another, less attractive, chauvinist aspect. Doornbos wonders which aspect will dominate in the pluralist, competitive political process that is the goal of democratization.

Poluha takes issue with the principle upon which the Ethiopian experiment is based. She questions the assumption that ethnicity overshadows other forms of association and identity in all circumstances, and that ethnic-group interests have priority over all others. She maintains that other forms of association, and the identities and interests that derive from them, may predominate, depending upon the context. Consequently, to recognize ethnicity as paramount, as in Ethiopia currently, is to deny the right of individuals to decide for themselves which identity is most relevant in a given situation, while at the same time legitimating the right of an amorphous ethnic entity to impose its choice on the individual. Poluha also questions the wisdom of identifying ethnic groups with political parties. Very seldom, she points out, will all those who share the same ethnic identity join the same party. Consequently, delegating power to a party identified with an ethnic group creates problems of accurate representation. Poluha sees danger in the preference accorded to group rights at the expense of individual rights, the cornerstone of liberal democracy. Arguing that both should be equally respected, she fears it will be impossible to pursue "ethnification" in Ethiopia and promote democracy as well.

O'Brien and Salih analyze different facets of the process of identity-formation in the Sudan. O'Brien examines the concepts of race and ethnicity introduced into the Sudan by the British during the colonial period, and traces their continuing influence after independence. The coupling of race with civilization is one legacy, and it persists in the distinction made between Arab/Muslim/northerner on the one hand, and non-Arab/Pagan/Christian southerner on the other, despite the fact that many "southerners" live in the north and are Muslims. O'Brien also describes how ethnic identities were formed during the colonial period when communities came to occupy distinct niches in the labour market. Employers associated ethnic groups with certain types of work and, for those who sought such work, the choice of the appropriate identity had, as it were, opportunity costs.

Salih examines the current dominant discourse on identity in the Sudan, carried out in the middle of Africa's longest war and under the oppressive shadow of the National Islamic Front, the ideological mentor of the military regime in Khartoum. This discourse fuses Arabism and Islam in the cultural foundation of a projected Sudanese national identity. Salih examines this ideological construct in the twin context of power domination and nation-building. According to him, the association of Arabism and Islam has forced non-Arab Muslims to resist a nation-building project premised on that cultural foundation. The latter is recognized and rejected by the African population, both Muslim and non-Muslim, as an ideological instrument designed to safeguard the economic and political dominance of the Arabs in the Sudan. Africans in the south and north comprise the majority of the country's population, and they naturally reject an ideology that excludes them from the regime's definition of Sudanese national identity. The regime's *jihad* to Islamize and Arabize them strengthens their resolve to resist, and the assertion of their own identity is part of such resistance. In southern Sudan, this assertion has led to an apparent contradiction between the ideological claims of the main resistance movement led by the Sudan Peoples Liberation Army and the ethnic aspirations of the groups that support it.

Baxter and Adhana address the dynamic relationship between culture and power in the political assertion of ethnic identities in Ethiopia. Baxter argues that while the foundation of identity comprises a number of shared cultural features, the assertion of identity owes more to feelings and desires—the moral component—than to history or culture. According to Baxter, in the context of Ethiopia, where the Oromo have been politically dominated, economically exploited and culturally oppressed, the assertion of this identity in recent years is proof of the existence of an Oromo nation. Furthermore, this assertion is inextricably linked to a political struggle for emancipation which, for some Oromo, aims to establish a sovereign nation-state. Adhana takes the national identity of the Tigray for granted, as well as the desire of this group for national emancipation within the imperial Ethiopian state. He traces the conception of Tigray nationalism through a long and tortuous historical gestation. According to him, at various stages of history its birth was aborted by the opposition of the Amhara rulers of Ethiopia with the complicity of the Tigray elite themselves, who pursued their own narrow interests. It was only very recently, under the leadership of the Tigray Peoples Liberation Front, that Tigray nationalism emerged triumphant.

Ocholla-Ayayo examines the role of ethnicity in conflict generation and conflict regulation. He focuses on its role as the key variable in political competition in Kenya, and in the miasma of corruption that has destroyed public confidence in that country's political system. He sees ethnicity as a tool that has been manipulated by the political elite who, despite public awareness of their venality, continue to draw on ethnic support. In this sense, and because the resources of the state are unequally distributed, ethnicity becomes the object of animosity and provokes conflict. Ayayo also considers ethnicity as a plausible conflict-regulator. He finds that it does function as such at the local level, especially among groups involved in certain types of interaction. However, it has failed to regulate conflict at the national level, where it is most needed.

The second part of this volume is devoted to case studies, four of which concern Ethiopia. In contrast to Baxter, Chanie focuses on the fragmented nature of Oromo identity and the highly divided political behaviour of its elite. He notes that the first manifestation of this identity occurred in the form of a voluntary development association in the 1960s—one instance that links ethnicity to development. However, there is no continuity in this sense, and Chanie concludes that the concept of an Oromo nation is illusory, and that Oromo nationalism is little more than the ideological weapon used by one group of the elite in the struggle for power. Another group of Oromo, he notes, chose religion for the same purpose.

Ali Said presents the case of the Afar, a small but by no means politically insignificant group in Ethiopia. While there is no doubting the coherence and salience of Afar identity, its political expression has been as segmented as the social structure of the pastoralist Afar society. As a result, the Afar relationship with the Ethiopian state has been manipulated to their great disadvantage. Ali attributes this failure to the Afar elite, whose political horizon does not extend beyond personal and clan interests. In this context, ethnicity appears as a hindrance to the development and welfare of the Afar population. In the present Ethiopian constitutional structure, the Afar region enjoys considerable autonomy. However, self-government has done little for development. Regional power has become the bone of ferocious contention among several political factions claiming to represent the Afar, leaving little energy or resources for development.

Markakis presents the case of the Gurage in Ethiopia, focusing on the interaction between internal and external factors in the process of identity formation, and on the impact of decentralization on ethnicity. The forging of a Gurage identity during this century is traced to the incorporation of their homeland into the Ethiopian imperial state, the exigencies of migrant labour in the urban sector, as well as to the policies of the imperial government. A recent dramatic change in the economic and political situation, especially the politicization of ethnicity as part of the decentralization of the Ethiopian state, has resulted in the unravelling of the Gurage identity and the assertion of rival identities attaching to smaller groups. According to Markakis, the unravelling is explained by the changed function that ethnicity is required to perform in the new situation. This implies not only that the contours of identity can change according to circumstance, but also the functions that ethnicity performs.

Tegegne Teka views the Ethiopian experiment with a critical eye. He agrees with Poluha that ethnic identities are not necessarily the most important attributes people assert in social and political interaction, and that to impose them is to deprive people of the right to choose. Tegegne warns against making ethnicity the defining principle of political life, because it precludes the emergence of a unifying national identity that transcends the parochial and divisive tendencies of ethnicity. He focuses on the Amhara, the group that dominated the Ethiopian state until recently. His argument is that this group failed to develop a strong ethnic consciousness, partly because it has no clear ethnic identity, but mainly because it identified with the state that it regarded as its own. Tegegne believes it would be regressive to encourage this group to assert an ethnic identity in line with the current policy of the Ethiopian state. On the contrary, he believes the Amhara and others who have developed a pan-Ethiopian consciousness should be encouraged to construct an appropriate all-inclusive national identity.

Sharif Harir's case study of the Zaghawa, who straddle the Sudan-Chad border, is unusual because it depicts the simultaneous interaction of one ethnic group with two sovereign states, and describes how both became involved in an intratribal dispute over resources. Some tribesmen sought to exploit the presence of state borders to claim exclusive control of pastures, in violation of customary rules, and they involved state authorities in the ensuing clash between Zaghawa clans. This implied the breakdown of traditional systems of resource management and conflict resolution. However, a complete breakdown was avoided because the rulers of Chad, themselves of pastoralist origin, resorted to traditional methods to resolve the conflict and prevent recurrence.

Jerman analyzes the weaving of various strands to fashion an identity by the Bagamoyo in Tanzania. She distinguishes between two types of and roles for ethnicity, which she terms objective and subjective. In precolonial Tanzania, ethnicity was an objective phenomenon denoting cultural differentiation, but not necessarily social integration, or ethnic consciousness. Ethnicity was a cultural attribute, not a social identity: the latter was variously designated by clan, village, age-group, etc. By contrast, in the colonial context and afterwards, ethnicity becomes a subjective phenomenon, in the sense that it is based on consciousness. This is due to the colonial administrative practice of segregating people into ethnic units, as a result of which cultural differentiation acquired added meaning and people became more conscious of it. After independence, Tanzanian nationalism extolled traditional values while, at the same time, seeking to submerge ethnic identities in an all-embracing Tanzanian national identity.

Uganda is another state in Eastern Africa whose postcolonial history is marred by ethnic conflict. Byarugaba's examination of Ugandan politics follows the development of what Ali Mazrui (in, *Soldiers and Kinsmen in Uganda*, 1975, Beverly Hills: Sage) called the "military ethnocracy". He traces the ethnification of the military in the colonial period and describes how the struggle for power after independence took an ethnic form, inevitably drawing the military into the political fray. He shows how each successive political convulsion magnified the role of the ethnic factor in politics, until it emerged as dominant. With every political upheaval, the ethnic profile of the army changed, without, however, in the least reducing its political importance. Quite the contrary, Byarugaba ruefully concludes: for someone to become president of Uganda, the army must support him, and the head of the army must be of the same ethnic origin.

Muhereza and Otim examine the relationship of ethnicity and the state in Uganda after the advent of a new regime in 1986 under Yoweri Museveni. Since then, Uganda has been conducting an experiment of its own, designed to exorcise the spell of ethnicity. Unlike Ethiopia, where ethnicity has gained political prominence, the Ugandan experiment aims to insulate the political process against ethic contamination. Various means have been employed to this end, including the banning of political parties from participating in elections. This stands in sharp contrast to Ethiopia, where ethnic groups have been encouraged to form their own political organizations. Muhereza and Otim provide ample evidence that ethnicity is far from eliminated in Uganda, despite the regime's efforts. Nevertheless, they believe its divisive influence is being mitigated by the efforts of the new regime to forge a national unity.

Generally the essays in this volume demonstrate that the varieties of ethnicity explored here represent modern modes of political mobilization which will continue to shape and reshape Eastern Africa's political life. The mediating role of the state will continue to play a significant part in fostering cooperation as well as confrontation between ethnic groups, and between those who represent them or those who mobilize them in the struggle for power and resources. However, both processes of cooperation and confrontation will be based on and governed by a variety of organizational principles that are employed to achieve certain ends. These organizational principles differ greatly from one state to another and are prone to produce a variety of results—identical as well as contradictory—a fact which makes theorizing about ethnicity a daunting if not an impossible task. This task will be further complicated as ethnicity-based political organizations continue to oscillate between internal segmentation and conflict, and strong ethnic solidarity. In this respect, the Ethiopian experience is unique and particularly valuable for exploring whether ethnicity, as a principle of political organization, is capable of securing stable self-government where imported Western political concepts have failed. Will ethnicity persist as a source of fragmentation along economic, political, regional, linguistic, religious, and sub-ethnic lines or become a rallying point for positive engagement in public life? Will the Ethiopian experience encourage other Eastern African countries to more openly assign a prominent political role to ethnicity? Or will they continue to suppress ethnic sentiments—which is just as dangerous as letting ethnicity loose. Given all these questions, and more, it is hoped this volume will inspire others to explore in greater detail the newly emerging patterns, contexts and manifestations of state-ethnicity relations and the political forces that perpetuate, neutralize or suppress them.

PART I

NARRATIVES OF ETHNICITY

Linking the Future to the Past—Ethnicity and Pluralism

Martin Doornbos

Ethnicity—the resilient paradigm

Among the various themes that have constituted discourse on African states and societies, ethnicity has been noted for its remarkable record. The "resilient paradigm", as Timothy Shaw (1986) calls it, was part of the stock in trade at the very genesis of modern African studies. It has, however, been a controversial theme, its existence and legitimacy in frequent dispute over the years. Held up in some quarters as the final explanatory variable of just about everything happening in African politics, ethnicity has often been discarded with equal vehemence by radical researchers as an irrelevant conceptual obstruction to proper analysis of the politics of transformation, or simply as an American invention. Over the years this theme has, thus, definitely drawn its share of debate, resulting from changing waves of academic interest, from new political circumstances and preoccupations, and from the interplay between them. Significantly, though, at the end of each cycle of debate, ethnicity, the elusive factor, has often simply reemerged chameleon-like: featuring new colours and a different guise, it provoked new questions and debate as to its true nature and proper conceptualization.

For some time now, a new wave of questions about ethnicity has been in the making, following the drastically changed political conditions within and around African states in the wake of structural adjustment and its repercussions. Specifically, with the declining hegemony of the centralized state, the pressures to go multiparty, and the moves to adopt new forms of decentralization in various countries, questions are being raised with increasing frequency as to how ethnicity will evolve and manifest itself within these changing parameters. The questions have been echoed from Kenya to Cameroon, from Tunisia to Tanzania and from Zaïre to Zimbabwe. And evidently the echoes—or possibly some of the original queries—have been actively transmitted among Africa-watchers in Europe, North America and elsewhere. The questions come in different versions and, just as in previous rounds of debate, answers to them are likely to vary significantly, reflecting respondents' perceptions as to what is at issue and/or their inclination to highlight particular concerns while, intentionally or unintentionally, down-playing others. This chapter will attempt an initial exploration of the terrain by considering current questions and tendencies against the background of potentially changing state-civil society relationships.

Current questions

There is no doubt that recent events in eastern Europe and the disintegrating Soviet Union are being followed with keen interest in many multiethnic or multinational African states. Manifold uncertainties about the present con-juncture and future trajectories of African political systems are reflected in the nature of questions that are currently mushrooming about the role and significance of ethnicity. Are party formation and political mobilization likely to take shape along ethnic lines under conditions of political plural-ism? Will Africa see a kind of ethnic resurgence and militancy, a spurt of ethnically based mini-nationalisms, and/or a pervasive rethinking of ethnic consciousness and identity? Will there be increasing demands for the right of self-determination by African nationalities, starting with those that got squeezed in colonial or postcolonial territorial arrangements, but possibly also with other groups? Can ethnic expression take any "fundamentalist" turn, however this should be exactly understood? Or is it conceivable that radically different ways of structuring ethnicity might be emerging in vari-ous African political contexts? What are the implications for the postcolonial state and for the nature of politics? Is one perhaps witnessing today the pre-liminary steps in a broadly analogous process of basic restructuring of African state systems, beginning with the most ancient of them all, Ethiopia? Or are most of these queries addressed to simply transient phenomena, likely to disappear soon enough as they are satisfied, partly perhaps through their very articulation? What is one observing in the first place and how should we interpret it?

A sharpening of the questions posed is essential if we want to gain greater clarity about the processes concerned. Cautious questioners, there-fore, might well first ask whether or not there is in fact any likelihood of ethnicity becoming articulated and politicized more vigorously under multipartyism or decentralization than under previous or alternative condi-tions. What if multipartyism were not on the agenda? Would this leave articulations of ethnicity comfortably dormant, "neutral", or alternatively more easily contained and controlled? Or would they follow their own logic and evolution in any event, shaped as has often been the case by forces of domination and control and already marred in many instances by a pro-longed history of ethnic conflict? Raising these questions is to begin to answer them and to suggest that too narrow a focus on ethnicity per se, without due attention to its political context, may not be very helpful. But if there is no a priori reason why ethnic mobilization must necessarily increase in pluralist and decentralized frameworks, one cannot assume either that there will be no relationship or effect. In part, the move towards pluralist systems and decentralization may itself be a response to, and an attempt to accommodate, growing ethnic pressures resulting from unequal opportunities. More generally, any restructuring of existing institutional arrangements, such as the present impulses towards political pluralism and decentralization, may contribute to changes in state-civil society relationships and thus to a shift in the political context of ethnicity. What possible forms of ethnic articulation could this then induce and what significance should be attached to it?

Some questions about the relative significance of ethnicity vis-à-vis the retreat of the central state and the prospects of multipartyism, however, appear to deserve as much attention as the phenomena they enquire about. This would be true of questions which bluntly ask "will tribalism be unleashed again?", or of the simple assertion of the inevitability of ethnic conflict under a pluralistic system (the defence-line of several regimes—Kenya, Zimbabwe, Zambia until recently—anxious not to lose their carefully nurtured power base). It might be recalled that the latter kind of arguments are not exactly new. Independence itself was delayed in a number of instances on the strength of similar forebodings of "tribal" conflict and the argument has since been advanced in different guises in more than one place at more than one time.

But questions in this vein about ethnicity are problematic. Their very phrasing seems to anticipate specific answers, such as the expectation that multipartyism will degenerate into erratic, irrational "tribal" sentiments, thereby revealing a preoccupation with certain, mainly "visible", emotive and violent aspects or phenomena only, while tending to ignore concrete social issues and grievances which may underlie ethnically expressed political action. Again, for those in power advancing the argument, playing the "tribalist" card usually amounts to emphasizing a single "threatening" emotive dimension, as if this had an autonomous role, while at the same time hoping to avoid confronting inequities in the exercise of power or the allocation of resources which may have given rise to the expressions of frustration and consciousness in the first place.

Problems with conceptualizations

A few preliminary points, not unlike those that were pertinent during earlier phases when ethnicity was gaining attention, will be useful. One is that ethnicity as such does not explain anything; it needs to be explained. If this requires re-emphasizing, it will be evident that such reiteration is addressed to two otherwise quite opposite modes of thinking. One is that of any latter-day adherents to the primordial loyalties school that entertain an a priori expectation that the dissolution of the one-party state will naturally lead to multiethnic multipartyism and, through this, to a blossoming of ethnicity generally. The other is that of various Marxist researchers who, from an overriding preoccupation with the harder facts of political economy, have tended to dismiss ethnicity as just an instance of false consciousness, positing that manifestations of ethnic identity, ethnic ideology and ethnic conflict are mere epiphenomena not really worthy of serious attention. Modernization developmentalists and orthodox Marxist analysts at one time also shared another perspective. Both conceived of ethnicity as an anachronistic mode of thinking soon to be surpassed and engulfed by either—and here they differed again—the spirit of rationality and modernity or by mature class consciousness, itself also a token of rationality. The primordialists, however, should understand that various groups will try to strengthen their position and claims by invoking tradition, mythical charters of origin, or what not—and that not a few examples of these have been especially invented for the purpose (Ranger, 1983). Marxist researchers would have rendered greater service by exercising more conceptual flexibility, which might have allowed the recognition of certain expressions of ethnicity as protests against subordination and others as attempts to underpin positions of power and hegemony (Stavenhagen, 1991).

Closely related is another similarly elementary point. Ethnicity as such, or the so-called ethnic factor, does not exist independently: it essentially represents a single element, aspect or dimension lifted from a more complex reality. It derives its meaning and significance from the interplay between other variables such as class, state and power, while it in turn can (but does not necessarily) infuse such dimensions with meaning and political significance. Discussion of ethnicity per se does not make much sense, therefore, as there is no way of establishing what orientation or underlying motive any ethnic consciousness-raising may have without first understanding the context of the social forces and the issues concerned. Any "blind" discussion of ethnicity may in fact entail some of the most risky and dangerous forms of reification. Thus, ethnicity should always be considered in its dynamic relation to and interaction with other social factors.

Finally, if expressions of ethnicity, whether as identity, ideology or competitiveness need to be contextualized, it is also necessary to recognize their essentially fluid and manipulable properties. Ethnicity as constructed identity is one set of multiple potential identities and itself usually has multiple facets and faces. Whether any one or more of these will actually be called upon to give expression to current social demands or to a political front, is again merely a matter of contextual variables—which may explain quite unexpected changes in asserted identities, allegiances or coalitions by particular groups. Thus, novel identities may be asserted, or new coalitions

entered into under a common label in response to the changing requirements and opportunities in the political arena. It can indeed be striking to
note how "rediscoveries" of common interests can at times be clothed and
rationalized from a well-stocked supply of, at times quite original, "cultural"
attributes. Ethnic consciousness, in short, is not fixed.

Generally, ethnic configurations, the generation of ethnic consciousness
and the impetus to ethnic protest, must all be understood in the context of
the changing relationships between state and civil society from which they
derive significance and orientation. One key problem in understanding ethnicity, however, lies in the wide mix of tendencies, strategies and reactions
embraced by the "ethnic" phenomenon and, therefore, in the virtual impos-
sibility of associating ethnicity, unlike class for example, with any singular
kind of social or political thrust. Inkatha is one expression of ethnicity, but
so is both the Amhara resistance to the assertion of equality and self-determination by Ethiopia's other nationalities, and the latter's struggles for pre-
cisely these goals. Today, also, Tuareg demands for independence, recently
in lieu of enhanced autonomy; the instalment of a new Buganda council and
moves towards the reinstatement of Buganda kingship; the articulation of
protest in the dispute over the Dagomba paramount chieftaincy in northern
Ghana; the ethnic defence line of vulnerable communities in the Cameroon-
ian and Zaïrian rainforests; and similarly, the political networking of pastoralist groups in the Horn—all represent different instances of ethnicity at
play. Numerous other examples abound. Other than signifying an ethnic
articulation of something political, however, they do not necessarily have
much in common.

What must be appreciated is that the social basis and structuring of
ethnicity in Africa comprises widely different forms, including potentially
self-standing nationalities, ethnic strata, small vulnerable communities and
various clan and kinship networks. Besides, and above all, ethnicity and
class articulate to give shape to new ruling strata in various countries. All
this tends to stretch the category to a rather amorphous and seemingly
meaningless catch-all. Still, to restrict the analysis to the category of
"nationalities" (Mamdani, 1983) is to preclude consideration of the critical
problems that have arisen in connection with ethnic stratification or restrati-
fication in different parts of the continent, or with the struggle for survival
by distinct but vulnerable groups. Using a broader concept, then, one must
expect entirely different issues to arise in each case.

It should also be noted, though, that while in many cases (such as
struggles over access to resources or over political representation) a political
strategy—offensive or defensive, as the case may be—may be pursued with
explicit reference to ethnic identity, even such choice is contextual. Some
groups, collectivities or social movements at particular junctures will have
good grounds for emphasizing ethnicity, or to ethnicize issues, while others
instead may seek to de-emphasize it. Moreover, the motivation for choosing

different forms of identity articulation are likely to vary in crucial respects and may often be diametrically opposed.

The specificity of the African case

An understanding of ethnicity in context first requires a proper grasp of the specificity of its configuration in the African case, as compared, for example, to its occurrence in the Andean region and in central America, or in various countries of south and south east Asia. In several Andean countries, for instance, indigenous ethnic peasant communities are largely differentiated from the dominant urban-based national middle classes and other social forces associated with the state, while also remaining largely unrelated to the massive numbers of urban poor. Ethnicity here has a more overt class dimension, though it does not link with a single, comprehensive class structure (Stavenhagen, 1991). In India and other south Asian countries, by contrast, ethnicity is essentially taken to refer to the articulation of cultural identity and diversity among a whole range of minority communities, such as language, religious and tribal groupings and nationalities. Many of these communities, it is felt, stand to lose their cultural distinctiveness in the face of homogenizing technological forces and their pluriformity or coexistence is endangered by what Kothari calls the politics of majoritarianism (Kothari, 1988). Articulations of ethnicity thus tend to be partly related to the processes by which cultural distinctiveness and diversity are threatened. At the same time, however, there are also opposite and assertive forms of ethnicity, seeking political dominance and exclusive rights for particular communities. Promoted by the forces of majority politics, these include chauvinist Hinduist movements such as Shiv Seena in India and the movement towards constructing an exclusive Sinhalese-Buddhist identity in Sri Lanka.

In Africa, however, ethnicity is rarely confined to minorities vis-à-vis nationally dominant social strata that identify and assert themselves in similar fashion. Nor is ethnicity in Africa predominantly an expression of traditional distinctiveness vis-à-vis technologically and culturally homogenizing forces. Rather, it figures, and is perceived to figure, as one basic constitutive element in and throughout virtually all societies. Essentially, it underscores how, in one respect, the social fabric of most African countries comprises a fairly complex and fluid ensemble of different peoples, nations and nationalities, ethnic strata and in some cases, caste-like divisions. At the same time, there has been rapidly accelerating urban and rural class differentiation in most parts of Africa, at times articulated with ethnic differentiation, though generally cutting across the ethnic matrix. Thus, while social differentiation is in some instances coterminous with ethnic differentiation, there is no necessary one-to-one correspondence between them.

Nonetheless, perhaps one of the most significant long-term social transformations affecting the nature and focus of ethnic articulations in various parts of Africa has been the emergence and manifestation of a protonational bourgeoisie. Members of these strata may themselves selectively downplay ethnic backgrounds, identifying more strongly instead with national characteristics and points of orientation—from which they often have benefited a good deal. Alternatively, if they are largely drawn from one dominant ethnic category, as is often the case, they may be inclined to project the cultural identity of that group on to the multiethnic state as a whole. In either case, one important consequence of the crystallization of a dominant national bourgeoisie is the possible gradual peripheralization of various weaker ethnic communities. Ultimately these communities may resemble the indigenous peasant communities of Guatemala, Mexico or Bolivia, or several minority groups in India, thus adding new political significance and meaning to the reality and articulation of their ethnicity.

Ethnicity and the politics of pluralism

Also at stake today is the wider search for a redefinition and restructuring of the relationships between state and civil society, which has been dubbed problematic, dichotomous or precarious by various observers (Rothchild and Chazan, 1988). Recently the need has frequently been expressed to achieve a different balance within this duality in favour of societal rather than state forms of organization, and giving more concrete content to the concept and reality of civil society in the African context. However, the range of possible state-civil society relationships in Africa is itself a highly variable complex, which has, moreover, by no means been fully crystallized conceptually (Doornbos, 1990). To complicate matters further, the politics of ethnicity has in many places blurred rather than accentuated the civil society-state equation, precisely through the pervasive infusion of ethnic calculus into the control and operations of the state. A key question now is to what extent ethnicity may provide a basis for future, relatively autonomous sociopolitical organization and alternative development strategies (Hettne, 1991). All general predictions are hazardous. Still, it is conceivable that ethnically defined social entities will come to figure, perhaps even fairly prominently in some places, as one possible basis for new politicoorganizational forms, even though in many instances these will be based on coalitions and are likely to be very fluid. After all, ethnic mobilization and patronage provides one of relatively few possible bases for party formation and decentralized political organization. Particularly in decentralized operations and actions through NGOs, ethnic communities may serve as a basis for organization and self-help action. In so far as civil society denotes grassroots organizational forms, clan, kinship and other forms of local community association may increasingly present themselves as ready-made points of departure.

Generally, with so many self-help organizations springing up based on ethnic constituencies, it seems possible that the concept of civil society will gain increasing specificity. But those for whom grassroots organizations and civil society imply participatory processes and voluntary action will do well to remember, and to anticipate, that a move to local and supposedly traditional forms of social organization may also signify the emergence and proliferation of (male) chauvinistic roles, outlooks and ways of exercising power, with little scope for open exchange and popular involvement or liberal/progressive, relativizing and gender-neutral perspectives. Time will tell.

With respect to the possible effects of the articulation of ethnicity on changing African political structures (notably the abandonment of the one-party system, the shrinking of central state involvement and—in varying degrees—their replacement by substantially decentralized structures), at least two broad problem areas stand out.

One is the search for new organizational forms which could bridge the state-society divide and for institutional alternatives to the structures and linkages provided through the single party and centralizing state. It can hardly be predicted at this time whether any particular pattern will emerge as dominant. Conceivably more than one pattern may develop. Two broad possibilities, however, are likely. One is that dominant ruling groups hitherto represented in single-party structures will split into two or more wings, though in essence representing "more of the same" and jointly continuing to control and run the state apparatus. The other is that, given generally weakened central state structures and the consequent need to accommodate and recognize vocal constituent units, stronger ethnic groupings, language communities and nationalities may emerge as possible constituencies within the changing political framework. A case in point is the new Ethiopian regime's initiation of negotiations for a new constitution based on representation by nationality. Another is the rapid proliferation of new, ethnically defined parties in the Zaïrian context, totalling 205 at the time of writing. Central to all such initiatives is the search for an adequate fit between state forms, societal configurations and popular aspirations and involvement. Wherever this fit is found, one might, to borrow current donor community parlance, speak of conditions for "good governance" (though this does not exactly seem what the term is meant to convey).

Whether the new state forms that are currently being negotiated, such as decentralized structures or multipartyism, will actually represent more *democratic* forms and practices, is a question of evident interest, and one likely to remain topical for a long time. The manifest external interest in the measurable aspects of democracy, as in the insistence on counting more than one party as a yardstick for progress, stands in contrast to the relative silence on the more qualitative aspects of democracy. These latter include how popular involvement and feedback might have been, or might be, enhanced in existing political structures and policy practices at local and national levels. Presently, however, the various attempts at reform currently under way in several countries signify notably weakened central structures, inviting, as it were, alternative ways of filling the political space.

The other problem area almost certain to come into play with any modification of central party and state structures derives from the accommodations and political settlements made in the past among different ethnic groups, or more usually imposed on them. In many instances, conflicting interests and demands regarding issues like access to land and other resources, representation, the location of roads and services, or the award of other benefits, have resulted in political settlements which have strongly favoured some ethnic groups or strata, or at least some of their members, while being detrimental to others. Often, the development and growth of central state and party structures has been based on a kind of pecking order among competing ethnic groups and a freezing of these differential privileges and entitlements among them—or again, among their notables. Many enduring ethnic grievances and expressions of protest are essentially about such inequities in the distribution of public goods. Clearly, one must expect any loosening of state structures to be accompanied by the resurfacing of quite a few old grievances and by numerous demands and pressures to redress perceived ethnic inequalities and disadvantages. In some instances, no doubt, the relative positions of power and privilege will themselves be up for revision. The outcome of such challenges and struggles will inevitably be determined by the relative strength of the social forces at the local or regional level, now operating without the potential intervention of the central state.

The facade of one-party unity was hardly possible without the cement of patronage. By offering rewards to and through influential elites, patronage served to offset not a few inequities between ethnic winners and losers. It was thus instrumental in institutionalizing multiethnic representation in single-party structures. A potential class factor, to the extent that it was present, has often been neutralized in the process. However, with a move to other more pluralist state and institutional forms, patronage is likely to be equally, if not more, salient in the mobilization of followers and coalitions. One should not be too surprised if, in a number of instances, political entrepreneurship leads some former regional party notables to change allegiances and form new "ethnic" constituencies (one of several patterns currently manifested in the former Soviet Union).

The future of ethnicity

In trying to anticipate future forms of ethnic articulation, it is important to note that not only have the political structures through which interests have been expressed been transformed, but also that the stakes themselves have changed. Some twenty to thirty years ago a key route to individual wealth and aggrandizement was through political or bureaucratic office, based largely on ethnic patronage. Political and bureaucratic positions could then be translated into business and wealth. Today, this route no longer holds out such promise. Business wealth has begun to reproduce itself without political interference. Though connections are invariably helpful, overt emphasis on ethnic identity and patronage is no longer called for and may actually constrain the scope of business transactions and expansion. Second generations, meanwhile, have grown up in the urban milieu or abroad, and hold very different images of the ethnic linkage. In this sense, there would seem to be a reduced chance of ethnicity being politicized at the national level. Nonetheless, these trends may trigger unexpected ethnic responses elsewhere, as we note below.

At the opposite end, various categories of activist and urban worker may seek to avoid and de-emphasize ethnicity as a basis for social action, as indeed they have done in many cases. Politically, for example, the ANC in South Africa until now has been the major example of a consciously nonracial and nonethnic organization. In different areas of industrial activity, the scope for collective bargaining may be impaired by fragmentation of union strength along ethnic lines. Similarly, human rights actions and safeguarding essential freedoms generally demand transcending ethnic and racial frames of operation and the mobilization of broader social solidarity. Here too, there is no logic to ethnic mobilization and action, either before or after any institutional moves towards political pluralism. Nor, for all the inevitable emotive reactions they provoked, have the spontaneous bread riots following structural adjustment programmes in Khartoum, Lusaka or Tunis been particularly noted for articulating their protests in terms of ethnicity (Seddon, 1989).

A resurgence of ethnicity may come in basically two, again opposite, ways. One will emanate from ethnic communities under threat and from groups that have lost out in their dealings with the state or with more powerful neighbours and rivals. Here one should note that it is by no means certain that the currently proposed political reforms towards multipartyism and decentralization will replace of politically dominant groups, locally or nationally. Most ruling groups are actively trying to prevent this from happening. If, somehow, such a momentum did develop, however, then many disadvantaged ethnic groups and strata will no doubt voice demands for redress of their grievances. Under these circumstances, ethnicity cannot but flourish: few things are as favourable for ethnic or national self-identity as freshly remembered suffering linked to the prospect or expectation of redress and justice. Under such circumstances, ethnicity may be seen as a framework and source of solidarity and liberation. There would be a sense, then, of how relations with rival groups and the centre might be renegotiated, perhaps in treaty fashion (as is being attempted in the Soviet Union today), on the basis of parity and mutual recognition. Visions of alternative arrangements and relationships between constituent groups, ethnic or otherwise, based on equity, reciprocity and mutual respect for cultural distinctiveness could develop (Hettne, 1991). If fulfilled, these visions would give rise to dramatically different political forms and formations in Africa.

Some groups, even under these circumstances, however, would face difficulty in articulating their most basic concerns and, indeed, their very identity. This is the problem of weak cultures being interrogated by dominant cultures. This is made more problematic by the fact that the interrogation is conducted, and inevitably distorted, in the language and conceptual categories of dominant social forces, either colonial or postcolonial. Ashis Nandy (1987) has asked, "What are the obstacles a culture faces which seek to redefine its identity?" The answer is given, in part, by Mudimbe with reference to Africa when he points out how "the forms and formulations of the colonial culture and its aims were somehow the means of trivialising the whole traditional mode of life and its spiritual framework" (Mudimbe, 1988:4).

It is possible, if not probable, that the problems and contradictions in this respect will become more rather than less manifest in the years to come. As noted already, the emergence of a protonational bourgeoisie may well entail a further peripheralization of various ethnic communities from the mainstream of development. But it is not just that cleavages between dominant and subordinate groups may widen and be increasingly reflected in novel forms of cultural differentiation—often, incidentally, based on narrowing and formalistic extrapolations of Western-derived dominant culture on the one hand as against increasingly eroded forms and expressions of marginalized traditions on the other. It is also that many of Africa's new bourgeoisies have not been noted for their empathy towards the cultural distinctiveness of weaker ethnic groups. Pastoralist groups in the Horn of Africa and elsewhere are a case in point. Perceived as an embarrassment to the national identity of new "modern" ruling elites, the latter have often been quick to devise policies of "sedentarization" to remove the pastoralists' "backwardness" from sight (Doornbos and Markakis, 1991). Generally, *ethnic* pluralism and coexistence—as Africa has in fact known for most of remembered time in most of its regions—requires and presupposes a give-and-take attitude on the part of all the social groupings and strata concerned. In its absence, insistence on conformity to the emerging cultural standards of the new national elites is likely to engender increasingly embittered articulations of ethnic consciousness and the expressed need for cultural survival on the part of peripheralized groups.

Conclusion

If ethnicity can indicate a route to the rediscovery of meaning, a recapturing of cultural identity and the recreation of solidarity, there can be no dispute about its enigmatic force and its liberating potential. Such in any case seems to be its promise and revitalizing power for various social movements currently seeking escape from oppression and arbitrary rule in different parts of Africa. These movements might further gain in significance and depth if they were to link up to other "new social movements", such as ecological, human rights and spiritual movements. But the other uglier face of ethnicity is one that, while purporting to achieve such ultimate ends, actually presents itself in narrowly parochial terms over which powerful political patrons claim to be the sole legitimate interpreters.

Not unlike "liberation ethnicity", this more parochial "chauvinist" alter ego tends to share several universal features, which are also pursued by similar groups in Asia and Europe: the search for and re-emphasis of roots, the true tradition and the reconstitution and salvation of the community. The divide between liberating and chauvinistic ethnic perspectives on a just future can be extremely narrow and at times only careful analysis of the chosen language and symbols may give a clue as to the social basis from which a particular perspective is being advanced. Basically, this is the consequence of the different and shifting social realities concerned: opposition groups as well as dominant forces, even within a single political context, may both draw from one and the same body of spiritual traditions to generate support for the particular position they advocate, which in the final analysis amounts to either a challenge to or an effort to uphold the status quo. What makes analysis even more precarious is that the positions themselves may shift almost imperceptibly from one to the other. As with nationalism, articulations of ethnicity and ethnic identity may go through cyclical processes: emerging as populist, tentatively progressive forces, they may increasingly come to represent narrow conservative tendencies and the dominant stratas' interests in maintaining the social order. The politics of pluralism is thus likely to engender not a few misreadings of coded ethnic messages in years to come.

Perhaps one major cause of the failure of the postcolonial state in Africa has been its gross neglect of its cultural basis. In the urge to create political unity, the tendency has been to negate ethnic, regional and cultural diversities rather than to recognize them as the building blocks of a civil society. The result has often been a facade of seeming unity at the cost of many unsettled wounds and denied identities. Fatally in the long run, the state project had no meaningful or alternative sources of cultural inspiration to draw on, finally leaving it without a vision and empty-handed in the face of impending crisis and disintegration. "Official nationalism", to use Benedict Anderson's (1983) term—extremely narrowly conceived from the start—simply ran out of steam.

In reaction, the current trend is to opt for political pluralism, decentralization and possibly for according ethnicity a prime place as a basis for political organization. This pendulum swing in the other direction reflects and stimulates expectations that such an alternative will provide a superior basis for long-term political projects. This could be a grave misconception, though this is not an argument against pluralism per se, and certainly not against seeking democratic alternatives, nor against the basic need to overcome past and emerging ethnic inequities and to respect ethnic identities. However, if ethnicity is to be assigned any paramount constitutional role in this scheme of things, renewed disillusionments will be difficult to avoid: ethnicity can only provide an alternative basis for political organization at the cost of a whole new wave of misrepresentations, distortions and inequities.

Bibliography

Anderson, Benedict, 1983, *Imagined Communities: Reflections on the Origin and Spread of Nationalism*. London: Verso.

Doornbos, Martin and John Markakis, 1991, "The Crisis of Pastoralism and the Role of the State", in Jeffrey Stone (ed.), *Pastoral Economics in Africa and Long Term Responses to Drought*. Aberdeen: Aberdeen University, African Studies Group.

Doornbos, Martin, 1990, "The African State in Academic Debate: Retrospect and Prospect", *Journal of African Studies*, 28, 2.

Hettne, Björn, 1991, "Ethnicity and Development, An Elusive Relationship". Paper presented at the Nordic Conference for South Asian Studies: Ethnicity, Identity and Development in South Asia, Denmark 11–13 October 1991.

Kothari, Rajni, 1988, *Rethinking Development in Search of Humane Alternatives*. New Delhi: Ajanta Publications.

Mamdani, Mahmood, 1983, "The Nationality Question in a Neo-colony: An Historical Perspective", *Mawazo*, 5, 1.

Mudimbe, V.S., 1988, *The Invention of Africa: Gnosis, Philosophy and the Order of Knowledge*. London: James Currey.

Nandy, Ashis, 1987, *Traditions, Tyranny and Utopias: Essays in the Politics of Awareness*. Delhi: Oxford University Press.

Ranger, Terence, 1983, "The Invention of Tradition in Colonial Africa", in Eric Hobsawm and Terence Ranger (eds.), *The Invention of Tradition*. Cambridge: Cambridge University Press.

Rothchild, D. and N. Chazan (eds.), 1988, *The Precarious Balance: State and Society in Africa*. Boulder and London: Westview Press.

Seddon, D., 1989, "Riot and Rebellion in North Africa: Political Responses to Economic Crisis in Tunisia, Morocco and Sudan", in B. Berberoglu (ed.), *Power and Stability in the Middle East*. London: Zed Press.

Shaw, T., 1986, "Ethnicity as the Resilient Paradigm for Africa", *Development and Change*, 17, 4.

Stavenhagen, Rudolfo, 1991, "The Ethnic Question: Some Theoretical Issues". Geneva: United Nations Institute for Social Development.

Ethnicity and Democracy—A Viable Alliance?*

Eva Poluha

The delegation of state power to ethnic groups is based on several assumptions that need to be made explicit. First, most people belong to an ethnic group or "nation" by virtue of the language they speak. Ethnic groups are, in this sense, enduring—they do not change over time. Second, people belonging to the same ethnic group usually live together in geographically distinct communities, a phenomenon that makes the delegation of power to such units possible. Third, ethnic groups tend to be homogeneous and the people who belong to the group have similar interests. Thus delegation of power to them becomes relevant. Fourth, ethnic groups can be compared to organized political entities, whose members fit certain social criteria but do not have any social relations with each other. Fifth, democracy is based on respect for language and culture. Therefore democracy ought to rest on ethnic communities which have these attributes. Sixth, ethnic group rights are more important than individual, class or gender rights. Therefore, democracy should be based on power sharing among ethnic groups. The following pages will relate these assumptions to the theoretical discussions on both ethnicity and democracy and, in the light of experience in Ethiopia, try to assess their relevance.

Ethnicity and religion in Ethiopian history

Over the centuries, major population movements have taken place in Ethiopia. Large-scale migrations and the creation of a unified territory under Ethiopian rule resulted in the mixing of ethnic groups. People with different ethnic backgrounds came to live side by side, and sometimes new groups appeared through integration. Living as neighbours, people also learned from one other, developing similar survival strategies, and elaborate forms of cooperation developed between individuals and households. Frequent

* The author wishes to acknowledge the financial support from SAREC/Sida and useful comments from Gunilla Bjerén, Elehu Feleke, Karin Norman and Mona Rosendahl.

intermarriage resulted in ethnic permeability with loose borders between the respective groups. This feature has come to characterize the Ethiopian ethnic landscape. This trend has been strengthened by an often closer adherence to religion than to ethnicity, since most ethnic groups have both Muslim and Christian adherents. Interethnic marriage among people of the same religious persuasion has, for instance, usually been favoured over intra-ethnic marriage across religious divides.

This flexible relationship between ethnic groups was encouraged by the loose organization of the Ethiopian state. Power and royal authority, often in the form of exaction of tribute, was exercised by an emperor over feudal lords and/or ethnic chieftains. At other times (1600–1850), these lords acted like independent rulers. They wielded power over the peasants who, upon proving themselves loyal clients by paying dues, were armed by the lords. During the reigns of Tewodros (1855–68), Menelik (1889–1913) and Haile Selassie (1930–74), there was an increased concentration of power and control in the central ruler.

Over the centuries, the provincial lords promoted their political positions through marriage. Thus, no stigma was attached to ethnicity; power remained important and access to power was not equal. The main dominant group during the last centuries has been the highland Christians, practising plough-agriculture and using Amharigna as the lingua franca. Although the rulers were mainly Amhara, with some Tigray, Oromo, Gurage and other elements, the large majority of peasants and pastoralists from these language groups were far removed from power. Nevertheless, a person aspiring to power usually had to be a man who had mastered Amharigna, adhered to Christianity and had developed a good relationship with a powerful patron. Without fulfilling these requirements, the chances of becoming a member of the ruling class were negligible. Over the centuries, whenever political alliances were entered, class interests remained a major factor.

At present, an ethnification process is going on in Ethiopia. More of the interactions between individuals and groups are organized around an ethnic idiom, and ethnicity has become the rallying point for government and opposition parties alike. The government has redrawn the map of Ethiopia in order, it is said, to fit more properly with perceived ideas of ethnic belonging. It seems clear that it is the government's perceptions of ethnic territory that are being followed, since other groups, parties or people have not discussed the issue. Many employees in the bureaucracy are being reinstated in their ethnic "home" areas, to make the regions ethnically homogeneous. Difficulties have been encountered, especially by those who were born out of interethnic marriages and those whose parents or grandparents moved to the area. While in many countries outside Ethiopia, religion is an important ethnic criterion, as it provides yet another tie between members of the same ethnic groups, this is not yet the case in Ethiopia where many ethnic groups remain religiously divided. However, there is a heightened religious awareness in the country among Muslims, as well as among Coptic and Protestant Christians. It is important to note that the ethnification process, although conspicuous in some places, is not universal throughout Ethiopia. Nor is it pursued with the same vigour everywhere. Those pursuing an ethnic agenda are mainly the urban elite, predominately in Addis Ababa. It is the politicians who express the most stereotyped image of their respective groups. Intellectuals, historians, sociologists, anthropologists and others treat historical facts with greater care, although they often also have an ethnic political agenda.

Ethnicity—an elusive concept

Early conceptions of ethnicity focused on its primordial qualities (Narrol, 1964): a common language, a collective name, a common myth of descent, a shared history and allegedly inherited characteristics common to the members of the group. Emphasis was placed on such cultural aspects as dress and hairstyle, which, apart from language and values, are distinctive among ethnic groups. Schermerhorn (1970) defines an ethnic group as a collectivity within a wider society, having a real or putative common ancestry, memories of an historical past and a cultural focus on one or more symbolic elements that are viewed as epitomizing their peoplehood. Schermerhorn mainly refers to the primordial aspects of ethnicity, as does Manning Nash (1988) who talks of "bed, blood and cult", meaning groups that are biologically self-reproducing, endogamous, with ideas about a common history and ancestors and a shared religion.

Individuals become members of an ethnic group through enculturation. From birth they learn to recognize similarities and differences and in this context develop a specific competence of behaviour, sometimes consciously and sometimes unconsciously. The conscious behaviour patterns and characteristics become a repertoire from which the individual can pick what is considered most relevant to the situation. The unconscious, on the other hand, is often made up of norms and values that have become part of our way of being. In this way, ethnicity is a form of social organization through which cultural difference is communicated (Eriksen, 1993).

It is important to stress that individual human beings express a tendency to be both similar to and different from other human beings. Individuals also do this within their own groups, at times emphasizing similarities and at others showing less acceptance of group behaviour. When group behaviour is found less attractive, a member may want to stress his or her distinctiveness. Group traits, whether considered good or bad, strong or weak, will vary according to both context and the people the individual meets. In this way, each human being can affirm identity both as an individual and as a member of his/her group.

If only primordial aspects are considered, ethnic groups readily appear as homogeneous and bounded entities. What is not covered by Schermerhorn's definition is the importance of interaction (Barth, 1969) and context (Young, 1976; Hettne, 1992). Having taken these aspects into consideration, it becomes clear that an ethnic group can never exist in isolation—it always exists in interaction with and in relation to other groups. Whatever primordial qualities exist, they are irrelevant unless compared to "an other" from which they can be distinguished. In other words, there must be a "significant other", because ethnic groups are always relational. There is always a "we" and "us" in relation to a "you" and "them". Furthermore, the relationship is usually in flux, rather than stagnant.

Ethnicity is relational in the sense of being a perpetual process of becoming either more or less important to relationships. Ethnic feelings can emerge in areas or countries where they did not seem to exist before. In Sweden, for example, it was not so important to stress being Swedish until the 1970s, because Swedes had few encounters with strangers. But with the influx of immigrants, "Swedish-ness" is developing as a separate identity in relation to the other groups from whom Swedes want to distinguish themselves.

Ethnicity is, thus, "socially constructed" and, depending on the situation and context, its content will change. The importance attached to ethnicity by a male Ethiopian farmer living in a homogeneous society will probably be negligible, as compared to that attached by a middle-class man who wants to build a political career and to whom ethnicity might be a valuable asset. Once a struggle over scarce resources ensues, the importance attached to ethnicity can be expected to increase considerably.

While some researchers underline the importance of primordial feelings as the glue that keeps ethnic groups together, others have given greater emphasis to ethnicity as a resource to be mobilized or as an instrument to be employed for further ends (Cohen, 1974a, 1974b, 1981; Björklund, 1989; Wanek, 1989) usually of a political and economic nature. The ethnic constituency then represents a "site of mobilization" for these ends (Smith, 1994:706–33), but what is mobilized is usually primordial feelings. Ethnicity as an instrument has also often been associated with separatist movements, and is usually harnessed by minority groups who see separation as a means to end oppression. However, even a majority grouping with political power may have recourse to history and myth when, as in the case of Sri Lanka, it wants to deprive the minority of economic and political influence (Tambiah, 1986).

It is important to recognize that ethnicity, like culture, is always formed in a process. It is never static. Thus new forms or characteristics are perpetually created, since what is considered important changes over time. This flexibility makes it possible for members of ethnic groups to communicate their ethnicity in different ways.

Difference can be intentionally under-communicated especially when other aspects like class (O'Brien, 1990) are more important. It can also be under-communicated when some kind of stigma or association of inferiority is attached to a group. An individual from a minority group looking for a job in the administration of the majority or hegemonic group will play down all possible signs of ethnicity and instead enhance the required criteria and qualifications. On the other hand, where there is no need, ethnicity may not be communicated at all. When positive rewards of different kinds are expected, ethnic difference is often over-communicated. This can happen when ethnicity is used as a basis for recruitment to jobs or positions, or in the distribution of ecological and other resources. Political and other leaders who seek support use ethnicity to gain it.

During an ethnification process, the leaders of each group seek to strengthen the image of the group, emphasizing the primordial aspects; who the group members are, from where they come, and what they are going to be. To do this, it becomes necessary for them to demarcate themselves in relation to other groups. Therefore, borders between groups must not only be maintained, but also sharpened to make one's own group distinct. In embellishing themselves, they also have to belittle and sometimes vilify the others. One common approach is to adapt the past to present needs. People often have to create, or recreate the past through new histories and myths so that it serves their present needs. In the words of Tonkin (1989:5), "to account for the present, to justify it, understand it, or criticise it, the past is used, selectively appropriated, remembered, forgotten or invented".

Another way in which ethnicity is promoted as the major criterion for defining ethnic encounters is through stereotypes. Individuals usually use some form of stereotype to create order in complex situations. But stereotypes are also used by politicians in order to homogenize ethnic signifiers, since this practise facilitates identification. As such, the stereotyping function is a means for establishing borders and facilitates the inclusion of our own people and the exclusion of others. To unravel the stereotypes and see the complex, changing nature of ethnic groups, it is important to understand how depictions of them as bounded, homogeneous, enduring societies originated, since this process often accounts for the reification or essentialization of ethnic groups.

Here I mention three sources of stereotyping, with emphasis on the last. An important source of inspiration for standardized conceptions of ourselves and others seems to be the genuine resentment that members of subjugated groups feel towards those who oppress them. Another that promotes the image of societies as homogeneous, thereby facilitating essentialization, is the oral histories of "how things used to be" which are told in most societies. Almost all written history in Ethiopia is in the liturgical language of Geez or Amharigna, apart from that recorded by foreigners. For non-Copts and non-Amharigna speakers, oral histories are sometimes their only source of information about past events. As such, these histories become important both to the people themselves and to historians writing about the past. There is, however, a tendency for oral histories to become standardized and homogenized as part of the process of being told and retold from generation to generation. They give a picture of a people with a distinct history, which seldom is the case, especially as ethnicity did not historically have the importance in Ethiopia that it has recently acquired. Zitelman is quoted by Baxter as saying "the written historical texts, distributed though the networks of OLF's mass-organisations, gave a uniform picture of a golden Oromo past, when democracy under the *gaada* [Oromo age-grade system] was flourishing, and when Ethiopian colonialism had not yet disturbed the peace of the green pastures" (Baxter, 1994:173, 174). Baxter himself notes that "it would be remarkable in the circumstances if a romanticised, primordial past were not being fabricated" (ibid.).

The texts of social scientists, especially anthropologists, are another source of inspiration for the reification of ethnic cultures. Anthropological studies have to a high degree focused on groups and how they perceive themselves, rather than on individuals (Wolf, 1982). Much emphasis has been given to how members identify themselves in relation to people of another group or other groups, and how this process of identification can be understood as a means of self-definition or self-construction. In studying groups, anthropologists have, however, always had problems delimiting them, since the borders between groups are often fluid, so that one group, or parts of it, merge with another. This has resulted in a focus on difference between groups rather than on sameness. What has further sharpened the focus on difference in anthropological studies is their comparative nature. Thus differences between ethnic groups have been stressed, as have similarities within each group. In monographs and articles, ethnic groups have been projected as homogeneous and bounded and their cultures have been reified.

Democracy—individual and/or collective rights?

Democracy originated in Athens where the citizens collectively determined laws and policies by direct vote. Those who were present could vote and nobody even raised the issue of representation. The citizens were all adult men. Women, male immigrants and their descendants and slaves were excluded. In this way, direct vote rather than representation, exclusive rather than inclusive citizenship, and neglect of minorities characterized Athenian democracy (Hansson, 1994). Thoughts of democracy only gained ground in the West during the French Revolution (see Phillips, 1992). In France, the revolution was a reaction against the special treatment enjoyed by members of the different estates, especially the nobility, by those who were excluded from power and oppressed by the feudal system. The growing, power-hungry bourgeoisie was the most outspoken critic of feudal prerogative. The whole revolution was, in this sense, an act against group privilege and group representation, and for an ideal of citizenship where each *man* was to count equally.

The transition in the early twentieth century towards universal suffrage again entailed a contest over the various group privileges that had developed, this time based on sex (since women had no representation), on property (where this had limited voting rights), on education and on race. The success of universal suffrage thus came to mean representative democracy with all-inclusive citizenship and respect for minorities, since nobody was to be discriminated against on the basis of sex, religion or ethnic identity. In European history then, democracy has come to be a challenge to interest groups and their special political privileges.

The belief that democracy elevates individuals above groups is contested by women and members of minority or aboriginal groups. Despite the fact that political forums are democratically elected, these forums, they argue, in no way mirror existing gender or minority group situations in society. To balance political representation, Young (1992) argues for a participatory democracy on the assumption that some groups are actually or potentially oppressed or disadvantaged and require representation on a group basis. According to Lukes (1976) and Gaventa (1987), some groups never even contend for political power because powerholders manipulate them through the use of myths, processes of socialization, monopolization of media and control of information. They are even able to influence and determine the very wants of individuals and subordinate groups by such subtle means. Disempowerment can thus be seen as a function of collective forces and social arrangements, and not simply as each individual's lack of initiative.

Ethnicity and democracy in the Ethiopian context

As was earlier shown, Ethiopian history is characterized by large-scale migrations. Kinship groups that have moved and settled together can often be found to be homogeneous, in the sense of having a common language, history, norms and values and common ancestors. Interspersed and mixed with these groups, are groups that have intermarried and whose members belong to more than one ethnic group. With regard to mixed marriages in the countryside, it is mostly the women who have moved to their husbands' homes upon marriage. In the towns, and especially among the upper classes, there has been what Smith (1994:713) calls a strengthening of the "lateral *ethnie*", a process of spatial expansion of *ethnie* at the cost of social depth.

Smith's "lateral *ethnie*" in the Ethiopian context would apply to an expansion of Christian highland Ethiopian society in space, towards the south, so that the boundaries between groups became diffuse and the sense of ethnic belonging does not run very deep. Instead, there was frequent exchange of upper-class members between neighbouring ethnic groups, especially through marriage and warfare, all predominantly within the same Christian faith. For the offsprings of this process, ethnic identity was not the most relevant category. Instead, they learned Amharic, the official language, in order to pursue a career.

The first assumption outlined at the outset of this chapter that everybody belongs to one ethnic group or "nation", whose language they speak and with which they identify, seems to be relevant for certain groups in Ethiopia. For others it would be remote from, even contradictory to their life experience, especially since the meaning and implications of ethnic belonging have changed over time and continue to do so. Likewise the second assumption, that people who belong to the same ethnic group live in geographically distinct and bounded communities, is relevant to only some parts of Ethiopia. At the same time, there are clusters of minorities everywhere.

The third assumption, that ethnic groups are homogeneous and their members have similar interests, is based on the belief that primordial feelings alone determine a person's interests. This may be the case in a situation of ethnic-group competition, where ethnicity is considered the most important criterion for determining one's alliances. The assumption that ethnic groups are homogeneous, however, does not take the contextual or relational aspects of ethnicity into account, nor the fact that ethnicity changes over time. Furthermore, it does not recognize that each individual has multiple status depending on gender, age, class and religious adherence, apart from ethnic belonging. In most projections of ethnic-group culture, a male gender bias is dominant, since the male conceptualization of what is relevant has come to count as the public culture (Das, 1994). In Ethiopia, this can be seen in the identification of Oromo culture with the *gaada* system, a system to which women had no access. Furthermore, religion is often taken to be more important than ethnicity in Ethiopia, making marriages between Christian Amharas and Christian Oromos more frequent than between Christian Oromos and Muslim Oromos. This again shows how mistaken it is to take the homogeneity and similarity of interests between members of the same ethnic group for granted.

The above refutation of the homogeneity of ethnic groups also shows that ethnic groups cannot be equated with political units, as is suggested in the fourth assumption. Members of ethnic groups share certain characteristics but seldom organize themselves for any specific purposes and have no shared goals. A group of people with the same ethnic characteristics may at certain stages mobilize as a political party. They then become an organization, a party, and the character of their collectivity changes. It is seldom that all who share the same characteristics will join such an ethnic party. Therefore, delegation of power to an ethnic group per se creates problems for both representation and accountability, because it is impossible to find representatives for such an amorphous category, and even more difficult to make them accountable to its members.

Democracy in Europe has emphasized individual rights. Nevertheless, part of the so-called democratic respect for the individual is the respect of that individual's right not to be discriminated against on grounds of sex, ethnic identity, race and religion. There is, therefore, an implicit respect for the rights of collectivities in the Western concept of democracy. This is underlined by Das (1994:119) who points out that "the subjects of [human] rights cannot be treated as isolated, atomised individuals, because in order for them to preserve and enjoy their culture, the collective survival of traditions becomes an important condition", and "collective existence is necessary because one's capacity to make sense of the world presupposes the existence of collective traditions" (Das, 1994:158). For democracy to exist, there must be respect for both the rights of individuals and of the collective—but not only for the latter, as is implied in the fifth assumption.

The final assumption that ethnic-group interests are more important than those claimed by other types of collectivities is partly refuted above. Only under certain conditions is ethnicity the overriding criterion guiding a person's acts and alliances. When the context and conditions are not ethnically defined, or are not the result of group contradictions, other interests may well take precedence. Thus, one cannot assume that one type of interests, like those deriving from ethnic identity, predominate over others in all situations. As a consequence, it seems that the right of the individual to decide which identity must be safeguarded and in what situation takes priority over the claim of an amorphous ethnic group to enforce its criteria on the individual.

Leaving these assumptions aside, it is important to understand what is happening in Ethiopia today, particularly how ethnicity came to the top of the political agenda. Ethnification in Ethiopia is not the work of one ethnic group or the government, but of intellectuals from all groups who have devoted much time and energy promoting it. However, the incumbent Ethiopian Peoples Revolutionary Democratic Front (EPRDF) has taken the initiative. This party succeeded in camouflaging the roots of all problems and all contradictions in Ethiopia in ethnic clothing. Most of the opposition parties and newspapers follow suit by reacting to what the EPRDF proposes, allowing it to dictate the political agenda rather than presenting their own. As a result, alternative schemes are not discussed.

It seems that the ethnic basis of the liberation movements from which most opposition parties arose facilitated ethnification. Being the largest and most powerful force in the transitional government, the EPRDF could satisfy the major ethnic demands of the other liberation groups by decentralizing the state administration and promoting the use of ethnic languages and communication in administration and education. The EPRDF also succeeded in creating a coalition of ethnic political parties, as described in other chapters in this volume. The opposition was disarmed and neutralized because the issues it had worked for, like ethnic regionalization and a multiparty system, were apparently resolved. By taking over the ethnic agenda, the EPRDF has been able to keep other key issues out of the political limelight.

What is the future of democracy in Ethiopia if the ethnic agenda is pursued? In order to achieve more ethnically homogeneous areas, more people will have to move away from where they now live. Ethnic stereotyping will be emphasized and spread to smaller towns with mixed populations, and to the countryside beyond. Stereotyping, in turn, will tend to enhance the dominant groups' real or mythical history and characteristics. Dominant groups will present themselves as unique, with all the positive attributes a group can have, and the contours of the image they present of themselves will be sharply etched and easily identifiable. In the process, minority groups will either be passed over in silence, or their group characteristics vilified. An essentialization of the dominant groups' cultures will take place and be used as a political weapon against any kind of opposition.

Such a process has been very convincingly illustrated by Marina Ottaway (1994). In her article comparing developments in South Africa, Ethiopia, Slovakia and Croatia, she asks whether the process of democratic transition contributes to ethnic conflict. Ottaway suggests that democratization in multiethnic societies requires the accommodation of ethnic identities in the political system. It is not enough to defend individual rights if one wants to promote democracy in multiethnic societies—some group rights have to be protected as well. Accommodation, however, does not mean partition on ethnic grounds, since that will immediately endanger the minorities living within the majority group's boundaries. In similar vein, Das (1994:155), in an article on cultural rights and community definition in India, shows how the Sikhs' promotion of their culture resulted in "reproducing the same hegemonic character of which the state stood earlier accused, [meaning that] this [was] evident from the fact that the militant discourse denies any possibility of alternative definitions of community".

An agenda of ethnification and ethnic decentralization is politically dangerous. Focus on one's own ethnic group to the exclusion of others is necessary in order to make demands in the name of the group. It entails enhancing the norms, values, virtues, history and homogeneity of one's own group. At the same time, by its own logic such behaviour means repressing the rights of minorities, even within their own areas, because there is no place on a majority ethnic group's agenda for minorities. As a consequence, the behaviour and discourse of those promoting their own culture becomes antidemocratic.

It follows from the above that it will be impossible for Ethiopia to pursue an ethnification process as defined above and to promote democracy at the same time. Yet, although decentralization on an ethnic basis cannot be expected to promote democracy—but will, rather, endanger it—it is also obvious that democracy cannot be promoted without respect for existing cultures—or the rights and interests of women in the various ethnic groups. The challenge is how to strike this delicate balance.

Bibliography

Barth, F., 1969, "Introduction", in F. Barth (ed.), *Ethnic Groups and Boundaries*. Oslo: Universitetsforlaget.

Baxter, P.T.W., 1994, "The Creation and Constitution of Oromo Nationality", in K. Fukui and J. Markakis (eds.), *Ethnicity and Conflict in the Horn of Africa*. London: James Currey.

Björklund, U., 1989, "Diaspora", *Antropologiska Studier*, 44, 20–35.

Cohen, A., 1974a, "Introduction and the Lesson of Ethnicity", in A. Cohen (ed.), *Urban Ethnicity*. London: Tavistock.

—1974b, *Two Dimensional Man*. London: Routledge and Kegan Paul.

—1981, "Variables in Ethnicity", in C. Keyes (ed.), *Ethnic Change*. Seattle: University of Washington Press.

Das, V., 1994, "Cultural Rights and the Definition of Community", in O. Mendelsohn and V. Baxi (eds.), *The Rights of Subordinated Peoples*. Delhi: Oxford University Press.

Eriksen, T.H., 1993, *Ethnicity and Nationalism; Anthropological Perspectives*, London: Pluto Press.

Gaventa, J., 1987, "Makt och deltagande", in O. Petersson (ed.), *Maktbegreppet*. Stockholm: Carlssons Förlag.

Hansson, S.O., 1994, "Demokratin har inte alltid varit demokratisk" (Democracy has not always been democratic), *Forskning och Framsteg*, 4, 94.

Hettne, B., 1992, *Economic Development and Economic Conflicts*. Göteborg: Padrigu.

Lukes, S., 1976 (1974), *Power: A Radical View*. London: Macmillan.

Narrol, R., 1964, "Ethnic Unit Classification", *Current Anthropology*, 5, 4.

Nash, M., 1988, *The Cauldron of Ethnicity in the Modern World*. Chicago: Chicago University Press.

O'Brien, O., 1990, "Perceptions of Identity in North Catalonia", *Critique of Anthropology*, Special Issue, 10, 2 and 3.

Ottaway, M., 1994, *Democratization and Ethnic Nationalism: African and Eastern Experiences*. Policy Essay No. 14. Washington: ODC.

Phillips, A., 1992, "Democracy and Feminist Theory", *The Political Quarterly*, 63, 1:79–90.

Poluha, E. (forthcoming), "Conceptualising Democracy—Elections in the Ethiopian Countryside", *North East African Studies*.

Schermerhorn, R.A., 1970, *Comparative Ethnic Relations; A Framework for Theory and Research*. New York: Random House.

Smith, Anthony D., 1994, "The Politics of Culture: Ethnicity and Nationalism", in T. Ingold (ed.), *Companion Encyclopaedia of Anthropology*. London and New York: Routledge.

Tambiah, S.J., 1986, *Sri Lanka Ethnic Fratricide and the Dismantling of Democracy.* Chicago: Chicago University Press.

Tonkin, E., M. McDonald and M. Chapman, 1989, "Introduction", in E. Tonkin, M. Mcdonald and M. Chapman (eds.), *History and Ethnicity.* London: Routledge.

Wanek, A., 1989, "Nationalism: some Theoretical Considerations", *Antropologiska Studier* 44, 3–12.

Wolf, E., 1982, *Europe and the People without History.* Berkeley: University of California Press.

Young, C., 1976, *The Politics of Cultural Pluralism.* Madison: University of Wisconsin Press.

Young, I.M., 1989, "Policy and Group Difference: A Critique of the Ideal of Universal Citizenship", *Ethics,* 99.

Tigray—The Birth of a Nation within the Ethiopian Polity

Adhana H. Adhana

Neither "ethnicity" nor the "state" has a fixed meaning. The content of each has varied throughout Ethiopian history. So has the modus vivendi between ethnicity and the state. Whether it is true that the character of ethnicity varied because the character of the state changed, or the reverse, it seems the character of the state played a decisive role in shaping the political content of ethnicity. Ethnicity can be merely an objective historical phenomenon without sentience, or may stir to life in various forms depending on the historical character of the state and the circumstances which impact on that character. In the case of Tigray throughout the entire period under discussion, the character of the state determined the political orientation of ethnicity.

Ultimately, the role of ethnicity in politics is shaped by class. It is the class character of the wielders of political power at the centre and the nature of the order they perpetuate, as well as the class character of those who wield power at the level of ethnic units, that determines the state of being and the political orientation of ethnicity. There is no ethnicity without a history behind it. The Tigray example also shows that ethnicity *is not necessarily* the bane of multinational statehood. For this reason, I believe that Ethiopian statehood has entered a brave new world since 1991. The phrase "brave new world" inherently implies a comparison of the present era with earlier ones. The latter comprise a period of formation and expansion, decline and reformation of the Ethiopian state, which displayed basic features of nationhood within the framework of linguistic (hence ethnic) diversity. Christianity provided the foundation for nationhood, while state support made this faith durable. Since Christianity did not define the territorial extent of the Ethiopian state, the state assumed the contradictory features of being simultaneously a nation and an empire. That was the case particularly during the heyday of the Ethiopian state, roughly from 1328 to 1529. Thus, Christianity accounted both for the durability and the fragility of Ethiopian statehood, because it was as exclusivist (particularly in the face of Islam) as it was inclusive. Defined by its predominant Christian character, Tigray formed not only a durable component of the Ethiopian nation but was also part of the backbone of the Ethiopian state.

This Ethiopian state was rooted in an earlier state known as Aksum, which was centred in Tigray and included much of Eritrea. The Aksumite state, which lasted from at least the first century AD to approximately 1150, was polytheistic to start with and became a Christian state in the fourth century, and it may have become a Christian society by the sixth century. Christian Aksum thus formed the cornerstone of the Ethiopian state from 1328 to 1889. In fact, Christian Aksum must be said to have comprehensively defined and anchored the Ethiopian state since it came into formal existence in 1328, if not since its inception in 1270. Everything that defined the Ethiopian state was a result of Aksumite invention and innovation.

For some 130 years after the end of the Aksumite state the Zagwe state held sway. This state was a continuation of Aksum, but with a dynasty that was distinctly Agau and located among a distinctly Agau population. The Ethiopian state that followed represented itself as the restoration of the primacy of the holy city of Aksum in Christian Ethiopia. An enduring myth was woven about the restoration of the so-called Solomonic dynasty and the primacy of Aksum both as the cradle of Ethiopian Christianity and of the state itself. The dream of all Ethiopian monarchs was to have their second coronation in Aksum. The rulers were Amhara and spoke Amharic. The literary and Church language was Geez, the Aksumite language, and it must have naturally challenged the Amhara much more than the Tigray to learn it. The monarchs had the power to appoint and dismiss provincial governors during much of 1328–1889, save for the period 1769–1855, when the throne was vacant. Normally, governors were from within the provinces themselves. This was at any rate the case for Tigray. Thus, there was nothing to prevent Tigray from being an integral part of the Ethiopian state, both in the political and the spiritual sense.

The imperial element of the Ethiopian state disappeared following the wars of Imam Ahmad of Harrar between 1529 and 1543. The Oromo population movements that followed precluded its immediate revival as an empire. The Ethiopian state was confined to northern Ethiopia, north of the Abay and the Beshilo rivers. Ethiopia had thus become the nation itself, and Tigray, which had also come to include the Eritrean highlands between 1607 and 1632, formed the best part of the state. The power of the monarchs declined sharply after 1706, but Tigray remained part and parcel of the Ethiopian state. Where there was a change was in the appointment of the governors of Tigray. As the monarchs increasingly failed to assert themselves in the provinces, the governorship of Tigray became a bone of contention among rival dynastic houses based in Adwa, Agame, and Inderta in Tigray and what is today Eritrea.

In middle of the eighteenth century, Mika'el Suhul of Adwa emerged dominant. Iyyasu II (1730–55), the last of the Ethiopian kings with some degree of authority, found Mika'el Suhul too powerful and simply confirmed him as the governor of the entire region, from the river Angereb in the northwest to the Red Sea in the east. Mika'el Suhul had shown the way for members of the Tigray political elite to prevail over the province through their military prowess. It was the resources of Tigray that enabled Mika'el Suhul to dominate the Ethiopian state itself from 1768 to 1771, when the elite of the other provinces combined to limit him to the rule of Tigray, which then made up half of the Ethiopian state. This Tigray was coterminous with the Aksumite core region and the Tigray linguistic region.

As regards Tigray, ethnicity remained an objective-historical phenomenon without sentience up to 1771. The Tigray political elite expressed its political conflicts with other provincial elites within the Ethiopian state in religious forms well up to 1831. If ethnicity played any political role during this period, it was in "religious-political" form. Mika'el Suhul failed to establish a Tigray dynasty. Upon his death, it was Weldesilase of Inderta who prevailed for sometime over the whole of Tigray. But he also failed to construct a provincial dynasty, and Subagadis of Agame succeeded him practically over the same regional entity. His rule was brief, because the political elite in the rest of Ethiopia once again combined to defeat him in 1831, when the governorship of Tigray passed on to an outsider, Wube of Simen.

The Tigray elite failed to make a comeback until 1865. During Wube's reign, the political premise was dynastic rather than ethnic. The situation was practically the same during the first decade (1855–65) of the "reformation" of the Ethiopian state. However, the end of that decade witnessed a resurgence of the Tigray political elite in the person of Kassa, who combined in himself the political claims of the dynastic houses of Adwa, Agame, and Inderta. He dominated the Tigray by 1867, and became the ruler of Ethiopia with the royal name of Yohannes IV in early 1872. His coronation was in Aksum. By 1878, Yohannes had also brought Wollo and the southern Christian kingdom of Shoa into the domain of the Ethiopian state. He thus completed the early phase of the "reformation" of the historic Ethiopian state begun by Tewodros II of Gonder (1855–68).

Yohannes IV presided over the Ethiopian state for seventeen years, (1872–89). Ruling the Tigray and the Gondar region directly, he kept Wollo under close supervision, while he ruled Gojjam and Shoa indirectly. In the case of Tigray, he unified all the local dynastic houses and his reign witnessed an expansion of the Tigray political elite. To that extent, it can be said that Yohannes forged Tigray into a protonation, but this protonation expressed itself in historical-political rather than ethnic terms. The focal points were Aksum and Ethiopia rather than the Amhara and the Tigray. The linguistic division between these two groups was still irrelevant, in contrast to some arcane doctrinal differences between them which proved politically contentious. Tigray had thus become a protonation, but one which expressed itself otherwise than as ethnicity per se.

It was the fate of Yohannes IV to attempt to reform the Ethiopian state and defend it from foreign aggression simultaneously. He successfully repulsed the Egyptians in their bid to dominate Ethiopia in pitched battles at Gundet and Gura'i in 1875 and 1876. Ethiopian victory over Egypt strengthened the power of the monarch domestically, and enabled him to bring the kingdom of Shoa under his authority in 1878. However, the Shoan kingdom proved a source of weakness rather than strength to the Ethiopian state between 1878 and 1889. An historic confrontation between two distinct polities led to intense rivalry on the Ethiopian highlands.

The kingdom of Shoa was part of the political culture of the historic Ethiopian state. However, it had existed separately under its own dynasty for some 150 years since 1696, until Tewodros II ended its independence in 1855. But it was only a nominal part of the Ethiopian state, and that only up to 1865 when it regained its independence under King Menelik. When Menelik submitted to Yohannes in 1878, it was only due to the latter's realism and the relative weakness of his kingdom. Yohannes left the power of the Shoan dynasty intact and kept the kingdom autonomous. King Menelik laboured hard to overcome the relative weakness of his kingdom by building an empire in the southwest, south, and southeast, and through collusion with Italy. The whole process created a difficult predicament for Yohannes in 1888–89, when Italy threatened the Ethiopian state from the direction of Massawa in the north, the Sudanese Mahdists invaded Gonder from the northwest, and King Menelik colluded with the Italians and rebelled in concert with the king of Gojjam.

The Ethiopian monarch opted to confront first the Mahdist army, which had retreated to Metema, near the Ethio-Sudanese border. The Ethiopian forces clearly had the upper hand in the battle of Metema in 1889, when a stray bullet claimed the life of Yohannes and Ethiopian success in the battle turned to rout. Meanwhile, Menelik was working on a treaty which ceded territory in the north to Italy. This became the Italian colony of Eritrea. Menelik declared himself the king of Ethiopia as soon as he received news of Yohannes' death. He was now the most powerful leader and had little difficulty in establishing his authority over the Ethiopian state, except Tigray. Under Menelik, the Ethiopian state expanded to cover its current territory, becoming an empire in fact as well as in name, and was ruled by the Amhara elite of Shoa. Shoa now became the prototype of Ethiopian nationhood.

After Metema, Tigray found itself politically orphaned, militarily battered, economically shattered and psychologically disoriented. The heir of Yohannes, Ras Mangasha, did not have the necessary resources to hold the Tigray political elite together. The death of such a personality as Ras Araya

Silasse the Elder (the uncle of Yohannes) in the aftermath of the battle of
Metema, contributed powerfully to the disarray among the political elite.
Militarily, Tigray was at its weakest since 1871. Mangasha could command a
puny army of only 5,000 men. The great famine of 1888–92 devastated
Tigray. Geopolitically, Italy, with the collusion of Emperor Menelik of
Ethiopia, pressed on Tigray from the north, where it had carved out its
colony of Eritrea by 1890. In the south, Menelik had established his mastery
everywhere. Early in 1889, he entreated the Italians to move their troops into
the region north of the Mereb, and after Metema he continued to implore the
Italians to guard against the supply of arms to Tigray.

Caught between the hammer and the anvil, Tigray manifested its political disorientation in various ways: periodic outbursts of fratricidal civil war,
were interspersed with temporary reconciliations and a common front
against Menelik and Italy, and tentative steps towards alliance with Italy in
Eritrea against Menelik. Moves to submit to Menelik were hampered by
divisions on the issue, and questions regarding the formation of a common
anti-Italian front with Menelik against Italy. These political manœuvres had
various authors, group and individual, and combined the genuine with the
furtive, the old with the new, the strategic with the tactical, the individual
and personal with the common protonational, emotion with reason, and
principled positions with outright opportunism. The political behaviour of
the Tigray political elite was in constant flux. This bewildering sequence of
political behaviour, occurring in quick succession, reflected the convulsions
of a protonation faced with odds far beyond its capacity to overcome.

During the period from 1889 to 1935, Tigray was confronted with an
unfamiliar polity. The premise of the imperial state was coercion and domination. In the case of the Tigray political elite, this coercive and militarist
approach invited only resistance, which reached its peak between 1889 and
1909. It was also during this period that ethnicity appeared on the political
scene in Tigray, along with dynastic claims and individual political ambitions. By the end of the first decade of the twentieth century, Emperor
Menelik had become too ill to attend to state affairs. The Tigray political elite
was also a spent force and was deeply impressed by the power of Shoa.
However, two decades of resistance had helped restrain the Shoan elite in
their approach to Tigray. The latter, therefore, strove to control Tigray
through its own elite in the period from 1909 to 1935. Thus, the dynastic
house of Yohannes survived in Tigray in two factions. Shoan politics in
Tigray involved pitting one faction against the other, and eventually produced a personality who dared to challenge Ethiopian statehood itself when
he allied with the Italians in 1935.

The Italian occupation of Ethiopia (1936–41), further marginalized the
Tigray political elite. The Italian gave the people law and order and security
of person and property. For the peasantry, this period was one of peace and
the good life. It contrasted sharply with the woes of 1889–1935. The Tigray

political elite therefore lost credibility with the people of Tigray. With the defeat of the Italians in 1941 and the full restoration of the Ethiopian imperial state in 1942, it was a section of the Tigray peasantry that collided with the state. Peasant class grievances were nicely mixed with ethnic resentment during the popular rebellion of 1942–43 known as *Weyane*. A descendant of Yohannes who had committed political suicide when he became an Italian puppet in 1935, tried to exploit the rebellion for his narrow aims, but to no avail. Other disgruntled elements from the lower strata of the Tigray political elite also attached themselves to the rebellion, but the rebellion was of the peasantry against all that was venal and overbearing in the Ethiopian imperial state.

Mangasha, another descendant of Yohannes, had submitted to the domination of the Shoan elite between 1909 and 1935. He fought against the Italians in 1935–36, but surrendered with the collapse of the Ethiopian state in early 1936. Afterwards, this branch of the house of Yohannes could only survive with Shoan tolerance. Thus, the house of Yohannes had no real political substance by the end of 1941. The popular rebellion, however, created conditions for the maintenance of the house of Yohannes in Tigray as an adjunct of the Shoan political elite, with a descendant of Yohannes serving as provincial governor. Its continuity gave a semblance of autonomy to Tigray, but that was more apparent than real. The dynastic obstacle to the emergence of a Tigray nation was basically removed by 1941. A stage was thus reached in the history of Tigray which could either culminate in the fragmentation and dissipation of this political entity, or, given new conditions, allow it to forge ahead and become a fully fledged nation.

Many things conspired against Tigray emerging as a fully fledged nation. The maintenance of the insubstantial house of Yohannes by the imperial state served to camouflage the subversion of Tigray's identity. The newly introduced system of state education, which promoted Amharanization, not only constituted an onslaught on the language and culture of the Tigray, but also worked to distance the Tigray from the Amhara concept of the Ethiopian nationstate. Tigray became notorious for its poverty, particularly after the famine of 1958–59. The preservation of relics of local dynasties at the district level also worked towards fragmentation rather than unity in Tigray.

Eventually Tigray triumphed over these obstacles, and forged ahead as a full nation. The 1960s opened with what can be seen as a patriotic revolt against a backward regime. The opening act took the form of an abortive coup d'état by a section of the armed forces of the imperial state. Though it failed, the attempt nevertheless generated a radical political movement (the Ethiopian Student Movement) which, by 1969, openly challenged the imperial state with the principle of the right of nations and nationalities to self-determination "up to and including secession". By challenging the foundations of the imperial state, the movement was looking for new and inclusive, therefore, democratic foundations.

Tigray university students participated actively in the student movement, in essence the first school of revolutionary thought and practice. There is no doubt that the movement produced a new cadre of Tigray nationalists. These were not a homogeneous body. Indeed, they belonged to three broad political tendencies. The first tendency exuded ethnic hostility and toyed with the idea of "Greater Tigray" that would incorporate the Tigray-speaking region of Eritrea. The second subsumed the liberation of Tigray in the liberation of all Ethiopia. The third tendency was novel: it focused on the liberation of Tigray as such. The issue of whether or not Tigray's liberation would coincide with the liberation of the rest of Ethiopia would depend on the historical process itself.

The three tendencies had the liberation of Tigray as their common denominator, but their divergences were basic. The first was exclusive and emphasized ethnicity, the second was pluralist and accepted multinationality, and the third was eclectic and leaned towards pluralism through a concerted liberation struggle. The first tendency, had its origins not in the Ethiopian Student Movement, where it was peripheral, but in the particular history of Tigray between 1889 and 1935, and was a relic of an utterly frustrated and defeated traditional Tigray political elite. The second was clearly a straightforward, and therefore uncritical, extension of the political approach of the Ethiopian Student Movement, with its emphasis on class. The Tigray identity was secondary. The third tendency, which was the golden mean between the first two, was clearly rooted in the entire history of Tigray, its Ethiopian identity and its own ethnic identity, as well as in the revolutionary vision of the Ethiopian Student Movement.

The practical and political implications of the three tendencies for the liberation of Tigray can now be appraised. The first tendency would have submerged the Tigray identity under the illusion of Ethiopia without its imperial trappings. This would have ended up simply as *ethnic politics*, a politics of hate and exclusiveness, a politics of settling scores, a politics of people against people. The advocates of this tendency had at heart the grievances of the traditional Tigray political elite, rather than the current problems and long-term interests of the Tigray people. The third tendency focused on the liberation of Tigray both in class and national terms, within the framework of an Ethiopian state if possible, and without it if necessary. The idea of an Ethiopian state common to all its nations and nationalities was not precluded, nor was the liberation of Tigray regarded as secondary to the liberation of Ethiopia. Thus the postliberation political status of Tigray—separation and independence, or a nation within a multinational Ethiopian polity, the bearer of a double identity, Tigray and Ethiopian—was not predetermined: it was to be determined by the liberation struggle itself.

The movement had to guard itself constantly against two dangers: submergence under Greater Ethiopia chauvinism, or the slide into the narrow nationalism in the direction of Greater Tigray. In other words, the movement had to guard against one form or other of elitist politics that would use Tigray only in the pursuit of interests that had nothing to do with interests of the people of Tigray—politics rooted in either old dynastic ambitions and grievances or in petit bourgeois emotions and ambitions for power. To succeed, the movement, had to be based on the political mobilization of the Tigray people, the overwhelming majority of whom consisted of peasant farmers.

The odds against the national and class liberation of Tigray were simply massive. The old Tigray political elite and the feudal culture had to be overcome. A military regime with a huge war machine had to be brought to its knees and the cancerous problem of sub-provincialism had also to be fought and subdued. The struggle had to eliminate all the constraints that had stood in the way of Tigray becoming a nation. Tigray finally emerged as a nation within the Ethiopian polity, not only after a struggle against incredible odds, but *because* it had to struggle against such odds.

Towards Identifying some of the Moral Components of an Oromo National Identity

P.T.W. Baxter

The Oromo are one of the most populous nationalities in Africa and are certainly the largest in the Horn. Census data are not reliable, but there must be well over twenty million Oromo, almost all of whom reside in Ethiopia, where they make up around 40 per cent of the population. They are, as Edwin Foot put it in 1913, after spending six years trading and travelling amongst them, "a most industrious, pastoral and agricultural people, who are also keen traders ... [and] inhabit, besides large desert tracts, some of the richest, most fertile and salubrious country in Africa, whose varied attractions to be appreciated must be seen". Commonly referred to as Galla by northern Ethiopians, this name has become hateful.

All Oromo political and cultural spokespeople assume there is an Oromo nation, the members of which share a distinctive culture. They experience and feel their own identity so intensely in their daily lives that they see no need to explain it: it is simply a given. Their distinctive and ancient culture has been "fashioned" over the years by their ancestors so that it has come to embody those evocative powers that are "the very means of survival" of Oromo nationality (Waller, 1993:302). Most anthropologists, on the other hand, "see national cultures not as discrete entities, but as rhetorical and political constructions ... [as] ex post facto rationalisations" (Handler and Segal, 1996)—that is, as myths or "inventions". Both "culture" and "morality", like "nationality", are wrapped in vagueness. However, these differing perspectives can to some extent be reconciled. There can be more to a national identity than just a political stance. A number of students of the Oromo accept that there is an Oromo moral, national identity and an associated Oromo culture. This culture consists of some distinctive cultural features or customary behaviours, which have morally binding aspects and which appear to be so widespread that they may be considered to be components of a pan-Oromo cultural identity.

In response to political and economic subordination within Ethiopia, this shared culture has become the core of a shared national identity, an extended version, that is, of what John Lonsdale (1992:466) has termed a "moral ethnicity". It is a moral ethnicity which "creates communities from within through domestic controversy over civic virtue ... [and] is the most intimate critic of the state's ideology of order ... and is not given its due in modern analyses of Africa". In his analysis of violence and ethnicity in Kenya, and more widely in Africa, Lonsdale argues that "Mau Mau was ... a moral war" concerned with "civic virtue" and the proper sort of relationships that should exist between man and man, young and old, and men and women (Lonsdale, 1992:453). This insight should be kept in mind in an examination of the components of Oromo nationality and Oromo conflicts with the state within which most are confined. Whilst part of the motive of any individual national activist may well lie in the search for power, the Oromo "struggle" is as much about moral feelings and the proper way of living and behaving and doing things as it is about political recognition.[1]

The words we must use are not only vague, which makes them awkward in academic discourse, but, even worse, they have become tainted and obscured by the rhetoric and actions of extreme nationalists. Full of jingoistic associations, "nation", "national" and "nationality" can sometimes be used in a fairly neutral way, but "nationalism" only rarely so. Even the word "nationality" presents increasing difficulties now that so many countries are twisting the term in their chauvinistic efforts to restrict immigration. For Westerners, it also carries all sorts of uneasy overtones which stem from some of its savage consequences in two World Wars, in colonial histories and the remembrance of dreams which it has tarnished.

One way out of the dilemma provoked by the words may be to try and think of "nation" and "nationality" in the ways recently proposed by David Miller. In his subtle and discriminating defence of the idea of nationality in his *On Nationality* (1996),[2] Miller argues that the sense of nationality is derived from belonging to a nation, and of sharing in a nationality. He also argues that having a national identity exists both extensively and very pervasively in the modern world, and is a common sentiment held by ordinary people. Such sentiments, even though they may be based on myth rather than history, and on emotion rather than rationality, have to be reckoned with as valid components of any practical analysis just because they are so widespread and are held so strongly.

That the words have become debased by misuse, as have "culture", "society" and "class", does not entitle us to ignore the fact that they have strong meanings in popular discourse. Simply, the belief in distinctive nationalities influences our behaviour in daily life. To deny the existence

---

1. See essays in Baxter et al. (eds.), 1996, *Being and Becoming Oromo*, by Gemetchu Megersa, Gufu Oba, Marco Bassi, Gudrun Dahl and Mario Aguilar. Also Asmarom Legesse, 1990; Bartels, 1983; van de Loo, 1991; Zitelmann, 1994.

2. See also an excellent review of Miller's book by Charles King in the *Times Literary Supplement*, 10 May 1996:4–5. It appeared under the appropriate heading "Fellow Feelings".

and importance of the belief in distinctive nationalities is like denying the existence of a religion because, to the observer, it appears to be woolly and based on myth and unable to provide what the observer considers to be a rational explanation of itself. Indeed, both religions and nationalities depend in good measure on the diffuse meanings of their core myths/truths for their existence and their durability. Once these are made absolutely clear and precise they become "cults", or "factions" or "survivals".

It is a commonplace but, nevertheless, true observation that the boundaries of nationality are always vague and vary with contexts and relationships. But, however hazy those boundaries may be, most people feel more intense obligations to those they perceive as their fellow nationals, their "countrymen", as Ghanaians say, than they do to members of other nationalities. Simply, "belonging" to a nation and sharing a common national identity implies shared moral and emotional commitments which mostly lie latent and only become apparent in times of conflict or of exile. Gatherings of Oromo exiles of the Diaspora, for example, which I have been privileged to attend in Amsterdam, Berlin, Melbourne, Washington and Toronto are emotional occasions of intensely heightened consciousness. Anyone who has ever lived as an expatriate has only to think of the pleasures that derive from hearing speech or music which recalls one's homeland, or the comfort derived from meeting somebody one would cross the road to avoid at home.

To be a member of a nation is more than just having an identity in a passport, or a simple stamp that marks your difference from others. It is, when need arises, to be a committed member of an "ethical community" (Miller, 1996:49) bound to other members by chains of inescapable moral indebtedness and obligation. Moral arm-twisting by a fellow national in such circumstances is hard to withstand, as any African student studying abroad will testify. The ties of nationality, though normally so light as to be unnoticeable, may sometimes become as excruciatingly tight as those of family. David Miller also accepts that claims to forms of self-determination based on nationality, though not necessarily in the form of a nationstate, are morally defensible. This recognition seems self-evident to most ordinary active members of a nationality, but it is denied again and again by the rulers of "nationstates" which incorporate different nationalities within their borders.

The Oromo "Nation"

It became increasingly clear during the 1980s, as the Oromo Liberation Front became more active, and as the sufferings of both peasants and the poor increased while the voices of the Oromo Diaspora became stronger, that the existence of the Oromo nation could no longer be ignored. The "problem of the Galla", as it used to be called by Ethiopian centralists, could no longer be politically insulated, disguised or sanitized by the use of cover-all terms such as "ethnic group" or "people", and certainly not by the local use of "nationality" as an adjectival appendage to groups of folk-dancers. A rapidly increasing number of Oromo had come to share strong feelings of national identity and of patriotism. Most schooled Oromo were nationalists who stressed that they were Oromo rather than Ethiopians. The Oromo emerged from being a series of closely related ethnic groups which happened to speak the same language, and had, quite clearly, become a "nation". For most Oromo their nationality had become "a powerful source of personal identity".[3] The Oromo demonstrated all the components that are considered to be essential for a nationality: an active and developing "common public culture" (Miller, 1996:25), articulate intellectuals, a common language, a history, a set of myths and symbols which denote their cultural distinctiveness,[4] martyrs, heroes, lively political and cultural organizations and the maturity to recognize the existence and importance of localized cultural variations.

The old patronizingly dismissive judgements of many Orientalists, "Ethiopianists" and colonialists that, a) the Oromo had never been a unitary "nationstate" and, therefore, could never aspire to be; and b) that the Oromo had never demonstrated internal unity and were merely a mixed bag of peoples of different religions united only in their opposition to Shoan domination, have both became scholastic irrelevancies although they are still whispered. By such criteria few, if any, "ethnic groups" would ever have come to be recognized as "nations". That all Oromo do not think alike or follow the same religion does not automatically disqualify them for recognition as a nationality—indeed, the very opposite. All nationalities, like all cultures, are hybrids. As Lonsdale has pointed out, one of the characteristics of all nationalisms is that they "have the power to unite people of otherwise divergent beliefs" (1992:443).

The creation and expression of a feeling of shared and distinct Oromo identity and nationality, which subsumes Booran, Arsi, Macha, Tulama and other intra-Oromo distinctions, is a relatively recent phenomenon. However, it has become a fact that now has political consequences beyond Oromo, indeed across the Horn of Africa, if only because the Oromo are by far the most numerous nation in the Horn. Further, because ethnicity and nationality are never static, and because boundaries are always shifting and open to argument and manipulation, it is not possible to exclude considerations of political advantage and power. Individuals and groups can, and frequently do, change their nationalities and their allegiances, and this is especially true

---

3. Christopher Clapham, on the other hand, holds that the "attempt in recent decades to mobilize an Oromo identity ... has ... been greatly impeded by the diversity of the Oromo experience of incorporation into Ethiopia" (1994:33).

4. Each nationality seems to need to invent its own equivalents to the Imperial Myth of Solomonic descent and of a past Golden Age which will merge into a golden future, and treats the leaden present as an unfortunate aberration.

of pastoralists.[5] Indeed, the adoption and naturalization of non-Oromo has been as distinctive and continuous a feature of Oromo expansion as it was of the Azande or the Alur.

Oromo nationality is recognized by the constitution of the Federal Democratic Republic of Ethiopia, as are those of the other sizeable nationalities. A demarcated territory is recognized within which Afaan Oromo, the Oromo language, is recognized as the official language for use in schools. Indeed, the constitution goes so far as to state that "nations, nationalities and peoples within the state ... shall have the right to establish, at any time, a state of their own." This recognition of national aspirations is a complete reversal of the policies of every previous government of Ethiopia. However, how aspirations to establish "a state of their own" can be achieved is not indicated in the constitution, or in any official document (Brietzke, 1995:28). Certainly, the Ethiopian government has resisted any attempts towards the establishment of an independent Oromia. Many Oromo argue that, in practice, Oromo who work for an independent Oromia run the chance of being arrested and even disappearing. But there are many proud Oromo with strong feelings of national identity who, with varying degrees of enthusiasm, participate actively in the work of government, if only because, like many people in the Horn, they are weary of strife. As Edmond Keller (1995:632) has put it, "although many Oromo have come to expect that they will finally be able to establish their own nationstate, others prefer to take their chances with Greater Ethiopia".

The development of an awareness of Oromo nationality has been extensively documented by the Oromo scholars Mekuria Bulcha, Mohammed Hassan, Asafa Jalata, and others. Herbert Lewis has described the development of Oromo political consciousness from 1958 to 1994 (1996:37–47) based on his experiences in Jimma and Ambo, as following a "classic trajectory" similar to that of nationalisms in many parts of the world. He argues that, though the development of a politically aware Oromo national identity has had its own distinctive attributes, it, nevertheless, shares major characteristics with that of other emergent nationalities. Lewis distinguishes three overlapping phases: the 1950s and early 1960s in which the Oromo were aware of their cultural distinctiveness but lacked "an arena" in which to act; the late 1960s and 1970s when young Oromo were drawn into the modern sector and became aware of the politics of the "Ethiopian nation"; and finally the emergence of an increasing awareness of being discriminated against, of alienation from the centre, and the growth of pan-Oromo political movements. The arrogant abuse of power by Shoan officials and Amhara landlords encouraged opposition from Oromo. Thus, there was a continuing movement in Oromo self-awareness from merely passively knowing that they were a distinctive people occupying a territory which had been colo-

5. See Helland, 1996 on the Gurre and Ajuran; Schlee, 1989 on the pastoralists of northern Kenya; and Bassi, 1997.

nized, to the creation of an active consciousness of being part of an Oromo nation.

Absorption of a localized group identity into that of a wider Oromo national identity seldom required its holders to relinquish residual feelings of Ethiopian identity. The educated had been excluded from participation in national affairs if they did not Amharicize themselves, that is, cease to be Oromo. The great body of Oromo were peasants or pastoralists who were only marginally incorporated into the state and "one couldn't really say that ... country people [in Imperial Ethiopia] participated in a national culture" (Lewis, 1993:165). The Ethiopian state, except as an arbitrary wielder of force and taxation, hardly impacted upon them.[6] Assumption of an Oromo identity hardly required anyone to shake off an Ethiopian one.

My own experiences among Booran and Arsi lead me to follow Lewis in discerning a similar "classic trajectory" to that which he discerned in Jimma and Ambo. When I was first working amongst the Booran in Kenya in 1951, it was my belief, from Tutschek's definition in his dictionary of 1844, that Oromo was "the name by which the Gallas call themselves", from which it followed that Galla was what they were generally known as by outsiders. I saw Galla and Oromo almost as synonyms and did not really take in that Galla was used pejoratively by the Amhara and other northerners. Hodson and Walker's Grammar, on which I largely depended, was entitled *An Elementary and Practical Grammar of the Galla or Oromo Language* (1922). The opening words of its preface are: "In Abyssinia the Oromo, or Galla, language is, perhaps, more widely spoken than any other". Hodson and Walker use the word order "Oromo or Galla" in their text but "Galla or Oromo" in their title, presumably because Galla was the word with which foreign officials and missionaries, for whom they were writing, were most familiar.

Galla was known to Arsi as a name applied to them and many other southern peoples by the Ethiopians. In Kenya, many elders knew "Galla" as the official name given to them by the Kenyan government, a name which they presumed to be just another example of the ignorant ways of that government. The word Oromo was often heard by Booran as Orma, the name of the related Oromo-speaking people of the Tana area of Kenya whom they normally referred to as the Warra' Dai. But they also knew the word Oromo as an indicator of their ancient ethnic ancestry which they shared with other peoples who spoke the same language, such as the Arsi and the Guji. Many men had travelled as far as Addis Ababa as cattle traders and herders and knew that their language was spoken across most of southern Ethiopia. Later I found that the Orma of the Tana River held similar opinions and were equally uninterested in the words Oromo and Galla. Both of these

---

6. It is probably universal that the "peasant looks upon outsiders (including officials) as his enemies" (Bailey, 1966), and especially so if those officials behave in an arrogantly superior way.

groups spoke of their own languages as being Booran or Orma respectively, and not as Oromo. Indeed Booran had an extremely strong sense of their own identity; for example, children and adults who were admonished for bad behaviour would be told that "Booran do not behave like that" or "Booran do not cry", and were instructed to "behave like Booran".

Since that time, which in some ways seems like a lost age of milk and honey, events have brought intense awareness to the Booran of their Oromo nationality. On both sides of the international frontier, they have suffered such damaging losses of grazing and of water that their very survival is threatened, and government interventions affect their lives at every turn (Hogg, 1993; Helland, 1996; and Gufu Oba, 1996). One dramatic indication of the new awareness of an Oromo identity which encompasses their Booran identity is the extremely popular poems of the martyred Booran poet Jarso Waaqo Qoot'o. Taperecorded versions are played and replayed on buses and lorries and in bars and coffee shops (Abdullahi A. Shongolo, 1996). Jarso calls upon the "Oromo masses, the Booran, Arsi and Jaanjamtu ... children of the same mother" to stop fighting each other, as they had done in the past, because "you are all brothers, beware of Goobana".[7] Jarso adapted a traditional Boorana verse form to urge all the Oromo to unite and remain united, as the short extracts below indicate.

> *Long ago social order was disrupted*
> *hence you all separated,*
> *but you are all brothers ...*
>
> *The trunk of Oromo is one,*
> *the branches are spreading wide ...*

The shady oda tree (*Ficus sycomorus*) is a favoured site for, and a potent symbol of, peaceful assemblies, and is the emblem of the OLF.

> *Oromo like a swarm of bees ...*

A recurring image in the poem and an evocative one to Oromo, who are represented as returning to and nurturing their hereditary divine leaders *Kaallu* on whom they all depend.

> *We the Oromo are never apart*
> *we are fathers and brothers and kinsmen.*
> *Bale and Harrar were once far away,*
> *but now they are nearer to Moiyale ...*
>
> *Then let us join hands*
> *to acquaint ourselves with each other,*
> *to rejuvenate[8] our laws,*
> *to rejoin our shoulders together,* [my emphasis]

---

7. i.e., The Quisling Goobana was the Oromo general who under Menelik, incorporated many Oromo areas into the Kingdom of Shoa.

8. *Baayyanachiisaa*, the Oromo word translated here, has the sense of "calming down, feeling better, getting back to normal" after a giddy fit or period of dehydration.

Are our masses aware
that Eritrea is a state,
with only one million inhabitants?

We whose backs have been depressed
by saddles, are thirty one million.

The Booran of the 1990s are fully, if reluctantly and not very successfully, involved both as Oromo and as Booran in current political affairs in Ethiopia and in Kenya. This is an extraordinary change from the early 1950s.

Events have imposed an active consciousness of being Oromo upon the Booran. An informant writes that when the Booran held their great assembly, *Guumi Gaayo*, in September 1996

> ... even the politicians recognised its symbolic and practical implications. The Ethiopian State president, Nagasa, and Oromia's president, Kuma, made themselves available at the ceremony. They came by two helicopters and the Booran were delighted. Nagasa and Kuma came with thousands of *ruufa*,[9] which the Booran saw as a gesture of peace and goodwill on the part of a government they do not care much about. But the educated Boorana were characteristically cautious to be overjoyed by the VIP presence.

Can we identify the cultural and moral components of nationality?

David Miller suggests that two essentials of national identity are shared historical experience and a shared "public culture". The Oromo have shared remarkably similar, though not identical, historical experiences. Their "public culture" has been shaped by "political debate" (Miller, 1996:68–69) for as long as we have records. Regular, periodic, wide-ranging and open discussion of points of public policy, law and custom are a prominent feature of Oromo life (Bassi, 1996a). Marco Bassi's recent monograph *I Borana: Una societa assembleare dell'Etiopia* (1996b) very aptly has on its cover a picture of *kora gosaa*, a clan meeting.

For Oromo, their distinctive national identity is an established fact which is accompanied by moral obligations. The items of shared identity most commonly cited by Oromo are the possession of a common language (whatever the dialect, all Oromo can converse with each other), a shared cosmology, and the respect paid to their generation-set system known as *gaada* and the democratic values it enshrines. "There is no question that the *gaada* system has been the foundation of Oromo civilisation, culture, identity and world view" (Asafa Jalata, 1995:32). Other distinctive features of Oromo culture are a strong democratic ethos and sense of human equality; the absence of strong secular leaders; models of society based on pervasive "levels

---

9. These are short turban lengths of chequered cloth. They are worn by adult men on sacred occasions in memory of the first divine leader *Kaallu*, who was swaddled in one when he was sent to the Booran as blessing from God. In 1951 a travelled Kenya Booran explained to me that the *ruufa* to them was like the Union Jack was to the colonial government.

of dualistic organization" as demonstrated in the *gaada* and moiety systems (Hinnant, 1989); close and enduring similarities of religious ceremony and the customs of sacrifice which underlie them; belief in one manifestation of God, *Waaka*; the maintenance of a flow of prayers and blessings; a tradition of pilgrimages to the Father of Anointment, *Abba Muuda*; the association of men with vigour and virility and the blood of enemies and big game, which complement the association of women with endurance and fertility and the blood of childbirth; clan and descent-group names which span the nation; similar modes of absorbing, adopting and fostering incomers and overrun peoples; very similar complex ritual calendars; a similar range of greetings, blessings and prayers; and distinctive styles of hairdressing according to gender and ritual condition.

The list could be continued, but just to list shared culture traits, and to indicate their presence or absence among the different ancestral subcultures which make up the Oromo, can only be a barren exercise both theoretically and practically (Baxter and Blackhurst, 1978). "It is not so much the objective presence or absence of such items of cultural heritage that matters, but the symbolic weight or presence that such items have" (Banks, 1996:75). If national identity and its associated moral obligations are cultural constructions, the interest and the power of the shared behaviours and beliefs lie in their contexts and their interconnectedness, an examination of which seems a profitable way forward.

Oromo intellectuals, having spent the last twenty-five years claiming and establishing their own national identity, are now turning their attention to ways "to centralise and consolidate the Oromo liberation movements and create Oromo national power that can reinvent an Oromian state and compete and survive in the capitalist world system" (Asafa Jalata, 1995:35). At a recent Oromo conference in Berlin,[10] Yohannes Noggo asserted the struggle was no longer simply to establish their identity and to explain their history to their own people. Their identity is now established and the present struggle is for organization and resources in order to renew and rejuvenate their culture (cf. Jarso's poem above). The extent to which Oromo debates have moved on since the 1970s and 1980s has become clear. Oromo are now confirmed and comfortable in their identity, which is probably why they can afford to have disagreements among themselves. At present, their discussion is on more practical issues, such as the rejuvenation and utilization of the values of the *gaada*, and the problems created by the presence of smaller nationalities both within and without the borders of Oromia.

---

10. I am grateful to Thomas Zitelmann for this information.

Bibliography

Abdullahi A. Shongolo, 1996, "The Poetics of Nationalism; a Poem by Jarso Waaqo Qoot'o", in P.T.W. Baxter et al. (eds.) , *Being and Becoming Oromo: Historical and Anthropological Enquiries.* Uppsala: Nordiska Afrikainstitutet.

Aguilar, M.I., 1996a, "Symbolic Integration to Oromia: Boorana Traditional Practice, Language and God in Eastern Kenya", *The Journal of Oromo Studies,* 3, 1&2: 62–67.

—1996b, "Keeping the 'Peace of the Waso Boorana'", in P.T.W. Baxter et al. (eds.), *Being and Becoming Oromo: Historical and Anthropological Enquiries.* Uppsala: Nordiska Afrikainstitutet.

Asafa Jalata, 1993, *Oromia and Ethiopia; State Formation and Ethnonational Conflict, 1868–1992.* Boulder and London: Lynne Rienner.

—1995, *"Reinventing an Oromian State: A Theoretical Analysis".* Proceedings of the Oromo Studies Association. Washington, DC:31–35.

Bailey, F.G., 1966, "The Peasant View of the Bad Life", *Advancement of Science*: 399–409.

Banks, Marcus, 1996, *Ethnicity: Anthropological Constructions.* London: Routledge.

Bassi, M., 1996a, "Power's Ambiguity or the Political Significance of *Gada*", in P.T.W. Baxter et al. (eds.), *Being and Becoming Oromo: Historical and Anthropological Enquiries.* Uppsala: Nordiska Afrikainstitutet.

—1996b, *I Borana: Una societa assembleare dell'Etiopia.* Milan: Franco Angeli.

—1997, "Returnees in Moyale District, Southern Ethiopia: New Means for an Old Inter-Ethnic Game", in R. Hogg, *Pastoralists, Ethnicity and the State in Ethiopia.* London: Haan Publishing.

Baxter, P.T.W. and H. Blackhurst, 1978, "Vercingetorix in Ethiopia: Some Problems Arising from Levine's Inclusion of the Oromo in his Delineation of Ethiopia as a Culture Area", *Abbay,* 9:159–166.

Baxter, P.T.W., 1983, "The Problem OF the Oromo or the Problem FOR the Oromo?", in I.M. Lewis (ed.), *Nationalism and Self Determination in the Horn of Africa.* London: Ithaca Press.

Baxter, P.T.W, J. Hultin and A. Triulzi (eds.), 1996, *Being and Becoming Oromo: Historical and Anthropological Enquiries.* Uppsala: Nordiska Afrikainstitutet.

Blackhurst, H., 1980, "Ethnicity in Southern Ethiopia: The General and the Particular", *Africa,* 50, 1:55–65.

—1996, "Adopting an Ambiguous Position: Oromo Relationships with Strangers", in P.T.W. Baxter et al. (eds.), *Being and Becoming Oromo: Historical and Anthropological Enquiries.* Uppsala: Nordiska Afrikainstitutet.

Brietzke, P.H., 1995, "Ethiopia's 'leap in the dark': Federalism and Self-Determination in the New Constitution", *Journal of African Law,* 79, 1:19–38.

Clapham, C., 1994, "Ethnicity and the National Question in Ethiopia", in P. Woodward and M. Forsyth (eds.), *Conflict and Peace in the Horn of Africa. Federalism and its Alternatives.* Dartmouth: Aldershot.

Debella, H. and A. Kassem, 1996, "Hawani's Story", in P.T.W. Baxter et al. (eds.), *Being and Becoming Oromo: Historical and Anthropological Enquiries.* Uppsala: Nordiska Afrikainstitutet.

Foot, E.C. , 1913, *A Galla-English, English-Galla Dictionary.* Cambridge: Cambridge University Press.

Gufu Oba, 1996, "Shifting Identities along Resource Borders. Becoming and Continuing to be Boorana Oromo", in P.T.W. Baxter et al. (eds.), *Being and Becoming Oromo: Historical and Anthropological Enquiries*. Uppsala: Nordiska Afrikainstitutet.

Handler, R. and D. Segal, 1996, "National Culture" in *Encyclopedia of Cultural Anthropology*. New York: Henry Holt: 840–44.

Helland, J., 1996, "The Political Viability of Boorana Pastoralism", in P.T.W. Baxter et al. (eds.), *Being and Becoming Oromo: Historical and Anthropological Enquiries*. Uppsala: Nordiska Afrikainstitutet.

Hinnant, J., 1989, "Ritual and Inequality in Guji Dual Organisation", in D. Maybury-Lewis and Uri Almagor (eds.), *The Attraction of Opposites: Thought and Society in the Dualistic Mode*. Ann Arbor: University of Michigan Press.

Hodson, A.W. and C.H. Walker, 1922, *An Elementary and Practical Grammar of the Galla or Oromo Language*. London: Society for the Propagation of Christian Knowledge.

Hogg, R., 1993, "Continuity and Change among the Boran in Ethiopia", in J. Markakis (ed.), *Conflict and the Decline of Pastoralism in the Horn of Africa*. London: Macmillan.

Hultin, J., 1996, "Perceiving Oromo. 'Galla' in the Great Narrative of Ethiopia", in P.T.W. Baxter et al. (eds.), *Being and Becoming Oromo: Historical and Anthropological Enquiries*. Uppsala: Nordiska Afrikainstitutet.

Keller, E., 1995, "The Ethnogenesis of the Oromo Nation and its Implications for Politics in Ethiopia", *The Journal of Modern African Studies*, 33, 4:621–34.

King, C., 1996, "Fellow Feelings", A review of David Miller's *On Nationality*, in *Times Literary Supplement*, 10 May, 4–5.

Lewis, H.S., 1993, "Ethnicity in Ethiopia: the View from Below (and from the South, East, and West)", in Crawford Young (ed.), *The Rising Tide of Cultural Pluralism: The Nation-State at Bay?* Wisconsin: University of Wisconsin Press.

Lonsdale, J., 1992, "The Moral Economy of Mau Mau: Wealth, Poverty and Civic Virtue in Kikuyu Political Thought", in Bruce Berman and John Lonsdale (eds.), *Unhappy Valley: Conflict in Kenya and Africa*. London: James Currey.

Mekuria Bulcha, 1996, "The Survival and Reconstruction of Oromo National Identity", in P.T.W. Baxter et al. (eds.), *Being and Becoming Oromo: Historical and Anthropological Enquiries*. Uppsala: Nordiska Afrikainstitutet.

Miller, D., 1996, *On Nationality*. Oxford: Oxford University Press.

Mohammed Hassen, 1996, "The Development of Oromo Nationalism", in P.T.W. Baxter et al. (eds.), *Being and Becoming Oromo: Historical and Anthropological Enquiries*. Uppsala: Nordiska Afrikainstitutet.

Richards, C.G., 1996, "No Carpet on the Floor", *African Research and Documentation*, 71, 1–32.

Schlee, G., 1989, *Identities on the Move. Clanship and Pastoralism in Northern Kenya*. Manchester: Manchester University Press.

—1994, "Ethnicity Emblems, Diacritical Features, Identity Markers: Some African Examples", in David Brokensha (ed.), *A River of Blessings*. New York: Maxwell School of Citizenship and Public Affairs, Syracuse University.

Triulzi, A., 1996, "United and Divided; Boorana and Gabaro among the Macha Oromo in Western Ethiopia", in P.T.W. Baxter et al. (eds.), *Being and Becoming Oromo: Historical and Anthropological Enquiries*. Uppsala: Nordiska Afrikainstitutet.

Tutschek, C., 1844 and 1845, *Dictionary of the Galla Language*. Munich: published privately.

Waller, R., 1993, "Conclusions", in Thomas Spear and Richard Waller (eds.), *Being Maasai; Ethnicity and Identity in East Africa*. London: James Currey.

Zitelmann, T., 1994, *Nation der Oromo: Kollektive Identitäten, nationale Konflikte, WirGruppenbildungen*. Berlin: Das Arabische Buch.

—1996, "Re-Examining the Galla/Oromo Relationship. The Stranger as a Structural Topic", in P.T.W. Baxter et al. (eds.), *Being and Becoming Oromo: Historical and Anthropological Enquiries*. Uppsala: Nordiska Afrikainstitutet.

Power and the Discourse of Ethnicity in Sudan

Jay O'Brien

This chapter considers the discrepant systems of ideas that Europeans and Africans respectively brought to their encounter in nineteenth and twentieth century Sudan. Specifically, the link between the dominant colonial European conceptions of race, culture and identity and the indigenous Sudanese conceptions and realities are examined, with particular reference to their embodiment in the ethnic structure assumed by the agricultural labour market. Although the colonial order did fragment society along ethnic lines and compose a corresponding discourse of difference, Sudanese communities responded with cultural creativity that preserved space for resistance. The struggle over the discourse of ethnicity and nationality continues to be a key part of Sudan's political conflicts.

British ideas of race and ethnicity

The conceptual framework that the British brought to understanding the peoples over whom they sought to rule in Sudan was essentialist and Darwinian. They were inclined to sort the Sudanese into a congeries of distinct, bounded and unique communities which could be classified along a series of social evolutionary stages (Johnson and Anderson, 1988). Thus, "hunters" were viewed as the most "primitive", followed by "pastoralists" and then "cultivators."

The social realities the British actually encountered in Sudan were, of course, a good deal more complex, and thus much interpretation was required before they could be made to fit this evolutionist schema. Groups were so fluid as to unsettle administrators when they attempted to impose a grid of fixed boundaries around "tribes" for purposes of administration through "indirect rule". The members of many communities engaged in varying mixes of the three subsistence types, rather than adhersing to the one corresponding to their supposed level of sociocultural attainment. The mixes varied locally, depending on climate, available resources and other factors. In some communities, all individuals might engage in cultivation, herding and foraging at different times. Elsewhere, communities tended to specialize in one subsistence mode and related communities specialized in complementary activities, while goods and personnel moved back and forth among them.

Europeans tended to see such situations as the result of various recent "outside" influences, and generally sought to determine the essential character of each group by working out which subsistence activity was properly theirs. Thus, Evans-Pritchard (1940) determined that the Nuer were essentially pastoralists, even if many Nuer communities derived much of their diet from fishing and cultivating crops. He then sought to explain their basic cultural values and fundamental way of life in terms of this pastoral essence, and presented their cultivation, fishing, hunting and collecting activities as temporarily necessitated by the intrusions of Arabs and British, or by ecological stresses such as floods, rinderpest, etc.

More generally, several processes were seen to operate among the Sudanese to cause such a mixing of subsistence activities belonging to different evolutionary stages and resulting in the blurring of cultural boundaries. The most significant of these were Arabization, Islamization, racial degradation, acculturation and civilization (or modernization). All these processes were seen to work through some sort of contagion. In general, contact with "advanced" cultures was thought to lead "backward" groups, more or less automatically, to become more like the advanced. Thus, pastoralists exposed to farmers on a regular basis would gradually become cultivators themselves, adopting the associated beliefs and behaviour and thereby achieving a higher level of advancement.

Implicit in this approach is a contradictory cluster of cultural conceptions. On the European side, "culture" was an aspect of "civilization". Accordingly, the concept embraced all those higher intellectual, moral and aesthetic processes still commonly referred to as "high culture". Not all peoples had civilizations in this sense, and Africans in particular were considered to lack them (see Asad, 1973). In the absence of great intellectual advancements characteristic of "civilization" and, consequently, the technology and other means required to elevate peoples above the daily struggle for subsistence, Africans were seen by Europeans to have a very different sort of culture, much simpler sets of ideas and lives based on their distinctive subsistence modes. Such cultures were not considered to embody a creatively conscious process, but were simply the extrasomatic accoutrements of the modes of subsistence corresponding to precivilization levels of sociocultural evolution.

With respect to the Sudan, the twin processes of Arabization and Islamization were seen as the most dominant, widespread, and potentially troublesome influences at the time of the British conquest (Spaulding and Kapteijns, 1991). While orthodox Western thought viewed Arab/Islamic civilization as stagnant and decadent, it nevertheless recognized it as a civilization far more advanced than the "backward" cultures of "subsistence-oriented" African communities. It thus regarded African groups as prone to become Arabized and Islamized more or less automatically by prolonged exposure to Arab Muslims.

Another process was seen to be working in reverse. "Advanced" groups, Arabs in particular, were thought to become degraded through intimate forms of intercourse with people of "lower" stock, that is, through miscegenation. MacMichael's books (1912, 1922) traced the Arabization of Sudan by investigating the pedigree of tribes claiming to be Arab. He judged the genealogies of some to be impeccable, but viewed others as degraded through interbreeding with Africans. He portrayed yet others as upstart Africans adopting a veneer of Arab culture in order to "pass" as their Arab "betters". Thus, the "Arab element" of the Gawa'ma'a, according to MacMichael, came to central Kordofan in the sixteenth or seventeenth centuries, but "the Gawa'ma'a are a much debased race and are flattered to an even greater extent than usual in Sudan by the denomination of Arab" (1912:76). The central idea here is that Arab "genes" or "blood" became diluted through mixture with the "genes" or "blood" of "lower" races, to the point that the supposed higher qualities of Arabness were lost.

British ideas about cultural and racial matters shaped the attitudes of most British individuals towards the Sudanese, and provided much of the rationale and intellectual framework for the administration of Sudan. But they also shaped academic discourse about Sudan and Africa in enduring ways. Johnson and Anderson (1988) have analyzed the lasting impact of crude Darwinism on academic understanding of African subsistence patterns and ethnicity. Spaulding and Kapteijns (1991) have shown the dominant role Orientalist notions of "Arabization" and "Islamization" played in the academic reconstruction of Sudanese history since the middle ages. While the crudely racist notions of racial debasement found in the works of early imperial apologists such as MacMichael have long been shed by respectable scholars, the critical studies just mentioned show the lingering legacy of the larger intellectual heritage.

While these ideas were also applied to other regions of the world (North America for example, see Pearce, 1988), it was Africa that became the field for the greatest elaboration of crude Darwinism. In Africa, as elsewhere, these ideas articulated with more general features of Western social thought. As Eric Wolf has shown, Western social science has been preoccupied with dividing its subject matter into distinctive cases, or societies, "each with its characteristic culture, conceived as an integrated and bounded system, set off against equally bounded systems" (1982:4). Wolf concludes from this that:

> By endowing nations, societies, or cultures with the qualities of internally homogeneous and externally distinctive and bounded objects, we create a

model of the world as a global pool hall in which the entities spin off each other like so many hard and round billiard balls. (Wolf, 1982:6)

What is missing is an appreciation of the interconnectedness of social and cultural phenomena and historical contingency, internal differentiation, and the fluidity of the units which present themselves for analysis at any particular moment.

Culture and identity in Sudan

The ethnic terms in which the agricultural labour force came to be structured in colonial Sudan were framed in the context of capitalist incorporation. The pattern of incorporation into the agricultural wage-labour force mirrored differences between groups which both participants and observers generally conceived in terms of cultural differences among them. If one knew a person's ethnic identification, one could fairly reliably predict what form her or his incorporation would take, including the type, pattern and intensity of work. The result was a highly segmented labour force structured in terms of ethnic identification.

However, it was not a simple matter of cultural determination of social forms. Indeed, once incorporation had become widespread, the process moved in the other direction, from social form to ethnic identity. Employers who sought labour of a particular type wanted first of all to know which ethnic groups provided it, and then tended to go to the villages where those ethnic groups were known to live in order to recruit. The labour files of the Sudan Plantations Syndicate in the Gezira Scheme are filled with messages from inspectors requesting workers of the particular ethnicity they deemed most suitable to the type of work needing to be done. Workers who sought work of the particular type found it necessary or convenient to be in the villages where they could expect potential employers to look for them. In this way, an ethnic template of a very particular sort was imposed on Sudan's social geography.

Not one but many ethnic processes were at work. The dynamics of each derived from the specific interaction of local characteristics and capitalist encroachment. In rural areas the social composition of a particular ethnic identity tended to be more or less heterogeneous, but took its central character from a predominant form of market participation. In urban areas and some rural trading centres, a more narrowly occupational definition of ethnic identity—or ethnic definition of occupational identity—occurred. In both situations, access to certain positions in the labour force and labour market tended to become regulated by ethnic identity, often involving substantial cultural change. Whether through coalescence and synthesis of a new identity, assimilation and accommodation of individuals and small groups to shifting established identities, or through other means, people came to participate in labour migration circuits and other markets as "ethnics" of a particular sort.

The ethnic segmentation of the Sudanese labour market and the ethnic processes associated with its development corresponded to specific conditions of capitalist expansion, and were not some legacy of age-old ethnic identities. Not only did new ethnicities arise and old ones change or disappear, but the very principles of their organization and differentiation underwent profound transformation. Much to the frustration of colonial and postcolonial administrations, Sudanese ethnic groups did not show the fixed and bounded nature of the billiard ball model.

Though it is hazardous to speculate about the nature of ethnic processes in precolonial Sudan, it seems likely that they were not subject to a single dominant social force such as capital, as was later the case. It also seems most likely that group identities were centripetal and hierarchical rather than boundary-oriented and horizontal (cf., Anderson, 1991:15): that is to say, they depended more on shifting linkages to power centres, than on ancient traditions of membership in a group with a fixed name and residence (see Abdel Ghaffar, 1977). Some identities, including Arab, were conceived genealogically and not in the "blood" metaphor of the British. Thus, it sufficed to count a bona fide male Arab, however remote in time, in one's ancestry to count oneself legitimately as an Arab.

Alternatively, many ethnic labels were used to describe ways of life: "Arab" referred to the nomadic pastoralists and "Baggara" referred to cattle keepers. Such openness was not incompatible with the prestige accorded to descendants of the Prophet or the more illustrious Arabian tribes. On the other hand, this situation also meant that people had several potential ethnic identities they could use, or genealogically defined social groups they could claim membership of, and hence, regional and occupational identities that could be mobilized in similar ways. Abdel Ghaffar (1977) has analyzed some of these phenomena for central Sudan, and Evans-Pritchard described something of the sort for the Nuer under the heading of the "children of the girls" (Evans-Pritchard, 1940:226-27). In contrast to the fixed notions of identity with which the British approached Sudan's social landscape, Sudanese ideas tended to emphasize genealogy and phenotype and to be very fluid. Racial classification was generally based on an individual's appearance rather than on biological parentage, and it would have seemed absurd to assert that a person who appeared one colour was really another.

Before the British imposed the system of native administration on rural Sudan, it was not difficult to change tribal or cultural identities. Anthropologists have often been told by Nuer, Gawa'ma'a, Baggara, etc., of members of their community who "used to be" Dinka, Fellata, Fur before they became Nuer, Gawa'ma'a, Baggara. The speakers were not speaking metaphorically: they literally meant that someone who was Fur is now

Baggara. It is only their essentialist, genotypical preconceptions that lead Europeans to regard such talk as prevarication or metaphor.

When I was carrying out research in a Gawa'ma'a village in north Kordofan in 1977, the village *shaykh* propounded a theory of power centres and affiliation remarkably similar to that outlined by Abdel Ghaffar (1977). He also defended the Gawa'ma'a's claims to Arab descent, in spite of MacMichael's contrary opinion based in part on the dark skin colour of most Gawa'ma'a. He attributed dark skin to long residence in harsh conditions, claiming that my Sudanese field assistants' colouration had darkened two shades, from red to green, that I had darkened from white to red, and that we would all grow darker yet if we remained long in the village (O'Brien, 1980). It is clear that popular Sudanese ideas about culture, race, etc., provide important clues about the way sociocultural processes in Sudan may have differed, and may now differ, from the Western models employed to study them.

There is more involved here than divergent European and Sudanese cultural models. Conceptions change over time: as the social realities are created to interpret change, they interact and influence one another. At any moment in time, contending social groups may embrace conflicting conceptions of the basis of identification. There can be no doubt, for example, that some Sudanese elites who were educated by the British and worked in close association with them developed cultural and racial conceptions that came closer to British ideas than to traditional Sudanese ideas. Indeed, such conceptions have dominated much of Sudanese public discourse since well before independence in 1956.

This was made clear in the first act the Sudanese legislative assembly was empowered to formulate, the 1948 *Nationality Act*. It defined citizenship in terms of membership (by descent) in ethnic groups living within the territorial boundaries established for the Anglo-Egyptian Condominium in 1898. In contrast to the policies of many countries, being born on Sudanese soil, even to parents born in Sudan, did not entitle a person to citizenship in the absence of the proper ethnic qualification. In practice, it often became sufficient to be acknowledged as a member of an Arab tribe to be accorded the rights and privileges of citizenship. In contrast, admitting to (or sometimes even being suspected of) membership of an ethnic group thought to have originated in West Africa and generally regarded as not Sudanese, was often sufficient to disqualify a claim to Sudanese citizenship, even for people whose families and lineages had established themselves in what came to be Sudan well before British conquest.

The Zabarma people of Um Fila and other villages in the Rahad region are a case in point. When tenancies in the new Rahad irrigation scheme were allocated to farmers in 1976, all Zabarma who had not already secured nationality certificates were denied them, despite the fact that their ancestors had settled in Sudan in the middle of the nineteenth century. When sympathetic officials encouraged Zabarma men to be listed as Arabs so that they might be eligible, they refused. When three adult men in Um Fila claimed membership of Arab tribes, they were granted tenancies without having to prove citizenship. Neither the abolition of native administration in 1964, nor the exclusion of questions about ethnicity from the 1973 census, altered the fact that ethnicity, defined in a rigid and essentialist way, was a fundamental aspect of postcolonial government policy.

It was under such pressure that some marginalized communities "discovered" their "Arabness" in the decades following independence. Their public declarations usually included reference to genealogical research allegedly showing that some wandering Arab holy man or merchant had at some point in the past settled in their community, marrying or otherwise fathering the offspring from whom group members are said to be descended. Observers sometimes scoff at such declarations in the manner of MacMichael, arguing that the people concerned have simply been tinkering with their genealogies in order to acquire more prestige. Without denying that such things happen, it should also be pointed out that knowledge of actual Arab ancestors could have existed within given communities for generations without prompting members to assume or promote an Arab identity. When being seen as non-Arab became a liability, communities might well reassess the significance of this aspect of their heritage.

Such reassessment is but one aspect of the dynamism of the processes of identification, ethnic and otherwise. The stuff of identities in any given context may also be read differently by different actors. What may to one person be nothing more than family ties, market relations, or occupational facts of life, may be read by others as marks—as indelible as tribal scars—of membership of a particular ethnic group. How many of the people in western Sudan who identified themselves to others as "Baggara" simply meant that they herded cattle for a living, but were heard instead to affirm an ethnic identity? Even when people on one or both sides are aware of the discrepancy in meanings, which meaning will prevail depends on the relationship of the discourse on ethnicity and identity to prevailing power relations.

Social crises and conflicts that focus attention on issues of identity and values complicate the dynamics of association and identification. So too does the perceived social position of interlocutors and audiences for identity statements. Mohamed Salih (1994) has argued that it is the perception by both supporters and opponents of the leadership of the SPLM/SPLA (Sudan Peoples Liberation Movement/Sudan Peoples Liberation Army) as ethnic Dinka that determines how their policy statements and actions are read. Despite official statements that the SPLM/SPLA seeks a unified Sudan, many rural Dinka see the movement as an organization defending their interests in opposition to the competing interests of other ethnic groups. Its opponents have from the start seen the SPLM/SPLA as a southern Sudanese separatist movement.

Under the current Islamist regime in the Sudan, religion has come to play the central role in discussion of identity, but still in a way that anchors identity to essentialist notions of ethnicity. This is perhaps clearest in discussions of the rights of non-Muslim people under an Islamic government. Members of historically Muslim ethnic groups are effectively Muslims in legal terms regardless of their beliefs (through the law against apostasy), and members of historically non-Muslim groups may be exempted from Islamic law in provinces which have been predominantly non-Muslim historically. Officially, these problems are found in the south and the exempted people are "southerners" whose rights are regarded as protected as long as "their" province is exempt. This is the case even if they are not personally able to enjoy that protection because they reside in the northern provinces where many may have been born.

Even liberal voices promoting Sudanese national reconciliation tend to conceive ethnicity and identity in essentialist and genetic terms. Francis Deng, for example, in fiction (1986) as well as in scholarly work (1995), portrays the identities embraced by dominant groups in Sudan and the repression of other identities as a case of collective false consciousness. He maintains that the Sudanese people and their culture are hybrids of African and Arab parentage, and that as soon as the warring parties realize this fact, forswear purist pretensions, and recognize their Afro-Arab brotherhood, conflicts of identity will cease. The vision that Deng expresses veers between the rigidly genetic and the messianic.

Imagining new communities

The principles for national reconciliation drafted at a meeting of Sudan's leading progressive intellectuals were laid down in broad strokes. They sketched the basis for a unified nation, which they call "The New Sudan". Here, a community "conceived as a deep, horizontal comradeship" (Anderson, 1991:7) was envisaged to replace the Sudanese nation that has been torn apart by decades of oppression and civil war. It was based on the principles that, 1) the Sudan has never historically emerged as one nation. It is a multinational and multicultural country. Thus no particular nationality, whatever its size, has the right to impose its own identity on the others; 2) national identity is not based on social, cultural or geographical locality but on the principle of citizenship; 3) successive regimes have failed to recognize the country's diversity. This failure has led to the one-dimensional nature of Sudanese nationalism as reflected in the political, economic, cultural and social dominance by one nationality that denies other nationalities the right to develop; and 4) thus the necessity emerges to promote of a new cultural outlook conducive to creating an environment for mutual interaction between the cultures of the various nationalities (Ambo Workshop, 1989:173).

According to these guidelines, national identity is to be based on the inclusive principle of citizenship rather than on exclusivist ethnic identities. Yet, as points 3 and 4 tacitly acknowledge, "citizenship" is a rather amorphous attribute that does not define any particular national identity when severed from the ethnic qualifications of the 1948 *Nationality Law*. Point 4 offers a "new cultural outlook" rather than a new Sudanese cultural formation, which remains ambiguous in its implications for national identity. Subsequent points set out the key rights and freedoms demanded for Sudan's citizens, such as freedom of religion guaranteed by a secular state, the emancipation of women, etc. Nevertheless, it remains unclear how the past exclusion of certain ethnicities from the Sudanese nation is to be rectified. Mohamed Salih's (1994) analysis of rank-and-file perceptions of an ethnic message behind nationalist forms of SPLA/SPLM rhetoric suggests that much work is needed to prepare the ground for a successful discourse on citizenship.

The Sudanese Peoples Liberation Movement, in a paper prepared for the same workshop, emphasized many of the same rights and freedoms of democratic citizenship in its formulation of a new Sudanese national identity. However, the paper is less ambiguous about culture, which it sees as central to the identity it wishes to promote. The SPLM/SPLA sees Sudanese culture as "essentially a product of historical development" (1989:84), and goes on to argue that

> ... its African and Arab identity factors, their respective cultures in addition to Islam, Christianity and other traditional beliefs some of the citizens observe and practice, are influences that do not exist in isolation from each other. These are elements which over the ages have been inextricably interwoven into the fabric of our society. They are strands that have fused together to form an integral whole that cannot be represented or denoted by any one particular constituent element ... The diverse nationalities making up Sudan can and will have to coalesce into a Sudanese Nation (National Formation) with its own distinct civilisation and with the capacity to contribute in its own right to the enrichment of Human Civilisation rather than merely serve as an appendage of other nations. (SPLM/ SPLA 1989:84-85)

Both documents emphasize building a national community free of domination and oppression and contributing to some sort of supranational, global civilization. It is understandable that the wording of the first document should emphasize citizenship and cultural "outlook" and tiptoe around the issue of national identity, while the second more or less asserts fusion of the many cultures of Sudan into a single national culture as accomplished fact, in this way resembling Deng's viewpoint. These are documents produced in an effort to end a civil war. They bear the mark of these origins in their programmatic and optimistic formulation, but they do represent promising starting points. Serious discussion of culture and identity can only begin when conditions for peaceful discussion have been created. When that time comes, much real work will remain to be done before the legacy of the modernist conceptions of culture and difference brought to Sudan by Western social thought can be effectively challenged. Notions of cultural identity as closed and exclusive and of cultural difference as radical and irreducible will not do. Open and inclusive conceptions of ethnicity, such as the ones articulated at the Ambo workshop and the traditional ideas of rural Sudan, provide more promising starting points for approaching cultural conflicts.

Bibliography

Abdel Ghaffar Mohamed Ahmed, 1977, "'Tribal' Elite: A Base for Social Stratification in Sudan", *Sudan Journal of Economic and Social Studies*, 2, 1:21–30.

Ambo Workshop, 1989, Annex 11, "Ambo Workshop on Sudan: Problems and Prospects", in M.A. Abdel Ghaffar and Gunnar M. Sørbø (eds.), *Management of the Crisis in Sudan*. Bergen: Centre for Development Studies, University of Bergen.

Anderson, Benedict, 1991, *Imagined Communities*. London and New York: Verso.

Asad, Talal, 1973, "Two European Images of non-European Rule", in T. Asad (ed.), *Anthropology and the Colonial Encounter*. London: Ithaca Press.

Deng, Francis 1986, *Seed of Redemption: A Political Novel*. New York: Lilian Barber.

—1995, *War of Visions: Conflict of Identities in the Sudan*. Washington, DC: Brookings Institution.

Evans-Pritchard, E.E., 1940, *The Nuer*. Oxford: Oxford University Press.

Johnson, Douglas and David Anderson (eds.), 1988, *Strategies of Survival*. London: Lester Crook, and Boulder: Westview Press.

MacMichael, H.A., 1912, *The Tribes of Northern and Central Kordofan*. Cambridge: Cambridge University Press.

—1922, *A History of the Arabs in Sudan*, 2 vols. Cambridge: Cambridge University Press.

Mohamed Salih, M.A., 1994, "The Ideology of the Dinka and the Sudan People's Liberation Movement", in K. Fukui and J. Markakis (eds.), *Ethnicity and Conflict in the Horn of Africa*. London: James Currey.

O'Brien, Jay 1980, "*Agricultural Labor and Development in Sudan*". Ph.D. dissertation, University of Connecticut.

Pearce, Roy Harvey, 1988 (1953), *Savagism and Civilisation*. Rev. ed. Berkeley: University of California Press.

Spaulding, Jay and Lidwien Kapteijns, 1991, "The Orientalist Paradigm in the Historiography of the Late Pre-colonial Sudan", in J. O'Brien and B. Roseberry (eds.), *Golden Ages, Dark Ages*. Berkeley: University of California Press.

Sudan Peoples Liberation Movement and Sudan Peoples Liberation Army (SPLM/SPLA), Department of Information, 1989, "On the New Sudan", in M.A. Abdel Ghaffar and Gunnar M. Sørbø (eds.), *Management of the Crisis in Sudan*. Bergen: Centre for Development Studies, University of Bergen.

Sudan Government, 1956, *The Laws of Sudan*. Khartoum: Sudan Government.

Wolf, Eric, 1982, *Europe and the People without History*. Berkeley: University of California Press.

Political Narratives and Identity Formation in post-1989 Sudan

M.A. Mohamed Salih

Introduction

This chapter is concerned with the policies of the National Islamic Front (NIF) and their consequences for post-1989 identity formation in the Sudan. It attempts to describe and explain the ways in which a variety of discourses (Islamic, non-Islamic, Arabic, Afro-Arab and African) have been consciously used in the Sudan as pointers to specific identity forms. The historical background against which this occurs is, of course, the turbulent relationship between north and south in the country.

The history of this relationship is one of increasing hostility and escalating violence. At the beginning, in the early 1960s, there was the so-called *Anya nya* rebellion which was brought to a negotiated end in 1972 by the Addis Ababa Agreement. This granted the south regional autonomy within a united Sudan, and a semblance of stability prevailed for a decade.

Civil war resumed in 1983, following the introduction of Islamic *sharia* laws by the Numeri regime (1969–85), which violated the spirit of the Addis Ababa Agreement. The subsequent division of the south into three regions (Equatoria, Bahr Al-Ghazal and Upper Nile) was a further gross violation of the letter of the Agreement, which granted the whole of the south regional autonomy under a single regional government. The government was dominated by northerners, leading to the accretion of grievances. Accumulated southern grievances included the lack of serious attempts to implement socioeconomic development programmes in the south and the decision to build the Jongolei canal in the south: this would have diverted the White Nile waters away from grazing lands and permanent settlements. Finally, there was the refusal of the northern regime to consult with the south over the exploitation of oil in that region. The civil war resumed in 1983 when a new southern movement, the Sudan Peoples Liberation Army (SPLA) was founded under the leadership of Colonel John Garang. Unlike the *Anya nya*, the SPLA presented itself as a Sudanese national movement whose goal was to liberate the Sudan political system by eliminating northern dominance.

The collapse of the Numeri regime was followed by a brief period (1986–89) of parliamentary rule, which came to an end in June 1989 with the military coup inspired by the National Islamic Front (NIF), the political wing of the Muslim Brotherhood which has been active in Sudanese politics for years. A few months later, the displaced political forces in the north coalesced in opposition abroad in a movement called the National Democratic Alliance (NDA). The NDA consists of a dozen political parties and many professional associations and trade unions. After several years of tortuous negotiations, it was joined in 1995 by the SPLA and four regional movements representing the Beja, Nuba, Fur and Zaghawa ethnic groups in the north. By this time, the SPLA had suffered several splits in its ranks, when some of its leading figures formed their own breakaway factions (see below). Subsequent confusion reigned in the south. The main body of the SPLA remained under the leadership of Colonel Garang and entered into an alliance with the NDA. The breakaway factions initially advocated southern secession, but later allied themselves with the NIF regime in Khartoum.

Peace declarations and agreements notwithstanding, the nature of the opposition to the NIF regime is anything but clear. The northerners, dominant in the NDA, obviously seek to overthrow the NIF regime because it seized state power by force and is using Islamic fundamentalism to create a new base for political mobilization from which they would be permanently excluded.

The initial credo of the SPLA was to reform the political system of the Sudan radically by ridding it of the political forces that had dominated the country since independence, to wit, the very same forces banded in the NDA. The SPLA under Garang has not renounced this goal. However, it has also brought the issue of self-determination for the south to the top of its political agenda and succeeded in persuading the NDA to accept it. The basis for cooperation in opposition seems to be agreement on the restoration of democracy and the right to self-determination for the south. Ironically, confronted with military setbacks in the south, the NIF also paid lip service to the principle of self-determination as a basis for solving the problem of southern Sudan.

Arabism in NIF narrative and the African Sudanese response

This section treats the discourse of Arabism as it appears in the NIF political narrative. It refers to writings, political speeches and pronouncements by the NIF leadership, and explores their implications for a multicultural, multiethnic and multireligious country like the Sudan. It also treats attempts by the non-Arab, that is, African elite to engage and hence subvert the discourse of Arabism.

On 30 June 1989, the Revolutionary Command Council for National Salvation declared that "the coup has a pan-Arab orientation, not to the left nor to the right; non-partisan and non-factionalist; non-May [Numeri], non-tribalist and non-racial". In an interview with the newspaper *Al-Khlij* (15 July 1989), the leader of the military junta, Lt. Gen. Al-Bashir stated that

> I would not object to the separation of Southern Sudan if the people so de-
> cided. If the southern parties failed to agree on a solution to the problem of
> the South, it means that we will not reach a final settlement. If they agree on
> separation, we will not object to that. If they agree on a federal system, we
> will not object, or if they agree to a regional system, or think that the South
> could be one province, we would not object to that. What is important is that
> they should agree on a formula for a solution, and we are ready to accept it.

The NIF government is keen to correlate the division between north and south with the distinction between Arab and African, while also associating Islam with Arabism. It proclaimed 1990 as the "Year of Africa" in the Sudan, the implication being that Sudan's status as an African entity is not taken for granted. In October 1992, the NIF appointed a council of nine members, known as *majlis al shura* (consultative council) lead by Hassan Al-Turabi, the leader of the National Islamic Front and the regime's chief ideologue. The only non-Arab member was Ali Al-Haj Mohamed, an African from Darfur.

The NIF reliance on Islam (as an ideology) was evident in Turabi's London lecture on Nationhood (1992a), in which he argued that

> ... the ideal of *Islam is one of freely associating social groups united by common de-*
> *scent, custom, domicile, interest or moral purpose* [emphasis original]. These
> should be federated as social constellations or as geographic conglomerations
> with due regard to the particularity of each and the integrity of the whole,
> and with intricate equilibration of the immediate local community, the inter-
> mediate regional composite and the distant universal collectivity. Islam in this
> particular case is seen as an ethnic faith which differentiates clearly between
> Muslims according to their race.

Al-Bashir's and Al-Turabi's remarks assume that pan-Arabism is nontribal and nonracial, a false assumption that ignores the consciousness of the oppressed that the NIF uses military force to translate the cultural domi-nance of Arabism into economic and political dominance. In this situation, the definition of where cultural dominance starts and where political and economic dominance ends is very blurred. According to Deng (1995: 411), the result of these ambiguities is that an unacknowledged racial cleavage remains unbridged and is indeed deepened by the elites on both sides, one building on a fictional notion of Arabism, the other responding by an equally fictional notion of Africanism, both overlooking the realities of Sudanism.

As to the association between Islam and racism in the Sudan, Harir has illustrated this by narrating the story of Bolad, a long-time friend from Darfur, who left the NIF and joined the SPLA in the struggle for the "New

Sudan". Bolad was captured by the government-allied Baggara Arab forces (in the warzone in Darfur), tortured and killed. Harir (1993:307) argues that the NIF did not spare Bolad's life because, as an African from Darfur he had decided to abandon an anti-African, exclusive and racist northern Sudanese river project .

It is the association of Arabism and Islam, the cornerstone of NIF policies, that has persuaded many non-Arab Muslims in the north, among them the Fur of western Sudan, the Nuba of south Kordofan, and the Beja in the east to resist the regime's nation-building project. While NIF ideology may resonate among ethnic groups that claim Arab ancestry, it is seen by African Muslims and non-Muslims as an attempt to maintain the economic and political dominance of Arabs in the Sudan.

Significantly, the NIF Arab-Muslim narrative has strengthened the resolve of the African element, the majority in the Sudan, to counter the project which would deny them claims to a Sudanese identity. The marginalized ethnic groups that joined the SPLA took up arms against the regime as part of the struggle of the oppressed for an alternative Sudanese identity outside the Arab-Islam framework of the NIF. In a sense, force has become an important factor in current Sudanese identity formation. Deng (1995:482) has rightly argued that

> ... because of the decisive role of power in shaping identities, the equations of military power in the civil war are in themselves significant factors in the prospects of redefining the national identity. The fact that the South has fought for nearly forty years and has become militarily strong over the years gives credibility to the identity for which it is fighting.

It is not surprizing that the regime's call for *jihad* (holy war) elicited a military response from its intended victims. Southerners consider the very notion of *jihad* as a form of military imposition of an Arab-Muslim identity on African non-Muslims and African Muslims alike. The marginalized groups, therefore, struggle to subvert the NIF project in order to free themselves from Arab-Muslim hegemony. According to the late Ruay (1994:176), an activist from southern Sudan, "the fundamentalist regime has vowed to wage a *jihad* against the South. But at the end of the day, the Southerners are destined to win for no power under the sun can wipe out the will of a determined people, although it will be a very costly victory".

At the discourse level, it is argued elsewhere (Mohamed Salih, 1998) that as part of the struggle for recognition of distinct identities, marginalized ethnic groups are resistant to political integration into the dominant ethnonationalist identities. The marginalized ethnic groups negate NIF Arab-Islamist discourse for fear of losing out in the "national" definition of the identity according to which Sudan would be reconstructed on a different ideological and political basis. In short, the NIF's insistence that Sudan should constitute a homogeneous political entity as part of the Arab nation, with Islam as its ideology, has sparked political and military resistance, thus contributing to the further militarization of the country. The more northern politicians define the Sudan as an Arab nation with Islam as its religion, the more the Africans, Muslim and non-Muslim, continue to develop their military capacity to resist (Mohamed Salih, 1995). In the absence of a meaningful dialogue to solve the nationality question, military power will continue to play a significant role in the formation of diverse Sudanese national identities.

Militarization and the significance of narratives

Although the NIF regime inherited the current civil war from its predecessors, a full-fledged militarization of Sudanese society began in earnest with the promulgation of the Popular Defence Forces (PDF) Law in 1989. This set up a paramilitary force whose objectives are to train men and women in civil and military tasks, to raise their level of security consciousness, and instil military discipline so that they can cooperate with the regular armed forces and security services. The establishment of the PDF followed a practice initiated by the government of Sadig Al-Mahdi (1986–89). Tribal militias were formed in 1986 to serve in the war against the SPLA and were responsible for atrocities committed against communities in southern Sudan (Mohamed Salih, 1989, 1995; Mohamed Salih and Harir, 1994).

The PDF recruited officers among young professionals and students associated with the Muslim Brotherhood. According to the regime's propaganda, the PDF is waging *jihad* to halt Christian expansion in central Africa (El-Affendi, 1993). The reconstruction of the concept of *jihad* in the NIF's narrative is illustrated by the so-called wedding of the martyr (*urs al shaheed*). Members of the PDF refuse to marry in the expectation of marrying in paradise; that is after they become martyrs. They reject marrying earthly women, *huur al-dunia* (dark-eyed virgins of the earth), in their eagerness to marry *huur al jinana* (dark-eyed virgins of paradise). Families are expected to treat the death of their loved ones in the *jihad* with jubilation, and should not mourn, since death is *urs al shaheed* (the wedding of the martyr), which should be celebrated.

The creation of PDFs has drastically changed the composition of the Sudanese military establishment. By 1996, the PDF vastly outnumbered the regular army, whose officer ranks were drastically depleted by repeated purges. Table 1 below shows that the PDFs represent more than 50 per cent of the Sudanese armed forces.

The invocation of *jihad* by the NIF regime is not directed solely at the south, where Christianity was introduced during the colonial period and later became associated with southern resistance to northern domination. Nor is it solely directed at the SPLA, which has made the abolition of *sharia* a precondition for peace negotiations. PDF forces have been active against suspected dissidents in north, including regions where the majority of the population is Muslim but non-Arab, such as Darfur, Kordofan, the Nuba mountains, and the eastern region. To that extent, the declaration of *jihad* has more to it than simply the invocation of an Islamic tradition. Its association with the NIF, whose followers are predominantly Arabic-speaking ethnic groups, means that Islam has a distinct Arabic character superimposed on it by the regime.

Table 1. *Sudan armed forces*

	1989	1996
Regular army: Troops	100,000	80,000
Commissioned officers	10,000	7,500
NIF trained officers	–	3,500
Popular Defence Forces	–	150,000
Total	110,000	241,000

Source: *Africa Confidential*, 15 November 1996.

One area in which meaning in this sense has played a significant role is the NIF's position towards women. As in other Muslim Arab states, women's visibility in the public domain has become a political issue, a testament to the pervasive role of the state in the war of the sexes. In the eyes of the NIF fundamentalists, the political meaning of women dressed in the Islamic style (not necessary veiled, but covering head and limbs) is the visibility of faith, an expression of a much deeper level of social control. For instance, in November 1991, the Khartoum governor issued an administrative decree which required women to wear Islamic dress in all state offices, public buildings and schools. Subsequently, the Civil Aviation Authority issued a rule banning female employees who did not wear Islamic dress from entering the airport building, because, the NIF-dominated governor's council had announced that the airport represents the image of the Sudan to the outside World and that image should be Islamic. Schools were instructed that female students should wear Islamic dress. When these rules were largely ignored by the public, they were reintroduced in 1996. This time, the Khartoum governor's office decreed strict sexual segregation in public, in line with the NIF's puritanical vision of an Islamic society.

It was decreed by parliament (22 October 1996) that men and women must not share the same seat on public transport, and men may not watch women playing sports. Sportswomen are prohibited from wearing sexually revealing clothes or clothes which expose the body. The decree reiterated a ban on coeducation in schools. In higher education, men and women students must sit apart in class. At public gatherings, theatres, cinemas, etc., a curtain must separate the sexes, and on public marches they must walk separately. Furthermore, women may not sit next to a non-close male relative (literally stranger) driver on public transport or in private cars, and may not go shopping at night without the company of their husbands or close male relatives. Men must have good reason for walking along streets leading to girls schools or women's gathering places. Not all Sudanese women wear Islamic dress through compulsion. Women members of the NIF known as Muslim Sisters and other religious orders wear it out of Sudanese tradition. However, because the NIF has issued administrative decrees forcing people to wear Islamic dress, resistance has increased among some women, particularly those in urban centres who do not share such devotion to Islamic tradition.

In Sudan's highly charged political milieu, the Islamic discourse has become an indispensable ideological instrument in laying claim to the ethnonational nature of the state and the society which it governs. The construction of meaning is informed by the multiplicity of Sudan's diverse cultures, ethnic groups and languages, as well as the economic and political circumstances which produced the longest civil war in Africa. (Mohamed Salih, 1998). Identity construction is not a simple assertion of difference, but also of the narratives that give meaning to the ideology of dominance. In the search for identity in this conflict-ridden society, narratives are very important to reaffirming the political boundaries which serve to reproduce or negate cultural subjugation.

Elite discursive narratives

Since the NIF regime seized power in 1989, a modest change has occurred in the discursive narratives which inform the north-south divide. The change is largely influenced by the SPLA's effort to promote a Sudanese national identity based on its vision of a "New Sudan". This is the first time the ideological scope of a southern resistance movement has encompassed the whole Sudan, not just the south. Some Sudanese outside the south, particularly those from the marginalized regions of the north (Kordofan, Darfur, southern Blue Nile, eastern region) have expressed sympathy with the SPLA's political programme, and distanced themselves from the dominant discourse (Khalid, 1988; Harir, 1994, and 1993; Mohamed Salih, 1985, and 1989). Others have remained within the dominant Arabist discourse with its strong ethnonationalist sentiments.

In the post-1989 period, a number of treatments of Sudanese identity can be identified. The Islamist narrative is represented by El-Affendi (1990: 182) who sees the NIF "as the carrier of the banner of 'northern nationalism', thus assuming a comparable role to that played by the SPLA/SPLM in the South", and maintains that "the role of the NIF is to defend Islam and Arab culture and frustrate Western attempts to use the South as a Christian bridge between Muslim North Africa and Eastern and Central Africa". El-Affendi

(1993:43–7) offers a discourse based on what he calls Islamic perspectives and traditions of knowledge, justice and conflict resolution.

> The basic Islamic principles regarding human relations which condemn all forms of aggression recommended that aggression should be fought back with just enough force to repel it and cause the conditions of peace to prevail ... The more basic question is, therefore, not what Muslims can or cannot accept, but what human beings can tolerate. It so happens that Muslims are more attached to their religion, and take it more seriously, than the average resident of planet earth.

The characterization of Muslims as more serious than the average resident of planet earth may be an exaggeration, but it is also an uncompromising definition which is ideologically constructed to serve NIF's political ends. This could explain why the role of Islamic ideology in Sudan has been presented by Islamist authors as a divine narrative not to be questioned, and why it should, therefore, be treated as an expression of what Islamists consider to be the assumed, and most desired, political reality.

The "New Sudan" narrative form is presented by Mansour Khalid (1988), the most prominent northern Sudanese committed to the SPLA's image of Sudan's future. Khalid's book, entitled *Garang Speaks*, presents the political programme of a southern political leader. This represents a major breakthrough in the discourse devoted to Sudanizing, rather than Africanizing, Arabizing or Islamizing, the Sudanese. The New Sudan, according to the SPLM (1989:84)

> ... strives to establish a new cultural order in the country. It takes as its point of departure the notion that human beings in any society have equal rights and obligations regardless of race, beliefs, colour, etc. The establishment of the New Sudan cultural order demands of necessity a radical restructuring of state power to establish genuine democracy and to follow a path of development that leads to far-reaching social change.

Evidently, the ethos of "New Sudan and of the NIF narrative are on a collision course, which can hardly be avoided given the type of ideology proposed by Al-Turabi (1992b) and El-Affendi (1990, 1991). New Sudan challenges the core values of NIF discourse and its efforts to expand an Arab-Muslim cultural order and political and economic dominance.

The unity-in-diversity narrative has been mainly adopted by a small number of southern and northern authors. In *War of Visions: Conflict of Identities in the Sudan* (1995:388), Francis Deng argues that in

> ... the Sudan, a country that is defined in terms that connote race, ethnicity, culture, or religion, there is no way discrimination can be avoided. The competing identity models are Arabism, Africanism, Islam, Christianity, and traditional religions. Arabism defined in racial and cultural terms, and Islam, crystallised in *sharia*, which in Islamic doctrine is a comprehensive way of life embracing public and private domains, are clearly the dominant models. Southerners generally believe that the differences between them and the

Arabs are genetic, cultural and deeply embedded. They also acknowledge that their prejudices are mutual. As a young Dinka put it, "the Arabs despise us and we know it; we despise them, but they do not know it". The Southern scorn of the Arab lies in the realm of moral values, which they believe to be inherited in the genetic and cultural composition of identity.

Deng (1995:483) concludes that "short of imposition by force, the only way to resolve the dilemma is to design a system of mutual coexistence in nominal unity or through outright partition".

Abel Alier (1990) in *Southern Sudan: Too Many Agreements Dishonoured*, and Abdel Ghaffar (1994) in *El Sudan baina Arabiatuhu wa Afrigyiatuhu* (*Sudan between Arabism and Africanism*) also see the possibility of unity in diversity, without defining the parameters upon which this could be based. The difference between southern and northern Sudanese who hold this position is that the latter still largely operate within the core values of Sudanese state nationalism, although they consider it possible and desirable to moderate differences in order to promote national consensus.

Separatism is represented by Ruay in *The Politics of Two Sudans* (1994), with his review of more than fifty texts dealing with colonial and postcolonial state policy towards the south. He concludes (p. 181):

> The Southern People are one people in culture, way of life and in everything, except the diverse languages that they speak. They are Black African people and they occupy a territory endowed with rich and varied resources ... A sovereign power in Southern Sudan, would govern its people in a way that would enhance everything that unites the people and exclude everything that divides them. The tribalists ... would have no voice in this system of the union of hearts in the future independent Southern Sudan.

But the case for separation is not grounded in the reality of southern Sudan, which is both ethnically and culturally divided. The reconstruction of a southern Sudanese national identity is as much at odds with southern reality as it is with the reality of the whole of the Sudan. The fragmentation of the southern movement in the early 1990s is proof of this fact, and it could prove beneficial for the south to discover this reality before a separate southern political entity is created.

Post-1989 narratives on negotiating identities

The NIF seized power in order to forestall an agreement between the National Democratic Unionist Party (NDP) and the SPLA on the revocation of the *sharia* laws. It would seem that the regime is more concerned about *sharia* than the prospect of the secession of the south. Its negotiating position now includes acceptance of the principle of self-determination. In response to the Al-Bashir statement cited earlier on the regime's willingness to countenance separation, John Garang was moved to say that "Bashir's comments could bring disaster". And one observer declared, "there is a danger that Al-

Bashir, a Muslim, would seek to partition Sudan" (*Indian Ocean Newsletter*, 16 August 1989).

The principle of self-determination was also accepted by the northern opposition parties grouped in the National Democratic Alliance. Joined by the SPLA in 1991, the NDA gained more acceptance in the marginalized regions of the Sudan and also improved its military capacity by establishing a presence in eastern Sudan. The NDA's most crucial political decision was to accept the right of the south to self-determination. At a meeting in Asmara, the capital of Eritrea, in November 1996, it was agreed that following the overthrow of the NIF regime the NDA will form a transitional government for five years. The parties at the meeting also pledged to hold a referendum on self-determination for the south and for certain other regions (Abyie and southern Blue Nile) within four years.

After the 1991 collapse of the military regime in Ethiopia, which had provided significant support and bases for the SPLA, the NIF took advantage of rampant factionalism within the southern resistance movement to neutralize some armed factions and to forge alliances with others. Schisms in the SPLA followed ethnic (Dinka, Nuer) and regional (Upper Nile, Bahr Al-Ghazal, Equatoria) lines. However, these lines of division do not represent clear-cut categories. The SPLA mainstream retained the support of diverse ethnic groups and regions. And while ethnicity has played a part in fragmentation, ethnic alliances were also forged.

Certain issues achieved prominence in the chaotic period that followed, including the leadership of Colonel Garang, who was accused of authoritarianism and arbitrariness. Another issue was the ultimate goal of the southern movement and the war of liberation (Mohamed Salih, 1994; Badal, 1994). Some of Garang's leading southern opponents argued that a "New Sudan" which includes the north as a partner is an illusion. They hold that historical experience has show that the north will never concede equal rights of citizenship to the south. Therefore, it is pointless to continue a struggle that cannot be won. Separation, they argue, is the only possible choice for the south. Although some of those who advocated this position were soon embraced within the NIF, they succeeded in placing self-determination on the political agenda. An agreement concluded by five southern factions (opponents of the SPLA) with the NIF regime in April 1997 includes the following statements:

1. During a four-year interim period south Sudan shall enjoy a special status as defined in this peace agreement.

2. The interim arrangements shall be preceded by a declaration of permanent ceasefire and a general amnesty proclamation.

3. The people of south Sudan shall exercise the right to self-determination through a referendum.

Among the important factors that persuaded the NIF to soften its position was the military setbacks it suffered in the mid-1990s, as well as mounting pressure from neighbouring states under the aegis of the Inter-governmental Authority for Drought Development (IGADD). After a long and tortuous period of consultation and negotiation, IGADD adopted certain principles as the basis of restoring peace in Sudan, and self-determination for the south was one of them.

For its part, the SPLA under Garang responded to the crisis with internal reforms and, most importantly, by redefining its notion of the "New Sudan". In May 1994, Garang announced the creation of a political and administrative entity called New Sudan. Geographically, this entity encompasses the three regions of the south, south Kordofan and southern Blue Nile. A parliament and an executive council were formed, with Colonel Garang as speaker of the first and chairman of the second. The executive council is empowered to:

1. Work for self-determination using all means including armed struggle.

2. Use the resources of "New Sudan" to support the war if this is necessary.

3. Separate the civilian administration from the military.

4. Form the necessary infrastructure for the civilian administration.

5. Ensure respect for the rule of law and human rights.

6. Issue a general amnesty to those who defected from the movement.

A year later, a "New Sudan Brigade" was established jointly with the NDA, signalling the extension of the war to eastern Sudan. The NIF saw the SPLA decision to create a "New Sudan" as a declaration of independence. In essence, the NIF's pact with the southern opponents of the SPLA was a desperate measure designed to prolong its hold on power. Hence, it can be argued that post-1989 identity formation in the Sudan has taken three main routes: 1) NIF imposition of an Arab-Islamic ideology irreconcilable with the tolerant values held by the majority of the Sudanese people. Specifically, this has reinforced the southern peoples resolve to 2) counteract the NIF attempts to reinvent Sudan as an Arab-Muslim nationstate. In my view the militarization of society and the intolerance that comes with it have contributed to fatally undermining the process of negotiating a common Sudanese identity. As I have shown in this section, conference after conference have failed to produce any meaningful dialogue to stop the carnage that has been inflicted on the southern peoples for more than four decades. Caught in a harsh militarized environment, itself a response to NIF aggression, NIF has become hostage to fear of the consequences of the violence which it has masterminded, should it lose its grip on power. The NIF has taken 3) a route marked by confusion and limited political repair, including delaying tactics and manoeuvring, which have neither silenced the agony nor provided a credible solution for the Sudan question. The south seems to be enduring much suffering in the knowledge that the days of old Sudan are numbered, and that this sacrifice is worth making in the face of the sad fact that the northern elite are also responsible for what has been taking place in the Sudan since 1989.

Conclusion

The recent political events in the Sudan demonstrate that the affirmation or contestation of ethnic and national histories is not just an affirmation or contestation of events and stories, but a statement of the economic, political and cultural claims the narratives attempt to justify or negate. Narratives gain significance from the political meanings given to them by power-brokers and nationalities (Mohamed Salih, 1998). This chapter has shown that in the Sudan, the relationship between the dominant discursive forms and narratives is consciously used in order to support or negate the historical position claimed by contending nationalities.

However, counter-narratives are significantly more important in informing the opposing marginalized nationalities and must, therefore, be carefully examined in delineating the elements of the resistance identity and its quest for identity reconstruction. The political reality imposed by NIF policies on Sudanese political life has rendered conventional political positions within northern Sudan's sectarian establishment (Umma and Democratic Nationalist Parties) futile. The situation has taken a turn which is militarily determined by the oppressed marginal groups and their regional movements (Nuba, Beja, Fur, Zaghawa), supported by the SPLA/SPLM. The political mill has unpredictably taken the discussion beyond common Sudanese narrative forms and trends. It has imposed a new reality which cannot be separated from southern Sudanese struggles which have made prudent the current political rethinking of Sudan's future. As more of the marginalized groups both in the north and the south join the armed struggle against those who project the north as an Arab-Muslim nation, the more vulnerable will be the discourse of Arabism and its political implications. In that event, the decisive elements of Sudanese identity will shift to what the moral majority of the oppressed would project as a Sudanese identity, informed by a new political reality.

In short, regardless of whether the NIF and the NDA are genuine in pledging self-determination to southern Sudan or not, the acceptance of these two main northern Sudan-based political forces of this issue marks a considerable shift in south-north identity formation. This is the first time in Sudanese history that the same political forces which fought for decades to keep the south as part of a unitary Sudanese state have agreed to its right to self-determination, including independence. Post-1989 identity formation in the Sudan, might not have been possible without the sacrifices the Sudanese peoples have endured in their struggle against the extremist policies of the

NIF. These policies will have far-reaching ramifications for the future of the Sudan, including the possibility of the establishment of a separate southern Sudanese state, based on a southern rather than northern Sudanese vision of how and what type of state that should be within or outside the corrupt northern Sudanese polity.

Bibliography

Africa Confidential, 1996, 15 November.

Abdel Ghaffar, M.A., 1994, *El Sudan baina Arabiatuhu wa Afrigyiatuhu* (in Arabic). Cairo: Arab Research Centre.

Alier, A., 1990, *Southern Sudan: Too Many Agreements Dishonoured.* Exeter: Ithaca Press.

Al-Turabi, 1992a, *Pan-Islamism and the Nation-State, The Nationhood Lectures.* London: Royal Society of Arts.

—1992b, "Interview with Al-Qods", *Al Arabi,* 9 January.

Badal, K. Raphael, 1994, "Political Cleavages within Southern Sudan", in S. Harir and T. Tvedt (eds.), *Short-Cut to Decay. The Case of the Sudan.* Uppsala: Scandinavian Institute of African Studies.

Deng, F. M., 1995, *War of Visions: Conflict of Identities in the Sudan.* Washington, DC: Brookings Institution.

El-Affendi, Abdel Wahab, 1990, "Discovering the South: Sudanese Dilemma for Islam in Africa", *African Affairs,* 89:358.

—1991, *Turabi's Revolution: Islam and Power in the Sudan.* London: Grey Seal.

—1993, "Knowledge, Justice and Conflict Resolution: The Relevance of Islamic Perspectives and Traditions", in A. Hurskainen and M. A Mohamed Salih (eds.), *Social Science and Conflict Analysis.* Helsinki: Helsinki University Press, for Human Life in African Arid Lands, Uppsala and Department of Asian and African Studies, University of Helsinki.

Harir, Sharif, 1993, "Racism under Islamic Disguise", in H. Veber et al. (eds.), *Never Drink from the Same Cup: Proceedings of a Conference on Indigenous Peoples in Africa.* IWGIA document 74. Copenhagen: International Working Group on Indigenous Affairs (IWGIA) and the Centre for Development Research.

—1994, "Arab Belt versus African Belt: Ethno-political Conflict in Darfur and the Regional Cultural Factors", in S. Harir and T. Tvedt (eds.), *Short-Cut to Decay: The Case of the Sudan.* Uppsala: Scandinavian Institute of African Studies.

Indian Ocean Newsletter, 1989, 16 August.

Khalid, M., 1988, *Garang Speaks.* London: Routledge and Kegan Paul.

Al-Khlij Al Arabi, (Daily newspaper), 1989, 15 July.

Mohamed Salih, M.A., 1985, "National versus Regional: Some Methodological Problems in the Study of Nationalism and Nation Building in the Sudan", *Bayreuth African Studies Series,* 1, 1.

—1989, "New Wine in Old Bottles: Tribal Militias and the Sudanese State", *Review of African Political Economy,* 45/46.

—1994, "The Ideology of the Dinka and the Sudan People's Liberation Movement", in Katsuyoshi Fukui and John Markakis (eds.), *Ethnicity and Conflict in the Horn of Africa*. London: James Currey and Athens: Ohio University Press.

—1995, "Ethnocide and Genocide in the Nuba Mountains", *Geojournal, International Journal of Physical, Biological and Geography and its Applications in Environmental Planning and Ecology*, 36, 1.

—1998, "Other Identities: Politics of Sudanese Discursive Narratives", *Identities: Journal of Global Studies in Culture and Power*, 5(1), 1–27.

Mohamed Salih, M.A. and Sharif Harir, 1994, "Tribal Militias: The Genesis of National Disintegration", in S. Harir and T. Tvedt (eds.), *Short-Cut to Decay: The Case of the Sudan*. Uppsala: Scandinavian Institute of African Studies.

Ruay, Deng, A., 1994, *The Politics of Two Sudans*. Uppsala: Scandinavian Institute of African Studies.

Sudan Peoples Liberation Army and Sudan Peoples Liberation Movement (SPLA/SPLM), 1989, "On the New Sudan", in M.A. Abdel Ghaffar and Gunnar M. Sørbø (eds.), *Management of the Crisis in Sudan*. Bergen: Centre for Development Studies, University of Bergen.

Ethnicity as a Mode of Conflict Regulation

A.B.C. Ocholla-Ayayo

Ethnicity is often regarded as a source of conflict generation rather than conflict regulation. A recent statement by a leading Kenyan political scientist and member of the legislature, Anyang'Nyo'Ngo (1993:6), is a clear reflection of the problem. "I do not think our problems as a nation can be solved by political formulas worked out by elite politicians caucusing on purely ethnic agendas", he says and adds, "whatever ethnic gains were made under presidents Kenyatta and Moi, no proper redress can be carried out by installing yet another president who will simply ensure that his people eat while he is in power". While nearly every ethnic group may demand a degree of autonomy, they also want a place at the centre of the state and a share of the national cake, to the extent that if their leaders choose to ignore the centre, they are likely to be discarded (Ocholla-Ayayo, 1991:79–81; Igbozurike, 1976:21–35).

Recent political trends tend to confirm the above observation. When the opposition party, Ford Kenya, started to split along ethnic lines, many of its followers who began to see the consequences of isolation returned to the mainstream party. Most people in Kenya are frightened by the prospect of an opposition victory that would result in another round of ethnic division of spoils. "That is why", continues Anyang, "it is important that we identify as our national leaders people who are truly ready for qualitative change and democratisation" (1993:6). It is difficult to find such leaders. For most politicians, the state is an "eating place".

Eastern Africa is a great rainbow of tribes and races whose potential to live together and build a strong entity is enormous. Diverse relationships link the various groups. The most common interethnic relationship is found in marriage exchange, where women move in one direction and cattle in the other (Ocholla-Ayayo, 1976). This is a peaceful kind of interethnic interaction likely to contribute to conflict regulation. Maasai intermarriage with Kikuyu continues even at times when they are hostile towards each other. Chang (1996) views this kind of interaction as contradictory, given the fact that farmers despise pastoralists. This shows how important marriage exchange is as a mode of interaction and, possibly, as a conflict-regulating mechanism, as Odak (1988) points out for the Luo and Baluyia in western Kenya, and Ocholla-Ayayo (1981) for south Nyanza. Yet, although Odak maintains interethnic marriages can pave the way for better understanding, this did not prove to be the case in Rwanda where, in fact, it caused greater suffering among divided families.

The Maasai, the Kuria, and the Luo still consider cattle to have high value, because bridewealth takes the form of cattle exchange. Though a common value, cattle can provoke conflict in the interactions among the three ethnic groups through the practice of cattle raiding. The Maasai have shown that although they cherish cattle, they have a higher value, which is to marry and have children and maintain the "biological continuity" of the Maasai. In this case, while Maasai sociocultural ideologies make for hostile interaction with neighbours in order to acquire "cattle value", they also consider "sociobiological continuity" a greater normative value that must be maintained at all times.

Ideologies direct goals and fix values for interaction. Interaction may be peaceful, as in marriage and economic exchange, or hostile, as in cattle raiding, verbal abuse and economic sanctions. Everyone, however, wants peaceful interaction that can promote peace and function as a conflict-regulating mechanism. In Kenya, interethnic conflict is traditionally most often linked with cattle raiding and land disputes. As many studies show, cattle raiding is universal and often escalates into group conflict. However, such conflict is regulated by traditional norms. Intermarriage among conflicting groups continues. What regulates violence and conflict between the groups is not political manipulation of any sort, but rather the institution of interethnic marriages.

Table 1 suggests a few noteworthy and fundamental propositions. Most interethnic conflict in East Africa stems either from land disputes or cattle raiding. The more intermarriage there is, the less conflict. The higher the socioeconomic and political interaction, the higher the possible interethnic conflict. Lastly, the higher the economic dependency, the lower the interethnic conflict, although in the long run this could be the reverse.

What then are the advantages in interethnic marriage? The women-for-cattle exchange between the Maasai and the Kikuyu has the following advantages. A relatively poor Maasai is able to marry more wives and have more children and, therefore, raise his social status, because the bridewealth in cattle demanded by the agricultural Kikuyu is low compared to that demanded by the Maasai. Odak (1995) found this to be the case also for the Baluyia-Luo exchange, as did Ocholla-Ayayo (1981, 1982) for the Baluyia and the Suba. Lacking agricultural skills, the Maasai want to marry women with such skills. Finally, the Kikuyu, who greatly value land, can gain access to Maasai land for cultivation.

Table 1. *The interethnic modes of relation and interaction in Kenya*

Ethnic groups	Economic exchange activities	Land issue	Marriage exchange relationship	Cattle raids	Interethnic conflicts
Maasai-Luo	Low	Low	Very Low	High	High
Maasai-Kikuyu	High	High/Low	High	Low	High
Luo-Baluyia	High	Low	High	Nil	Low
Luo-Kisii	High	Low	High	Nil	Low
Luo-Kipsigis	Low	Low	Low	High	Low
Luo-Kalenjin	Low	Low	Low	High	Low/High
Luo-Suba	High	Nil/Low	High	Nil	Nil/Moderate
Maasai-Kuria	Low	Nil/Low	Low	High	High
Maasai-Kisii	Low	Low	Nil	High	Low/High
Luo-Maragoli	High	Low/High	High	Nil	Nil
Turkana-Neighbours	Low	Nil	Low	High	High
Luo-Banyala	High	Nil/Low	High	Nil	Nil
Luo-Kuria	High	Low	Low/Nil	Low/High	High/Low
Kuria-Suba	Low	Low	Low/High	High	High
Kipsigis-Gusii	Low	Low	High	High	High
Dinka-Baggara, Rizeigat, Messinya	Low	Low	Low	High	High

Ongoing trends are likely to destabilize this relationship. Ocholla-Ayayo (1982) hypothesized that "the more the Kikuyu acquire land to settle and cultivate, the more they become potentially in conflict with the Maasai. As population increases, Maasai dependence on cattle decreases, because land scarcity is forcing them to shift from livestock raising to cultivation in order to survive. We must not assume the Maasai are going to remain pastoral forever". There are "agricultural Maasai" at present who turned to cultivation after losing their animals in the great rinderpest epidemic at the end of last century, and the same holds true for the southern Luo. There will come a time when the Maasai discover their grazing land has become Kikuyu farmland. As the Maasai-Kikuyu interaction rates increase, so will the conflict rates because, sooner or later, the interaction will assume an asymmetrical form which one ethnic group will consider to be exploitation. This will become a source of ethnic conflict.

Ethnicity as a power idiom

How does an ethnic group see itself in the political spectrum of a multi-ethnic state? To a great extent this depends on how political actors exploit the situation. In Kenya, at the national level, talk of tribalism fills the air, with statements such as "we are being sidelined" and "we are being finished", from politicians who fail to secure important positions in the government, or are kicked out of it. Others exhort the Kalenjin to remain united within the ruling party, while the Baluyia see themselves as a people whose time has come. The political arena, as the editorial columnist of the *Nation* (15 May 1996) put it, is in a whirl about what everyone wants. The Luo, he says, have been identified with "opposition politics", while smaller ethnic groups feel that by following the ruling party they are protected from larger and more powerful "land grabbers". The fear of ethnic conflict is real.

Some politicians cry wolf, while they themselves are the real wolves. A recent cry in Kenya was that the government should prosecute without ethnic bias people implicated in looting public funds and plundering the economy. Others assert that political godfathers should assist their henchmen to repay what they have stolen, since they continue to enjoy political patronage. We also hear voices calling tribalism the product of the differential treatment meted out to some communities in the distribution of the national cake. Hardly anyone talks about the nation and its aspirations. How the national cake will be divided is all they want to hear. Anyang calls for leaders "ready for qualitative change and democratisation". The problem ordinary people have is how to find leaders who have these qualities. Kenyans have often changed their members of parliament, only to see their replacements turn out to be simply "grabbers".

The outbreak of interethnic conflict and even violence can be deliberately fuelled by poor leaders. It takes only one person to trigger interethnic violence where tension has already accumulated. Events in the opposition ranks prior to the recent elections in Kenya are a good example. The level of mutual hostility exhibited by the four main factions, Ford-K Raila led by a Luo, Ford-K Wamalwa led by a Baluyia, Ford-Asili Matiba led by a Kikuyu, and Ford-Asili Shikuku led by another Baluyia, are a sign of ethnic polarization. The degree of acrimony, intransigence, intolerance and self-aggrandizement shown by the four ethnically based opposition factions is an ominous sign.

Once such leaders are elected to positions of power, they begin to think they are born to rule and to impose their will upon the people they are supposed to serve. When their hold on power begins to slip, they appeal to tribal chauvinism by crying wolf—"we are being sidelined", "we are being finished", and "our ancestral lands are being grabbed to raise support". No ethnic group wants to be isolated, perhaps especially because the opposition parties have not proven themselves worthy—as someone observed, they are like "ships with blind captains". Kenya's ethnic groups appear to have learned something from their neighbours who have been torn apart that they will all suffer in times of conflict, irrespective of the group they belong to. They understand that when major economic institutions are mismanaged, and interethnic conflict escalates, all Kenyans stand to suffer collectively. They realize that the conflicts in Uganda and Somalia were not started by entire ethnic groups, but by politicians and the group leaders themselves.

In Eastern Africa there is no shortage of official declarations of good intentions. In Kenya we hear of the "philosophy of love, peace and unity", in Tanzania we hear of "*Undugu* philosophy", and in Uganda "comrade ideology". According to the constitutions of the states in this region, and the manifestos of their political parties, the security, integrity, equality and material well-being of all citizens, irrespective of ethnic identity, is guaranteed. One may well ask whether human suffering is alleviated by these declarations, or whether they are mere slogans that are never put into practice. One of the most important human needs is security of survival, but "unity" is necessary for the maintenance of peace and achieving the security needed for survival. Security or survival is valuable because it is fundamental to all human activities. Two questions likely to be asked are whether all human activities are directed towards security of survival, and second, how far freedom to express ethnicity can be tolerated if it jeopardizes the security of survival of a multiethnic nation. If we wish to include the three Western ethical values—freedom, justice and security of survival—and at the same time maintain the three indigenous values—love, peace and unity—the choice of supreme value would be very difficult to make in dealing with multiethnic groups. These two ethical systems have the same end, in so far as they have chosen security of survival as the supreme value. This should perhaps be the case in Africa. If, on the other hand, the end is freedom or justice, then we have an ethical dilemma. We would be confronted by individual freedom, ethnic freedom, group freedom and national freedom. What all these can mean for a multiethnic nation is chaos.

Bibliography

Anyang'Nyo'Ngo, 1993, *The Challenge of National Leadership and Democratic Change in Kenya*. Nairobi: Shirikon Publishers.

Chang, D.M.F., 1996, "Marriage Practices of the Maasai and the Kikuyu in Kenya". Mimeo 1–27. Nairobi: Department of Sociology, University of Nairobi.

Igbozurike, Martin, 1976, *Problem Generating Structures in Nigeria's Rural Development*. Uppsala: Scandinavian Institute of African Studies.

Ocholla-Ayayo, A.B.C., 1976, *Traditional Ideology and Ethics among the Southern Luo*. Uppsala: Scandinavian Institute of African Studies.

—1981, *Female Migration and Wealth Dissipation among the Patrilineal Exogamous Communities in East Africa*. Nairobi: Population Studies Research Institute, University of Nairobi.

—1982, *Ethnic Inter-Marriages in Ethnic Boundaries in Western and Southern Kenya*. Nairobi: Population Studies Research Institute, University of Nairobi.

—1991, *The Spirit of a Nation: An Analysis of Policy, Ethics and Customary Rules of Conduct for Regulating Fertility in Kenya*. Nairobi: Shirikon Publishers.

Odak, Osaga, 1988, "Ethno-Cultural Processes in Western Kenya: A Study of Inter-Ethnic Relations". Paper presented to Ethnic Boundaries, 12th Icaes, Zagreb, Yugoslavia, July.

—1995, "Inter-Ethnic Relations in the Bantu-Nilotic Ethnic Boundaries in Western Kenya", *Zeitschrift für Ethnologie*, No. 120.

PART II

CASE STUDIES

The Rise of Politicized Ethnicity among the Oromo in Ethiopia

Paulos Chanie

Introduction

This chapter attempts to analyze the rise of politicized ethnicity among the Oromo of Ethiopia. It begins by outlining the impact of the historical interaction of the Oromo with other ethnic groups before the emergence of the modern Ethiopian state. Following this, the interaction of the Oromo with the dominant groups in the Ethiopian state, as well as the development of politicized ethnicity among the Oromo themselves, will be considered. Finally, certain factors which have hindered the transformation of politicized ethnicity into a successful Oromo ethnonationalism will be examined.

The Oromo are one of the largest ethnic groups in Ethiopia. Some writers believe the original homeland of the Oromo to be in the Horn of Africa outside the current borders of Ethiopia, while others argue that Oromo had long resided in the southern part of present Ethiopia. The latter contention seems to be reasonable, considering Oromo traditional history and legends, linguistic evidence and Oromo traditional places of pilgrimage. The Oromo were not a close-knit ethnic group, but were divided into many distinct and autonomous units, as is typical of pastoralist societies in this part of Africa. Nor did they live in isolation, but had continuous and intimate interaction with neighbouring ethnic groups inside and outside present Ethiopia.

This interaction was facilitated by the historic Oromo movement which is said to have started before the sixteenth century, and reached its peak in that century. During this movement, the Oromo expanded and dispersed into a large area, and became involved in continuous interaction—both conflictual and peaceful—with other ethnic groups. This brought about many changes in the cultural, political, economic and demographic situation of the Oromo, as well as among the Abyssinian, Sidama, Somali and other groups with which they came into contact. Some Oromo groups altered their ethnic markers and attributes, such as language, dialect, religion, mode of production, social structure, political system and customs. Because of these developments, the Oromo did not unite as a single political unit from the six-

teenth century to the middle of the nineteenth century. To repeat Brass'
(1991) position and relate it to this case, Oromo was not "a subjectively self-
conscious community that establishes criteria for inclusion into and exclusion from the group, and instead of merging in one political entity, the various Oromo groups created their own states".

The period of interaction between the Oromo and the groups that controlled the centralized state after the second half of the nineteenth century
will be divided into three phases, in order to illuminate the gradual development of politicized Oromo ethnicity. The first phase will cover the reigns
of emperors Tewodros (1855–68), Yohannes (1872–89) and Menelik (1889–
1913). The second phase includes the first part (1917–60s) of Emperor Haile
Selassie's reign. The third phase will deal with the remaining period under
Haile Selassie (1960–74), the military regime (Dergue) that succeeded him
(1974–91), and the present government that took power in 1991.

The first phase

This was the initial phase in the creation of the centralized Ethiopian state.
The pattern of expansion and conquest by the three emperors was not uniform. Tewodros and Yohannes waged a series of battles to subdue traditional Oromo rulers in the northern region, where some Oromo had earlier
settled. Menelik's expansion covered a much wider area to the south, east
and west of Shoa, his home province. One Oromo group after another was
conquered, and the modern, centralized Ethiopian state began to emerge.
This was possible because of Abyssinian superiority in firepower, and the
failure of the Oromo elite to forge political unity. Some local elites strongly
resisted, while others found it to their advantage to cooperate with the alien
conquerors in order to maintain and enhance their own power. The majority
of the Oromo people in the southern region were reduced to quasiserfdom,
and were subjected to oppression and exploitation.

Generally, this was a period of conflictual interaction between an alien
conqueror and the various independent Oromo states and kingdoms. The
resistance waged by some groups seems to indicate the beginning of the
development of ethnic consciousness among certain Oromo groups.
Although the objective ethnic markers (religion, language, common ancestry, custom, etc.) were to some extent altered, it seems they had started to
acquire subjective and symbolic significance and were translated into an
ethnic consciousness among particular Oromo groups. This was manifested
when the political elite of different Oromo groups made use of ethnic markers to mobilize resistance against the domination of the alien elite.
Nonetheless, there was no marked feeling of ethnic solidarity among the
different Oromo groups, except to some extent in Arsi. Some writers argue
this cannot be due to inadequate development of objective ethnic attributes,
which are the bases of ethnic solidarity. Neither is it sound to contend that

the development of the objective attributes was thwarted by the Abyssinian conquest. The "level of development" of objective ethnic markers is not a critical factor in creating ethnic solidarity, as Brass (1991:24) noted in his writing about ethnicity.

The richness of a group's cultural heritage, the stage of development of its language, the distinctiveness of its religious beliefs do not of themselves predetermine that one group of people will have more internal solidarity than another, or would be more likely to perpetuate itself through time. Although no conclusive reason can be given, lack of solidarity could be explained by one salient factor, the weakness of the local elite to use any of the objective attributes to create ethnic consciousness among the different Oromo groups. In most of the cases—except the Arsi, who were the strongest ethnic group—the local elite was coopted and profited from the conquest probably as much as the northern officials and soldiers who sought their fortunes in the newly conquered regions.

Nonetheless, the hostile relationship between the Oromo and the three Ethiopian emperors was instrumental in the development of Oromo identity and hence the emergence of later ethnonationalism. This initial phase introduced one ethnic marker—shared experiences of subjugation among the Oromo groups—which has been used effectively as a tool by the modern elite in their competition for state power and resources.

The second phase

This covers the period between 1917 and the 1960s, the major part of the reign of Emperor Haile Selassie, who was regent from 1917 to 1930 and emperor from 1930 to 1974. During this period, the emperor consolidated the power and authority of the throne by subordinating the nobility, regional lords and other local elites who had previously maintained control over the local population in a relatively independent manner. Subsequently, a complicated pattern of contacts and a variety of conflictual and non-conflictual relationships emerged between the different ethnic groups and the state. Among the conflicts was the Azebo-Raya Revolt (1928–30) in the north. This was an attempt by these Oromo groups to gain more independence and power. It took the form of resistance to taxation and protests against corrupt government. Ras Gugsa Walie, a descendant of a leading Oromo clan, joined the rebellion in order to pursue his personal interests.

The relationship between Haile Selassie and the southern Oromo groups took different forms during this period. Opposition to Haile Selassie's rule occurred both during and after the Italian invasion. The invasion enabled some disgruntled elites in the southern region to show their hostility to the centralization efforts of Haile Selassie. The first movement that demanded independence from Abyssinian rule was in Wellega during the Italian invasion (1936). Some of the hereditary Oromo rulers in the southwest favoured the creation of an independent Western Galla Confederation under the leadership of Dejazmach Habte Mariam Kumsa. The refusal of the British to support it doomed this attempt. Later on, the emperor effectively coopted these same leaders, and stilled their agitation for a long time.

The most significant and protracted resistance struggle occurred in Bale, an area inhabited by Oromo and Somali groups. This lasted from 1963 to 1970 and involved continuous fighting. As Gilkes (1975:214) noted, "the outbreak was essentially personal in origin and started with a quarrel over the ownership of the salt works there". However, additional important factors intensified this uprising. As Gebru (1991) has indicated, there was a potent combination of grievances stemming from political and administrative oppression, land alienation, taxation, ethnic hostility, religious discrimination and ecological decline. Moreover, the movement was incited by the newly independent Somali Republic. Most of the rebel leaders were disgruntled minor officials and members of important families who were constrained by the Abyssinian settlers' domination of the local economy and frustrated by the state's unwillingness to allow a substantial devolution of power. They effectively mobilized discontented individuals both at the village and district levels. The uprising came to an end because of various factors, chief among them being the failure of the leadership.

The second phase also involved the process of ethnic interaction in the new, multiethnic Ethiopian state. It was at this stage that objective ethnic markers—language, religion, territory, common ancestry, shared experience—acquired subjective and symbolic meaning. Subsequently, they were used to promote ethnic consciousness among some Oromo groups and to support ethnic-based demands. In most cases, it was the local elite that was disappointed by the measures taken by the centralized state and that used different ethnic symbols as tools to mobilize support for their conflictual interaction with the dominant state elite. Territory and shared experience were used in the case of northern Oromo; language, territory, common ancestry, shared experience among the western Oromo; while language, territory, common ancestry, shared experiences and religion were used by the elite for purposes of mobilization in Bale.

During this phase, the politicization of ethnicity on a pan-Oromo level, or the feeling of Oromo nationalism, hardly existed. That is, the articulation of demands for the acquisition of social, economic and political rights for the Oromo people as a whole was nonexistent. It is commonly assumed that the dispersal of the Oromo over a wide geographical area was a major cause of this lack of solidarity. The implication is that the intermingling of the Oromo with other ethnic groups forced them to modify and even change their objective ethnic markers, and adversely affected their unity. One critical factor that accounts for this lack of ethnic solidarity is the overall effect of the elites' handling of the situation. The locally powerful political, economic and social elites, which could be expected to play a critical role in articulating and shaping Oromo ethnic demands, allied themselves with the dominant state elite.

Nevertheless, the second phase can be considered as the initial stage in the Oromo ethnic transformation. The ethnic movements during this phase seem to partially resemble what Brass (1991) described as a form of ethnic movement in preindustrial societies, where the struggle is for control of the local community and of land. As he indicated, this phase would lay the ground for the next phase, where ethnicity will be politicized and used by the elite in the competition for access to state power. Likewise, the Bale rebellion might be considered, as Baxter (1983:139) put it, "the first Oromo rebellion of Arsi patriot-cum-burgundies in Bale in the 1960s, [and] had national reverberations", or, as Ottaway (1978:93) noted, "the background to the resurgence of the Oromo nationalist movement".

The third phase

This is the period beginning in the twilight of Haile Selassie's reign (1960s–74) and continuing to the present day. It was during this period that the process of centralizing and modernizing the state reached a relatively advanced stage and the modernization of society was promoted. As in many developing countries, the modernization of state and society was a prominent factor in the development of ethnic consciousness among the various ethnic groups in Ethiopia. Education—the vanguard of modernization—was the most critical factor in politicizing ethnicity. In Ethiopia, the expansion of education produced two educated groups, the old educated elite and the new educated elite. The former comprised those educated in the 1930s, 1940s and 1950s. Members of this small group were easily assimilated into the nobility and aristocracy, and were provided with employment that offered high salaries, social prestige and opportunities for advancement in the hierarchy of authority. Although a few members became disillusioned and politically frustrated, politicized ethnicity was not apparent in this group.

The new educated group emerged in the 1960s. It was much more numerous and more heterogeneous in terms of ethnic composition. This group included those who were already employed in the lower and middle levels of the state administrative hierarchy, and those who were enrolled in the country's sole university. It was this newly educated elite which politicized ethnicity.

Two major conditions led to ethnic political behaviour among the new educated elite. The first was "the discontent of the educated unemployed," which Brass (1991) identified as the classic problem of developing countries. In the Ethiopian case, the new educated elite was faced with unemployment and underemployment, as well as discrimination along ethnic lines from the old educated elite in terms of recruitment into and promotion in the state apparatus. The second condition was the exposure of this group to secular ideologies, particularly Marxism, and its commitment to values such as enlightenment, progress, equality, efficiency and development. Initially, the new elite made use of these values to support demands for a share of power in institutions and arenas created by the modern state. Failing that, members of this group turned to politicized ethnicity as an instrument to achieve this end. Hence, the situation which promoted the politicization of ethnicity among the Oromo was not different from other ethnic groups in Ethiopia or elsewhere.

A landmark in the development of Oromo ethnic consciousness was the emergence of the Mecha-Tulema Self-Help Association. Initially intended to promote development, the association quickly became identified with the expression of basic grievances, including the ban on the use of the Oromo language on public occasions, the expropriation of Oromo lands, the limited number of Oromo reaching officer's rank in the army and entering higher education institutions, etc. Very soon, the association came to be seen as the dynamic expression of Oromo self-identity. It attracted considerable support among Oromo in Addis Ababa and other parts of the country, particularly the urban elite. Oromo civil servants, military officers and intellectuals played leading roles in the association. This support endowed the association with obvious political potential, and made the imperial regime wary.

Rural uprisings throughout the 1960s involving Oromo in Arsi, Bale, Harrarge and Sidama also contributed to the rise of Oromo ethnic politicization. Moreover, explicitly political organizations were created by the Oromo elite during the reign of Haile Selassie. One of them was the Ethiopian National Liberation Front (ENLF). Although shortlived, this organization established the first guerrilla base in the Chercher Mountains in eastern Ethiopia. The ENLF soon split in two, one faction retaining the name ENLF and the other taking the name Organization for Oromo Peoples Liberation Struggle (OOPLS). Neither survived long, and some of their members joined the Oromo Liberation Front in 1976. To summarize, it was *only* during the final period of Haile Selassie's reign that the politicization of ethnicity was discernible in Ethiopia. This moment also witnessed the surfacing of pan-Oromo feeling and the rise of Oromo ethnonationalist movements in Ethiopia.

The imperial regime was succeeded in 1974 by a military dictatorship, commonly known as the Dergue. The Dergue claimed credit for the popular uprising against the old regime and took control of the state. This pivotal development frustrated the new educated elites of all ethnic groups in Ethiopia who had been active in the uprising and who claimed the right to become the architects of the new Ethiopian state. Failure resulted in division within this group, with some factions choosing to cooperate with the Dergue, while others chose armed resistance. Having lost the contest for the centre, sections of the new elite group began using ethnicity as a weapon against the military regime. As a result of the Dergue's adamant rejection of power sharing with the elite, they went on to create ethnic liberation movements. In this situation, the new Oromo educated elite was divided among several antagonistic political and liberation movements.

One of the groups that waged war against the Dergue was the Oromo Peoples Liberation Organization (OPLO), an ethnic branch of the most prominent opposition political organization in Ethiopia, the Ethiopian Peoples Revolutionary Party (EPRP). Another was the All Ethiopia Socialist Movement (MEISON), which first allied with and later turned against the Dergue. MEISON was reputed to have a large following among the Oromo of Wellega in the west and around Jimma in the southwest. MEISON also created the Oromo National Democratic Movement (ONDM) to compete for ethnic support among the Oromo. The Ethiopian Oppressed Peoples Revolutionary Struggle (ECHAT) was another organization which first allied with the Dergue and later turned against it. While it collaborated with the Dergue, ECHAT posed as a pan-Ethiopian movement. When it broke with the military regime, most of its members joined the Oromo Liberation Front (OLF). The OLF was founded in 1974 and produced its political programme in 1976. The major aim of the struggle, it declared, was self-determination for the Oromo people, their liberation from oppression and exploitation, and the establishment of the Peoples Democratic Republic of Oromia. At first, the OLF proved ineffective and made little progress in mobilizing Oromo support for an armed struggle. This was mainly because many of the Dergue's initial reforms, particularly the land reform of 1975 that restored land to the working peasants, were welcomed by a large number of Oromo, especially the Oromo elite. This support was dissipated through the regime's subsequent measures, and the OLF was able to rally an increasing following, particularly among the younger urban population.

The Somali Abo Liberation Front (SALF), set up in 1976 under the aegis of the government in the Somali Republic, was a mixed Oromo-Somali alliance. The main objective of SALF was "to liberate the lost territories of Western Somalia"—which they claimed include Bale, Arsi and Sidamo. Its members included leaders of the Bale uprising in the 1960s, such as Wako Gutu and Aliyyi Chirri and others who were considered prominent Oromo nationalists. Nevertheless, the ethnic orientation of SALF was anything but clear, and the Somali component was, if anything, more prominent than the Oromo. The OLF first tried to absorb SALF, and later denounced it as a "Somali pawn". Meanwhile, SALF preached to the Oromo people that they were a Somali tribe called the Abo. Heads of family were told and warned to teach their families "not to identify themselves as Oromo but as Somali of the Abo branch" (Gadaa, 1988). At a later date, much of the Oromo element of SALF joined the OLF.

The Islamic Front for the Liberation of Oromo (IFLO) is another political organization whose operations are limited to the Oromo-inhabited areas of Harrarge and Sidama. The founder and leader of the IFLO is Abdulkarim Ibrahim, better known as "Sheik Jara", who was a military commander in the OLF until he formed a splinter group in 1985. There were armed clashes between these two factions on several occasions, and IFLO units ambushed and killed some members of the OLF. Oromo movements were also organized outside Ethiopia. Among these is the Tokkumma Oromo Organization in the United States and various Oromo student groups in Europe and North America.

After the collapse of the Dergue in May 1991, the Tigray Peoples Liberation Front (TPLF) took control of the Ethiopian state. The TPLF sponsored several satellite ethnic movements and grouped them into a multi-ethnic coalition known as the Ethiopian Peoples Revolutionary Democratic Front (EPRDF). The Oromo elite, divided among several competing ethnic political organizations, was reduced to a subordinate role in the EPRDF state. The most important Oromo political force in the intricate manoeuvres that followed was the OLF, which had fought against the Dergue in the southwest and contributed to its downfall. Until the mid-1980s, relations between the TPLF and the OLF were ambivalent. The relationship worsened towards the end of the decade, when the TPLF created an Oromo affiliate called the Oromo Peoples Democratic Organization (OPDO), which was incorporated into the EPRDF. The TPLF also refused to recognize the OLF's claim to self-determination for the Oromo people, because this implied secession. Nevertheless, the OLF initially joined the transitional government that was formed in mid-1991. It held twelve of a total of eighty-one seats in the council of representatives and held four ministerial positions in the cabinet.

Subsequently, the relationship between the OLF and the EPRDF deteriorated rapidly. Localized armed clashes, secret and open discussions, and the signing of accords which were never implemented were typical of the period. Charges and countercharges were made daily, particularly as elections approached. There was widespread intimidation of party supporters, and killings and kidnappings of party militants. The EPRDF openly supported the Oromo Peoples Democratic Organization (OPDO), formed in 1990 under the aegis of TPLF. While also claiming the right of self-determination, this party is against secession and a close ally of the TPLF. One of its leading members became the first president of the restructured Ethiopian state. There was antagonism and tension between the OPDO and OLF from the moment the former was formed. The OLF claims the OPDO is a "weapon of Abyssinian hegemony—Tigrean in this case". For the OPDO, the OLF is a "narrow-nationalist" faction whose claim to represent the Oromo people is bogus. Finding itself outmanoeuvred as the elections

approached in 1992, the OLF withdrew from the government, and its leadership went abroad, from where they declared war on the EPRDF regime.

There are others who claim to represent the Oromo people. Among
them are organizations which were represented in the transitional government formed in 1991, such as the Islamic Front for the Liberation of Oromo
(IFLO), the Oromo and Abo Liberation Front (OALF), and the United
Oromo Peoples Liberation Front (UOPLF). The last Oromo organization to
appear is the Oromo National Congress, which announced its formation in
1996. The relationship among the different Oromo groups and the EPRDF
was confusing. At one point, the three groups (IFLO, OALF, UOPLF) signed
a cooperation agreement with OLF. At a later time, the same three organizations and the OPDO resolved to work as part of one programme. There was
similar division and confusion among and within organizations abroad
claiming to represent the Oromo. By the mid-1990s, only the OPDO remained in the ruling coalition. It dominated the regional government of the
Oromo region, and one of its leading members became the first president of
the Federal Republic of Ethiopia.

Summary and conclusion

In the above analysis, politicized ethnicity is the outcome of ethnic group
interaction with the state. During the first phase, it was found that ethnicity
was a political factor in the interaction of independent Oromo groups with
other groups that were creating the new, multiethnic Ethiopian state.
Though in a different context, the second phase witnessed the coagulation of
Oromo ethnic consciousness among some Oromo groups, after various
Oromo groups came under the centralized Ethiopian state.

Unlike the first two phases, where Oromo ethnic identity-creation was
on a regional basis, the third phase witnessed the development of Oromo
ethnonational consciousness. Two interrelated situations explain this development. The first was competition of the new educated Oromo elite with
elites of different ethnic groups for control of state power and resources. The
elite challenged the entire distribution of resources and the division of
power in society. The question posed by the elite was *not simply* who shall
have certain jobs, but who shall determine how jobs and other resources are
distributed. The second situation that fostered the development of politicized ethnicity was the reaction of the dominant state elite to the demands of
the elites of other ethnic groups. The dominant state elite lacked the political
will to accommodate the demands of the contending ethnic elites. The state
elite denied the Oromo elite its right to be a part of the highest state apparatus and confined it to a subordinate role. Hence the Oromo elite was not in a
favourable position to further its own as well as Oromo interests.

It was as a result of the above situations that the creation of a common
Oromo identity was observed, especially among the elite. This was in con-

trast to the distinct identity created by the different regional Oromo groups during the previous phases. Although most of the objective ethnic markers underwent some alteration, the newly educated elite was successful in creating an Oromo identity. The creation of this identity was possible because the elite effectively selected symbolic resources which proved politically useful: language; the historical hostility and the grievances the Oromo had accumulated while interacting with the state during the era of Tewodros, Yohannes, Menelik and Haile Selassie; the potency of some political and cultural symbols, like the *gaada* system; the claim to common ancestry and common history; and plunder of the rich resources of Oromo land by different dominant groups.

The fact that the new Oromo elite have created political organizations to claim group rights in the existing political system, or to be recognized as a sovereign nation, is proof of the development of ethnopolitical consciousness among many Oromo, especially among the elite. Irrespective of this fact, this group consciousness did not produce political solidarity or a successful ethnonationalist movement among the different Oromo groups. A reason for this could be the deep cleavages within the Oromo elite and the subsequent weakness of the political organizations they created. The Oromo elite, whose potential constituency is the largest ethnic group in Ethiopia, did not live up to its promise. The different Oromo elite factions have never been capable of effectively mobilizing the many Oromo groups living in Ethiopia around a mass-based nationalism. Rather, the history of the Oromo elite is the history of discord and fracture which has adversely affected Oromo solidarity.

From Yohannes's reign up to the present, the dominant elite was capable of coopting part of the Oromo elite and making it play a key role in the suppression of other Oromo. This pattern of fracture among the Oromo elite was further aggravated during the Dergue regime and under the current government. The different political organizations and liberation fronts which were formed by the new elite groups have been in opposition to one another. Even those which seem to consider the dominant state elite a common rival displayed a confusing pattern of alliance with the latter and among themselves. A group allied with the dominant state elite at one time would become an opponent at another. A strong adversary of the state would turn out later to be a strong supporter. There were instances where groups, especially those allied with the dominant state elite, used severe forms of repression against their rivals, killing and imprisoning members of rival groups and crushing rival political organizations. Implementing policies designed to undercut bases for ethnic group mobilization and using the media to make false allegations, were common.

One basic query needs to be answered. Within a certain range, intra-group differences and conflicts seem to be normal among any social group that strives for a common goal. But why is there such a tenacious rift between groups that claim to fight for the Oromo cause? In response to this query, the period during which politicized ethnicity has been prominent will be highlighted. This discussion rules out the common assumption that the Oromo elite are forced or manipulated by the dominant elite into submission. Given the level of education and consciousness of the new Oromo elite, it seems unlikely that they are forced or deceived in order to serve the interests of the dominant group at the expense of Oromo solidarity.

Nonetheless, the lines of fracture among the elite seem to follow differences in ethnic markers—region, religion, dialect, shared experiences and other cultural, political and economic attributes—among the Oromo groups. In fact the differences are not the objective markers per se, but the manner in which the various Oromo elite groups interpret and reinterpret them and the subjective and symbolic meanings they attach to them. In this respect, the Oromo elite divide into two trends. The first suppresses the differences and capitalizes on the common elements to create an Oromo identity. As has already been pointed out for the third phase (the 1960s), when politicized ethnicity started to take shape among the Oromo, the new Oromo elite was successful in promoting a common identity among many Oromo groups, especially the elite. The new Oromo elite was able to transcend differences and manipulate selected common symbols. It was this elite that made the objective markers acquire subjective and symbolic significance. However, this group did not survive for long. It started to fracture after the 1974 Ethiopian revolution, when the Dergue assumed full control of the state and the expectations of the intelligentsia to govern the country were shattered.

The second trend magnifies differences in the ethnic markers to justify the exclusivity of different ethnic groups. The tendency is to create a distinction between the Wellega Oromo, the Shoa Oromo, the Harrarge Oromo, the Jimma Oromo, the Arsi Oromo and the like. This fracture along regional lines has been underlined by incidents of violence between members of rival Oromo political organizations. This tendency is also reflected in the regional distribution of their members. For example the OLF has more members from Wellega, especially in leadership positions, whereas the IFLO, SALF, and WSLF have more members from Harrar, Sidama, Arsi, and Bale. The recently formed Oromo National Congress seems to have more members from Shoa. The new Oromo elite has a tendency to split along religious lines. It divides on the basis of religion and of denomination: Protestant, Orthodox Christian, Muslim. Although many feelings of religious difference were repressed, some were openly expressed. The difference between Christianity and Islam is vividly reflected in the presence of IFLO. Differences in dialect and shared experiences are also bases for splits.

The new Oromo elite also divide themselves according to what they demand from the political system. Some demand only some form of decentralization of political power, others press for outright secession, others yet, claiming to be the disadvantaged majority, demand power in the Ethiopian political system as a whole. Furthermore, there were ideological differences among the elites, especially during the Dergue period. There were Marxists, anti-Marxists and Islamists. Some saw the problem as a class issue, others as an ethnic issue. There are other socioeconomic factors which had a divisive impact on the Oromo elite: these include age, income, educational level, occupation, social class, interethnic marriage and others. To conclude, the newly educated Oromo elite groups have been capable of politicizing ethnicity. However, this group has fallen short of creating a successful ethno-nationalist movement. The basic reason for this is the cleavages within the elite group and the consequent lack of effective political organization.

Bibliography

Abir, M., 1968, *Ethiopia: The Era of Princes 1769–1855*. London: Longman.

—1980, *Ethiopia and the Red Sea*. London: Longman.

Addis Hiwot, 1975, *Ethiopia from Autocracy to Revolution*. Occasional publications, 1. London: Review of African Political Economy.

—1987, *A Certain Political Vocation: Reflection on the Ethiopian Intelligentsia*. Proceedings of the second International Conference on the Horn of Africa, 29–30 May. New York: New School for Social Research.

Africa Watch, 1991, "Evil Days: 30 Years of War and Famine in Ethiopia". Washington DC.

Asmerom Leggesse, 1973, *Gada: Three Approaches to the Study of African Society*. New York: Free Press.

Bahru Zewde, 1991, *A History of Modern Ethiopia 1855–1974*. London: James Currey.

Bairu Tafla, 1987, *Asma Giorgis and his Work: "History of the Galla and The Kingdom of Sawa"*. Stuttgart: Franz Steiner Verlag.

Bereket Habte Selassie, 1980, *Conflict and Intervention in the Horn of Africa*. New York: Monthly Review Press.

Bartels, L., 1983, *Oromo Religious Myths and Rites of the Western Oromo of Ethiopia: An Attempt to Understand*. Berlin: Dietrich Reimer Verlag.

Baxter, P.T.W., 1978, "Ethiopia's Unacknowledged Problem: the Oromo", *African Affairs*, 77, 308:283–296.

—1983, "The problem OF the Oromo or the Problem FOR the Oromo", in I.M. Lewis (ed.), *Nationalism and Self Determination in the Horn of Africa*. London: Ithaca Press.

Beckingham, C.F. and G.W.B. Huntingford (ed. and trans.), 1954, *Some Records of Ethiopia, 1593–1646*. London: Hakluyt Society.

Brass, P., 1991, *Ethnicity and Nationalism—Theory and Comparison*. London: Sage Publications.

Braukamper, U., 1980, *Oromo Country of Origin: A Reconsideration of Hypothesis*. Proceedings of the Sixth International Conference of Ethiopian Studies, Tel Aviv, 14–17 April.

Cohen, A., (ed.), 1974, *Urban Ethnicity*. London: Tavistock Publications.

Clapham, C., 1969, *Haile Selassie's Government*. New York: Praeger.

Crummey, D., 1975, "Society and Ethnicity in the Politics of Christian Ethiopia during the Zemene Masafint", *The International Journal of African Historical Studies*, 8, 2.

Darkwah, R.H., 1975, *Shewa, Menilek and the Ethiopian Empire, 1813–1889*. London: Heinemann.

Eriksen, T.H., 1993, *Ethnicity and Nationalism: Anthropological Perspectives*. London: Pluto Press.

Fukui, K., "Conflict and Ethnic Interaction: The Mela and their Neighbours", in K. Fukui and J. Markakis (ed.), *Ethnicity and Conflict in the Horn of Africa*. London: James Currey.

Gadaa Melbaa, 1988, *Oromia: An Introduction*. Khartoum.

Gebru Tareke, 1991, *Ethiopia: Power and Protest—Peasant Revolt in the Twentieth Century*. Cambridge: Cambridge University Press.

Gilkes, P., 1975, *The Dying Lion: Feudalism and Modernity in Ethiopia*. London: Julian Friedman.

—1983, "Centralism and the Ethiopian PMAC", in I.M. Lewis (ed.), *Nationalism and Self Determination in the Horn of Africa*. London: Ithaca Press.

Greenfield, R. and Mohammed Hassen, 1980, "Interpretation of Oromo Nationalism", *Horn of Africa*, 3, 3.

Greenfield, R., 1965, *Ethiopia: A New Political History*. London: Pall Mall Press.

Holcomb K. and Sisay Ibssa, 1990, *The Invention of Ethiopia: The Making of a Dependent Colonial State in North East Africa*. New Jersey: Red Sea Press.

Levine, D.N., 1974, *Greater Ethiopia—The Evolution of Multi Ethnic Society*. Chicago: University of Chicago Press.

Marcus, H.G., 1969, "Motives, Methods and some Results of the Unification of Ethiopia during the Reign of Menelik II." Proceedings of the Third International Conference of Ethiopian Studies, Addis Ababa 1966.

Markakis, J., 1974, *Ethiopia: Anatomy of Traditional Polity*. Addis Ababa: Addis Ababa University Press.

Markakis, J. and Nega Ayele, 1978, *Class and Revolution in Ethiopia*. Nottingham: Russel Press.

Mohammed Hassen, 1994, *The Oromo of Ethiopia: A History 1570–1860*. New Jersey: Red Sea Press.

Ottaway, M. and D., 1978, *Ethiopia: Empire in Revolution*. New York: Holmes and Meier.

Paulos Chanie, 1994, "Regulating Ethnic Based Conflicts: The Riddle of the Ethiopian Case". Unpublished M.A. thesis, Institute of Social Studies, The Hague.

Perham, M., 1969, *The Government of Ethiopia*. London: Faber.

Salole, G., 1979, "Who are the Shoans?", *Horn of Africa*, 2, 3.

Tessema Ta'a, 1980, "The Oromo of Wellega: A Historical Survey to 1910". Unpublished M.A. thesis, Addis Ababa University.

Waldron, S. R., 1984, "The Political Economy of Harari-Oromo Relationships, 1559–1874", *Northeast African Studies*, 6, 1 and 2:23–39.

Afar Ethnicity in Ethiopian Politics

Ali Said

Introduction

Ethnicity has always been a prominent feature of Ethiopian politics. The country's history is identified with ethnic tension and conflict. Ethiopian governments have not only failed to provide mechanisms for mediation and conflict resolution, but have also sought to manipulate ethnic differences to promote their own narrow interests. In fact, the downfall of successive regimes is by and large attributed to, among other things, their failure to give fair treatment to all nationalities and ethnic groups, especially minorities. Extreme centralization of power devoid of proportionate representation for the country's many ethnic groups, and denial of access to resources became breeding grounds for resentment among the marginalized groups and for armed confrontation with the central government.

This was the case with the Afar, a pastoral people who occupy a vast territory in the northeastern part of Ethiopia giving on to the Eritrean port of Assab on the Red Sea. Despite the geopolitical and economic importance of the Afar region, past Ethiopian governments ignored its people, who are in a worse economic and social condition than nearly all the other groups in the country.

Progressive encapsulation of the Afar land into the Ethiopian empire, coupled with the loss of the very resources the Afar and their animals relied upon, the critical dry-season grazing lands, left them destitute and vulnerable to the vagaries of nature. The exclusion of the Afar from mainstream Ethiopian development, the exploitation of their grazing resources for commercial farming, the failure to address key political issues and general neglect of their development needs planted the seeds of resentment among the Afar towards the central governments and ultimately led to ethnic conflict.

Afar history

The Afar occupy a vast area in Ethiopia, Djibouti and Eritrea. In Ethiopia, they are found in the northeastern lowlands, now delineated as the Afar region. Before 1991, the Ethiopian Afar were divided administratively among the provinces of Shoa, Harrarge, Wollo, Tigray and Eritrea. In Eritrea, the Afar live along the Red Sea coast and along the route which links Assab with Addis Ababa.

The Afar belong to the Hamitic stock of people, like the Somali, Oromo, Saho and Beja. They are traditionally divided into two tribes, *Assahimera* (reds, nobles) and *Adohimera* (whites, commoners). They are first mentioned by Ibn Sai'd in the thirteenth century by the name Dankal (Trimingham, 1952). Later, the Afar were aligned with the Muslim Adal who in turn were under the sovereignty of Ottoman Turkey. Afar pastoralists were in the armies of Imam Ahmed, better known as Gragn ("Left handed"), the Adal ruler, in his *jihad* that nearly conquered the Ethiopian kingdom in the sixteenth century. Gragn's armies were defeated with Portuguese assistance and Gragn himself was killed in battle.

A member of Gragn's family transferred the seat of the Adal sultanate from Harrar to the fertile valley of Awsa and began what Trimingham described as "the miserable history of the Imamate of Awsa" (Trimingham, 1952). The new state was overrun by "Nomadic Afar" towards the end of the seventeenth century, and the Afar Sultanate of Awsa was established. The collapse of the old sultanate and the beginning of Afar rule was an important event in the history of Afar, for it marked the beginning of a virtually new and more sophisticated Afar state.

Afar-Abyssinian relations passed through various phases before the twentieth century, sometimes hostile and many a time cordial. The strategic location of the Afar along the coast, the existence of trade routes to the hinterland and the location of saline lakes which were the source of salt, a medium of exchange, for the Abyssinian kingdom until the early twentieth century, coupled with the fact that the Afar land was the entrance point for external aggressors, made Abyssinia's rulers wary of antagonizing the Afar. In the nineteenth century, relations were by and large cordial, with minimal intervention by the highland kingdom in Afar affairs.

Ethiopian nation-building and Afar ethnicity

Prior to the assumption of full power by Emperor Menelik (1889–1913), ethnic political consolidation was impeded by religious, cultural and tribal diversity. This was particularly the case with the people of the south and the peripheral areas, including the Afar. Menelik's expansionist drive contributed to ethnic consolidation. The Awsan sultanate, which had not been accountable to the Christian kingdom, was now a vassal of Menelik and its sultan paid tribute to him. In turn, the sultan won recognition of his authority over his subjects, and this contributed to the consolidation of Afar ethnic identity. The encapsulation of the Afar into the Ethiopian empire marks late and advanced phase in the evolution of Afar ethnicity. The Afar were identified as a distinct group with their own mode of existence, predominantly nomadic pastoralism, and their own traditional hierarchy, culture and religion. Hence, Menelik's period can be identified with the consolidation of Afar ethnicity.

De facto recognition of the sultan's autonomy further consolidated the Afar ethnic identity. Menelik's interest in the Afar land was mainly economic, as it was the outlet to the outside world and the source of salt. This smoothed Afar relations with the central government. The Afar enjoyed a greater degree of autonomy than any other group, there was no infringement on their means of livelihood or any attempt at cultural or religious oppression. Ethnicity related to an identity based on kinship and did not translate into a basis for political mobilization.

Emperor Haile Selassie (1917–74) intensified the modernization efforts of his predecessor and also adopted a policy of assimilation into the culture of the ruling Amhara. The policy of assimilation was effected through marriage links, Christianization and the dissemination of Amhara language and culture. An economic development programme along the Awash River Valley in the early 1960s was the turning point in Afar-Ethiopian relations. The introduction of large commercial cotton farms and the subsequent establishment of the Awash Valley Authority (AVA), a government agency entrusted with the agricultural development of the fertile Awash River basin, meant that large tracts of Afar dry-season grazing land were lost to commercial irrigation schemes run by foreign concessions, members of the royal family and Ethiopian entrepreneurs.

The loss of resources proved a common source of resentment against the outsiders, which later developed into full ethnic conflict. One of the reasons why it took time for this resentment to become a political force was the friendly relations between the emperor and the sultan, who was not only the political chief of the Afar but also their spiritual leader. The sultan and other Afar notables became immensely wealthy through the ownership of cotton plantations. The emperor's cordial relations with the sultan and the prestige the latter enjoyed in the ranks of the Ethiopian ruling class helped Haile Selassie to check the early Eritrean rebels, and also influenced colonial politics in neighbouring Djibouti, where the Afar constitute a substantial proportion of the population. Haile Selassie hoped to incorporate what was then the French territory of Afars and Issas into Ethiopia, and used the sultan as his mediator in the area.

Despite friendly relations between emperor and sultan, the general feeling of ethnic resentment among the population moved the Afar elite, especially a small number of students abroad, to form the nucleus of the Afar National Liberation Movement (ANLM), just before the 1974 revolution in Ethiopia heralded the transformation of ethnicity into a political force.

The Dergue and the question of nationalities

Shortly after it came to power in 1974, the military junta, commonly known as the Dergue, committed itself to radical reform which would have serious social, political and economic implications. The land reform proclamation of February 1975, which abolished age-old feudal production relations, was the most significant of these measures. Nationalization of all rural land not only led to the expropriation of the holdings of Ali Mirah, the Afar sultan, but also deprived the pastoralists of their large tracts of dry-season grazing land, which were turned into large government irrigation schemes and state farms. An immediate result was the flight of Sultan Ali Mirah to Saudi Arabia. His flight marked the end of friendly relations between the central government and the Afar, which had helped contain Afar ethnicity. It ushered in a period of open ethnic confrontation between the Afar and the central government.

Following the flight of the sultan, Afar resentment sparked a rebellion which culminated in the burning of a cotton plantation and the killing of many outsiders. The closure of the Addis-Assab highway as a result of this uprising had serious implication for the country's economy. The Dergue reacted harshly and began what Shehim (1985) called an "Afar genocide". Asayta, the capital of the Awsa sultanate was destroyed and many Afar were murdered. The subsequent formation of the Afar Liberation Front (ALF) by the sultan's son, Hanfare Ali Mirah, gave ethnic resentment organized political expression and brought the ALF closer to the ANLM, despite ideological differences. The recognition of the sultan as a patriot by the ANLM marked the forging of a broader political forum for ethnic opposition. Increased politico-military activities by the Eritrean and Tigray nationalists also encouraged the politicization of Afar ethnicity.

After coming under increased pressure from various quarters, including ethnic-based movements of the Afar, Tigray, Somalis, Oromos as well as Eritrean nationalists in the north and northeast, the Dergue responded by producing the National Democratic Revolution Programme (NDRP) in 1976, which recognized the rights of nations and nationalities.[1] The programme theoretically heralded a democratic resolution of the ethnic issue, and initially won the support of many members of the ANLM and some of the AFL, who saw the realization of their demands for an autonomous Afar state.[2] A conference held in April 1977 began a dialogue between the various representatives of the Afar. Thus the Dergue succeeded in winning to its side a large segment of the Afar opposition, weakening and alienating the

---

1. Section five of the programme states: "The right of self-determination of all nationalities will be recognized and fully respected. No nationality will dominate another one since the history, culture, language and religion of each nationality will have equal recognition in accordance with the spirit of socialism." (PMAC, 1976)

2. Afar elders during the Haile Selassie regime periodically petitioned the emperor for the creation of an Afar state, which they argued would benefit the Afar and the people of Ethiopia as a whole.

ALF, a hardline group. A good number of ALF members soon joined the ranks of the ANLM to work with the Dergue. The government responded to this goodwill gesture offering members of the Afar opposition positions in the government and local administration.

Following the establishment of the Peoples Democratic Republic of Ethiopia (PDRE), the Dergue carved out an Assab Autonomous Administration from Eritrea. Since, the whole of Eritrea was under threat by Eritrean insurgents, this action was viewed simply as a security measure rather than a genuine response to the demands of the Afar for a united territory. The failure of the government to grant genuine regional autonomy frustrated the Afar and various political groups once again joined hands against the Dergue, employing ethnicity as a mobilizing factor. The successive victories of the Eritrean and Tigray insurgents over the Dergue gave the Afar opposition a further boost and increased its militancy.

Ethnicity and federalism in post-1991 Ethiopia

The collapse of the Dergue in May 1991 brought to power the Ethiopian Peoples Revolutionary Democratic Front (EPRDF), itself a product of ethnic conflict. The leading group in the EPRDF is the Tigray Peoples Liberation Front (TPLF), representing the political expression of Tigray ethnicity, or nationalism as they would put it.[3] The new regime convened a national conference in July 1991 to which all ethnic groups were invited to send representatives. The conference, in which the Afar participated, formed a transitional government. Subsequently, agreement was reached on a federal system as the best institutional framework to address the ethnic issue. Accordingly, Ethiopia was divided into nine regions, representing the major ethnic groups. These are Tigray, Afar, Amhara, Oromo, Benshangul/Gumuz, southern Peoples, Gambella, Somali, and Harari. The ALF, which held three seats in the legislature, was satisfied with this arrangement, mainly because the Afar were brought together under one regional administration. For the first time, the federal arrangement was designed to give ethnic groups maximum freedom to exercise self-rule. The constitution, adopted in 1992, gave all ethnic groups full power over regional administrative, economic, political and social affairs.

The first regional elections were held in 1992. In the Afar region, the elections involved several ethnic-based political organizations. The Afar Liberation Front Party (ALFP) and Afar Peoples Democratic Organization (APDO) were the major ones. The election was won by the ALF, which came to dominate the Afar regional council and the executive bureaux. The initial dominance of this political group can be explained by the long friendship and cooperation between the EPRDF and the ALF during the war against

---

3. See Adhana in this volume.

the Dergue. The ALF was the sole Afar political group represented at the July 1991 conference and it was this group that later claimed the three seats allotted to the Afar Council of Representatives. The Afar Liberation Front (ALF) is led by the sultan's family and claims the support of the large majority of Afar. Geographically, the ALF's strength derives mainly from the Awsa region, the historical seat of the sultanate. The ALF is led by the sultan's son, Hanfare Ali Mirah.

The Afar Peoples Democratic Organization (APDO) came into existence shortly after the fall of the military regime. This group is supposedly supported by Afar who were formerly part of Tigray province, and is an EPRDF affiliate. It claims to represent the interests of the cattle-keeping Afar, in contrast to the ALF which is associated with those of nomadic ancestry. Considering the close ties between APDO and EPRDF, it seems that the former largely represents the interests of the country's ruling party, instead of the interests of the Afar. The APDO is gradually breaking ALF's power monopoly, as is shown in the results of recent elections, when it won a majority of the seats in the Afar Regional Council (twenty-three out of forty-eight) and (three out of eight seats) in the Council of Peoples Representatives.

The Afar National Democratic Movement (ANDM) appeals to the Afar intelligentsia and considers itself a progressive political group representing the Afar people. The ANDM holds only one of the forty-eight seats in the regional council, and has one seat in the federal council. The party has recently complained about the fraudulent nature of elections at various levels. Whether the low level of ANDM representation is due to electoral fraud or lack of support among the Afar is hard to tell.

The Afar National Liberation Front (ANFL) secured eleven seats in the Afar Regional Council, one seat in the federal council and one in the Council of Peoples Representatives. It draws support from the Tigray-speaking Afar in the Berhale area bordering the Tigray region and is said to be a faction that broke away from the ALF; it is commonly known as northern ALF. In the recent local elections it came second to APDO.

Ugugumo (Revolution) is another militant group, which confronted the Dergue in the past, and is now challenging the EPRDF. This group claims to represent all Afar in the Horn and fights for what is known as Greater Afar. Since its operations are clandestine, very little is known about its leadership and social composition.

Realizing that the political right of self-rule is meaningless without economic support, the government hands over to regions a share of the central budget and the Afar region is among the beneficiaries. Unfortunately, economic management went wrong from the beginning. Corruption and embezzlement became watchwords of everyday life in the region. What funds remained were left idle and the proportion of the capital budget used during 1993 and 1994 was well below 30 per cent, one of the lowest in all the regions. The problems and needs of the people were virtually ignored, no significant development activities having taken place, except a few initiated by the federal government, and the general economic picture of the region is dim.

Conclusion

The new government's efforts to achieve conflict resolution and ethnic reconciliation—the adoption of the federal system, constitutional provisions for the right to self-determination up to secession, regional self-administration, political representation in the federal government—were encapsulated in a policy of democratization on an ethnic basis and other measures towards this end. However, corruption among local leaders, widespread embezzlement of public funds, inadequate development efforts by both central government and private sector, bitter power rivalry among different political groups and EPRDF manœuvres to change the local power balance all tended to frustrate the democratization process. This is a favourable ground for increased ethnic antagonism. The prevailing situation in the Afar region apparently endangers the peaceful and democratic resolution of the ethnic issue.

With relative autonomy within the Ethiopian state, the Afar have remained a closed society, with their culture and religion intact. Save for the traditional divisions largely based on geography (middle and lower valley Afar), and along tribal lines (*Assahimera and Adohimera*), there is a strong common ethnic identity among the Afar in Eritrea, Ethiopia and Djibouti. However, this ethnic identity did not translate into political solidarity until the early twentieth century. It was the encroachment on their means of livelihood as a result of the establishment of commercial farms and the later expansion of state farms that brought the Ethiopian state into collision with the Afar. It was only then that a common ethnic identity translated into a political force, and the Afar in the ALF rose as one ethnic group in opposition to the central government.

While the EPRDF is keenly aware of the ethnic issue and has tried to work out a policy framework to accommodate the issue, it would be difficult to conclude that it has met with success, for it has failed to address the root causes of Afar ethnic assertiveness, such as economic deprivation. As long as the new government fails to address the issue of regional economic development, feelings of ethnic hatred and resentment will remain, and the transformation of such feelings into full ethnic conflict will only be a matter of time.

Bibliography

Ali Said, 1994, "Resource Use Conflict between Pastoralism and Irrigation Developments in the Middle Awash Valley of Ethiopia", *East African Social Science Review*, 12, 2.

Ayele Gebre Mariam, 1986, "Economic Adaptation and Competition for Scarce Resources: The Afar in North Eastern Ethiopia". Unpublished M.A. thesis, Department of Social Anthropology, University of Bergen.

Bondestam, L., 1974, "People and Capitalism in the North-Eastern Lowlands of Ethiopia", *Journal of Modern African Studies*, 12, 3:423–439.

Dahilon Yasin, 1985, "The Rise and Fall of the Sultanate of Aussa with particular reference to the Reign of Ali Mirah". Senior essay, Department of Political Science and International Relations, Addis Ababa University.

Flood, G., 1976, "Nomadism and its Future", in Abdul Mejid Hussein (ed.), *Rehab: Drought and Famine in Ethiopia*. London: International African Institute.

Harbeson, J., 1978, "Territorial and Development Politics in the Horn of Africa: the Afar of Awash Valley", *Journal of African Affairs*, 77:479–98.

Lewis, I. M., 1969, *People of the Horn of Africa: Somali, Afar and Saho*. London: International African Institute.

—1983, *Nationalism and Self Determination in the Horn of Africa*. London: Ithaca Press.

Markakis, J., 1994, "Ethnic Conflicts and the State in the Horn of Africa", in K. Fukui and J. Markakis (eds.), *Ethnicity and Conflict in the Horn of Africa*. London: James Currey.

Pankhurst, R., 1992, "History of the Afar and the Afar country prior to the Nineteenth Century". Unpublished paper submitted to the Second National Conference on Ethiopian Studies, Addis Ababa.

Provisional Military Advisory Council (PMAC), 1976, "The Programme of National Democratic Revolution". Addis Ababa: Berhanena Selam.

Shehim Kassim, 1985, "Ethiopia, Revolution and the Question of Nationalities: the Case of the Afar", *Journal of Modern African Studies*, 23, 2:331–348.

Transitional Government of Ethiopia (TGE), 1994, "The Constitution of the Federal Democratic Republic of Ethiopia". Unofficial Translation.

Trimingham, J.S., 1952, *Islam in Ethiopia*. London: Oxford University Press.

Amhara Ethnicity in the Making

Tegegne Teka

Introduction

Since the take-over of political power by the Ethiopian Peoples Revolutionary Democratic Front (EPRDF) in 1991, the basis for organizing people in
Ethiopia so as to attain their political, economic and social objectives has become language/"nationality"/ethnicity. Politicized ethnicity has become the
ideology of the state and the guiding principle of the government. It is the
language groups that have become the nationalities, regions or states consti-
tuting the Federal Democratic Republic of Ethiopia (FDRE). People are
grouped and addressed on the basis of their ethnic identities; the delineation
of regional boundaries and regional administrations is based on ethnicity;
"multiparty" politics is based on ethnicity; and parliament is made up of
ethnic "parties", etc. In short, anything that has to do with government, politics and administration in Ethiopia is now governed by the politics of ethnicity or politicized ethnicity.

It is also important to note that although ethnicity may be the overriding principle at the level of the state, it may not necessarily be so at the popular level. Ethnicity has become the dominant feature of Ethiopian politics
only very recently. Referring to the role of ethnicity in Ethiopian politics in
the past, an historian has observed:

> Before the Ethiopian Revolution [1974] most discussions on regional sepa-
> ratism, ethnic nationalism and subject groups' identity in Ethiopia were con-
> fined to limited circles, mostly student unions and a few radical circles out-
> side Ethiopia, particularly in Europe and the United States. These were taboo
> topics among Ethiopianists and had no place in their public meetings and
> scholarly publications. (Triulzi, 1983:111)

Today, the contrary is true. The question of ethnicity is real and it has come
out into the open. Debates are conducted, scholarly articles are written, and
opinions are expressed in the media on ethnicity and society. However,
there are some people who prefer to assume this issue does not exist, and
others who are fearful and keep their distance. Such attitudes are not helpful

to the resolution of the problems at hand. Rather, we must face reality and explore the imagined and true nature of ethnicity in order to manage and regulate it for the good of society and the resolution of conflicts.

What is ethnicity?

There is no general definition of ethnicity that we can use as a benchmark and every commentator on the subject formulates his own. A definition by Hutchinson and Smith (1996:6) contains most of the familiar elements: an ethnic group is "a named human population with myths of common ancestry, shared historical memories, one or more elements of common culture, a link with a homeland and a sense of solidarity among at least some of its members".

If we use these criteria in the Ethiopian context and apply them to the ethnic group under consideration, the Amhara, there would be little agreement on the outcome. The Amhara do not have myths of common ancestry, shared historical memories, a link with a homeland (they have several homelands), but they do have elements of common culture, specifically a language, and a sense of solidarity among at least some members of their group. The one element that distinguishes the Amhara is their language. Even though it can be said that in terms of social identification the Amhara are perceived as an ethnic group, this identity is not clearly fixed according to conventional ethnic criteria. Just as it is difficult to have clear-cut definitions of ethnicity, it is also difficult to find groups of people with clear-cut identities. Jenkins (1997:169–70) has this to say:

> That there are limits to the plasticity of ethnicity, as well as to its fixity and solidity, is the founding premise for the development of an understanding of ethnicity which permits us to appreciate that although it is imagined it is not imaginary; to acknowledge its antiquity as well as its modernity. Rethinking demands that we should strike a balanced view of the authenticity of ethnic attachments. Somewhere between irresistible emotion and utter cynicism, neither blindly primordial nor completely manipulable, ethnicity and its allotropes are principles of collective identification and social organization in terms of culture and history, similarity and difference, that show little sign of withering away.

Ethnicity has become one of the most effective instruments for political mobilization in many parts of Africa. In Ethiopia, though such a policy has been adopted by the ruling party and other ethnic-based parties, it appears that the urban population does not seem to welcome it and it is not certain how the rural population feels and the extent to which it endorses ethnic federalism. Mesfin Araya (1991:29) states that "even though ethnicity in Ethiopia, as elsewhere in Africa, has its material and socio-psychological basis in the history of uneven development between regions and ethnic groups, it is also the instrument of the various ethnic elites to broaden their constituencies in their bid for state power." Sarah Vaughan (1996:339) adds:

> In the case of many of the liberation fronts who fought the Derge around Ethiopia's periphery, it is not clear that such "dissident nationalism" (Markakis, 1987) reflected the conviction of their populations that they were oppressed as a consequence primarily of their non-Amhara nationality. If the TPLF was able to argue this more convincingly in the case of Tigray, it took more than 10 years to forge a popular consensus, and that consensus, as already suggested, was underpinned by something more concrete: programmes which brought economic improvement to rural areas.

> If such programmes were a key reason for the success of the TPLF, and more recently of its EPRDF coalition partners, in mobilising peasant support, they suggest that nationality was less a primary contradiction in Ethiopia, than the most effective means of mobilising the population to combat uneven development. The notion of the pre-existing nation has been replaced as the parent of nationalism by the struggle against economic oppression. The old question remains at the heart of analysis of Ethiopian politics: which comes first—class or nationality?

Attitudes towards ethnicity in Ethiopia fall into two broad categories. The first sees the recognition of ethnicity at all levels of political life as part of the democratization process: recognition ensures justice and equality among ethnic groups and redresses the injustice of the past. The second regards ethnicity as divisive, and fears that the consequences of ethnicizing Ethiopian society will be grave.

I would like to add a third way of looking at the issue of ethnicity in Ethiopia. The third view recommends that while we recognize existing realities and emerging ethnic identities, we should at the same time pave the way for a collective identity, i.e., a pan-Ethiopian identity. This paper is concerned with the future. It suggests that we may not do any good to society if we continue to organize people in groups—by the language they speak, the culture they share, or the race they belong to. What will become of us if we ethnicize and balkanize our people? Is it an end in itself or a means to an end? It certainly cannot be the first, and if it is the second, it is indeed a fragile tool to depend on for social engineering. It is, therefore, very important to understand that what we do today serves the common interests of our people tomorrow.

The thesis of this paper is as follows. Promoting Amhara ethnicity/nationalism is neither necessary for this linguistic group, whose elites appear unwilling to cooperate in this project, nor good for the construction of a democratic Ethiopia. It is bad for national integration and nation-building. It is backward looking. It impedes the overall development of society, it spreads animosity among people and it does not advance the cause of peace.

Who are the Amhara?

Amhara is one of the Ethiopian "nationalities", as defined on the basis of language. The present Amhara state comprises the Amharic-speaking people of Ethiopia, who are not necessarily an "indigenous" people who always spoke Amharic. As currently defined, the Amhara are numerically one of the largest groups in the country. Levine (1974:118) observed: "In their home territory, Amhara rarely express a strong sense of belonging to the community of all Amhara. They identify themselves either on a regional basis, Gojjam versus Gondere—or else by means of the supra-ethnic term Habesha". The Amhara represent four regional provincial outlooks and sentiments; Gonder, Gojjam, Wollo and Shoa. In fact, the latter group claims preeminence over the others because it dominated the Ethiopian state since the time of Menelik. Most of the Amhara elite identify with this state and view themselves as Ethiopians, not Amhara.

Historically, the Amhara are thought to have occupied a region in southern Wollo, in the district of Amhara. Ludolf (1984:13–14) has this to say about the geographical location of Amhara: "Beginning from the 13th century, there existed an Amhara province which was bordered by Merhabete in the south, Yifat and Angot/Yeju/ in the east, Begemdir in the north and Gojjam in the west". Abba Gorgorios (an Ethiopian), in a letter he sent to Ludolf, describes the location of Amhara province as follows: "Amhara is located between river Beshilo in the north dividing it from Begemdir, and Wonchit river in the south dividing it from Shewa". Getachew Haile (1992:20) writes:

> Only those who spoke Amharic were called Amhara. For unknown historical reasons, the language of the Amharas started to spread outside Amhara, especially into Gonder, Gojjam, Last, and northern Shewa (notably Menz, Tegulet, Bulga). All these regions spoke other languages before they were overrun by Amharic. Other ethnic cultures gave way to the Amharic culture and language, influencing and changing in turn Amharic language and culture.

Presently, the Amharas inhabit the whole of Wollo (except some pockets in the east), the whole of Gojjam, Gonder and North Shoa. Since the Amhara that lived between Beshilo and Wonchit rivers went out and mixed with the neighbouring peoples and cultures, and this has been taking place for many centuries, it is difficult to find their primordial origins. This tells us that one's ethnic origin cannot be found in the language one speaks, and further proves that ethnic identities are shifting and changing according to historical and social processes.

The name Amhara is interpreted differently. It means "ploughmen" to some (Hudson and Tekeste in Takkele Tadesse 1994:176), free and proud people to others (Kidane Wold Kifle, 1956; Kessate Berhan Tessema, 1959; Desta Teklewold, 1970), highlander and Christian yet others. In his last speech, the head of the military regime (1974–91), Mengistu Haile Mariam, tried to explain what Amhara means:

> What does Amhara mean? Israeli travellers returned to their country after visiting Ethiopia. They wrote an account of their travels and reported to have seen the land of the Amhara. In Hebrew, *Am* means people and *Hara* means mountain, therefore, the name Amhara, means people living on the mountains. Prior to this, there was no group of people that carried this name or there was no language with this name. In Ethiopia, the correct meaning of Amhara is highland dweller. If this is the case, who then is Amhara? Is it the highland dwellers of Eritrea, Tigray, Gonder, Gojjam, Wollo, Oromo, Gurage, Kaffa, Gimira, Gammo, Hadiya, Wollaita, Kambatta, Argoba, etc.?

Baxter (1978:289) gives the Oromo perspective of the Amhara:

> From an Oromo viewpoint an Amhara is anyone who is either born into Amhara society and culture, or anyone who chooses to enter them, by speaking Amharic in domestic situations, by adopting an Amharic life style and by acting in public situations in support of Amharic values. ... An Amhara is one who, all in all, assumes that Amharic culture is so obviously superior to the other cultures of Ethiopia that all Ethiopians should seek to acquire that culture.

Apparently there is no consensus on the meaning of Amhara. This does not indicate that there is *not* a group of people called Amhara. Nevertheless, it supports the contention that, "ethnic identities are social constructs defined by the historical conditions in which they emerge" (Markakis, 1996:300).

Are the Amhara an ethnic group?

As mentioned earlier, the Amhara do not posses what people usually refer to as objective ethnic markers: common ancestry, territory, religion and shared experience except the language. The Amhara have no claims to a common ancestry. They do not share the same sentiments and they have no mutual interests based on shared understandings. It is, therefore, difficult to conclude that the Amhara belong to an ethnic group. But this does not mean there is no Amhara identity. As Clapham has said (1988:23–24) "like the English—their own [Amhara] ethnicity is weakly defined. Unlike the great majority of African peoples, they do not constitute a 'tribe'—a group ... defined by a methodology of common descent from a single ancestor". Levine (1974:117–18) asks:

> What are the boundaries of the community in which Amhara have traditionally identified themselves as members? The horizons of most Amhara are narrowly circumscribed. Most of their interest and energies are directed to the local units. Yet none of these complexes forms a corporate entity with which they are deeply identified and to which they remain steadfastly loyal. They look beyond their households to others which may offer greater economic opportunities or less restrictive regimes.

Speaking a single language is not enough to classify people as an ethnic group. Amhara identity has been influenced and changed by historical events. As a group they have travelled and settled far and wide in Ethiopia. The Amhara have gone to other territories, and others have come to Amhara territory, and a great deal of intermingling has resulted. Some see the Amhara as a fused stock. Clapham (1988:24) notes that:

> It is essential to emphasise the plasticity of Amhara—and hence, in a sense, of Ethiopian—identity in order to correct the very misleading impression that can be given by associating it with the descent-based ethnic identities characteristic of many other African societies. Being Amhara is much more a matter of how one behaves than of who one's parents were.

> In other words, since the indigenous Amharic speaking people have lost their Amharaness in their fusion with other peoples of Ethiopia, what remains as a marker is a language which has become part of the core culture of Ethiopia and can be regarded as national, not the exclusive property of a particular group of people.

Amhara ethnicity and the state

The Abyssinian/Ethiopian state is identified with the Amhara ruling class. This class did not encourage Amhara ethnicity when it had control of the state machinery with which to do so. The Amhara masses were not mobilized on that basis, because the elite had no interest in promoting Amhara ethnicity. One may ask why? The answer is that they did not need it. Because state bureaucracy was dominated by the Amhara ruling class, the elite felt they were the embodiment of the state. They were not subjugated as people, did not experience a feeling of inferiority and their culture was not suppressed. In fact, theirs is the national language, it is taught in schools, and has become the working language of the country. Politically progressive Amhara who championed the cause of freedom for the oppressed nationalities in Ethiopia did not raise the issue of Amhara ethnicity, mainly because it is nonexistent. The Amhara middle class and elite saw the Ethiopian state as their own state and identified with it.

Amhara "nationalism"/ethnicity has emerged gradually after the change of regime in 1991. This has happened as a result of state policies adopted by the ruling Ethiopian Peoples Revolutionary Democratic Front (EPRDF), and the subsequent need to protect the Amhara in the face of threats from ethnicist/nationalist elements in other groups. This is the time when politicized Amhara ethnicity began to emerge. In this connection, it is important to note what an ex-member of the EPDM/EPRDF has to say on organizing the Amhara along ethnic lines in a book which he published in Amharic. Andargachew Tsigie (1993:4–5) explains:

> Today politics in Ethiopia is based on ethnicity. There are ethnic groups that have very strong ethnic sentiments and very strong ethnic-based political

organizations. These ethnic-based political organisations have the capacity to design economic and political policies that will safeguard and promote their ethnic interests. This capacity is bound to get stronger because it is fuelled by ethnicity. In the face of this reality, those ethnic groups that are not organized, like the Amhara, will become underdogs and trail behind, and will not attain an equal level of development, however good their strategic objectives are. This is not good either for the Amhara or the other ethnic groups in Ethiopia. What must the Amhara do to surmount this problem? The only way out is to organize on the basis of ethnicity. If this Amhara ethnic organization is to have a meaning, it must be based on strong Amhara ethnic sentiments and ethnic identity. It is this Amhara ethnic consciousness that we call Amhara nationalism. (Translation mine.)

The fear of being marginalized in the economic and political sphere was one of the reasons for the emergence of ethnic-based political parties. Markakis (1996:303) has this to say about the proliferation of such parties: "Since the advent of a new regime in Ethiopia in 1991, dozens of political groups have emerged claiming to represent ethnic communities—'nationalities' in local parlance. Most of [these] are minuscule factions of urban petty bourgeois elements whose claim to represent the rural folk should not be taken for granted". Furthermore, Mesfin Araya (1991:27) commented on developments in Ethiopia in 1991 as follows: "What we see is not a struggle for social transformation whose beneficiaries would be the ordinary people. What we see is a crisis of inter-elite integration—pure and simple". This refers to the positioning of elites behind ethnic parties in the struggle for state power.

Two rival political parties claim to represent the interests of the Amhara "nationality". One belongs to the ruling EPRDF coalition, and the other is in the opposition. The first is the Amhara National Democratic Movement (ANDM). This party is what remains of the Ethiopian Peoples Democratic Movement (EPDM) after other minority nationalities left to organize their own ethnic parties. The EPDM had been a junior partner in the EPRDF along with the Tigray Peoples Liberation Front (TPLF), and took part in the campaign that brought down the military regime. The ANDM was created by the EPRDF during the transitional period in Addis Ababa. It was officially inaugurated at the Third Congress of the EPDM in January 1994. At this meeting, it was declared that "the multi-national character and objectives of EPDM is transformed into a democratic national movement of ANDM. The objectives of EPDM would continue to be the objectives of ANDM and would work for the people in the Amhara region" (*Addis Zemen*, January 1994).

The second party is the All Amhara Peoples Organization (AAPO). This was the first organization formed to represent the Amhara. An AAPO document (1994) states that:

The All Amhara Peoples Organization (AAPO) was established on 19 January 1992, i.e., over seven months after the establishment of the Transitional

Government of Ethiopia. It was established because of the acute need of the Amhara and to plead on their behalf in the context of the equality of all ethnic and religious groups within united Ethiopia. Thus, it is the need of the Amhara people, who constitute 40–45 per cent of the Ethiopian population, and yet were being denied all their basic rights, that necessitated the creation of AAPO.

This is not the occasion to discuss the two Amhara ethnic parties. However, one thing that can be said about them is that they have few followers, even among the elite, not to mention the rural population. This small following among the elite is also a feature of most other ethnic-based political parties in Ethiopia. The uninterest of the Amhara elite in nationalist/ethnicist mobilization is a positive trend in the construction of the new Ethiopia. Given the limited impact of the ethnic appeal to Amhara nationalism, we must seize this historical opportunity to begin the implementation of the nation-building agenda. At the moment, there is no collective action by the Amhara inspired by ethnic consciousness. How long this will remain will depend on internal developments and the policies of the state in Ethiopia.

Incipient Amhara ethnicity must not be encouraged, for it carries the danger of ethnicizing a large group of people with proportionately high representation among the elite and the middle class. If Amhara nationalism is allowed to mature, particularly among the elite, it is possible that the country will revert to the days we long not to see: conflict and a struggle for political power based on ethnic loyalties. If the Amhara elite embraces ethnicity as a tool of mass mobilization, this could be very dangerous for the creation of a post-EPRDF Ethiopia based on justice and social consensus. It would also take longer to fulfil the aspirations of the Ethiopian peoples to live in peace, equality and prosperity. It is for this reason that this group of people, the elite and the middle class of the Amhara and other nationalities, must be allowed to transcend ethnicity and embrace a pan-Ethiopian identity.

Framework for a pan-Ethiopian identity

The Institute for the Study of Ethiopian Nationalities (1978) recorded over eighty ethnic groups in Ethiopia and provided brief introductions to their history and languages. If, as a matter of state policy, ethnic groups were to become the basis of political organization through which the democratization process is to take place, are we going to have more than eighty regional government units and as many languages of instruction in schools? One can argue that the rights of people should not be compromised by the difficulty of implementation. Though one may agree with such arguments, implementation hardly looks practicable in view of the challenges that await us. Moreover, if we nurture exclusiveness and focus on the particularity of separate identities at the expense of their universal character, it is likely that we will provide opportunities for the elite and the middle class to exploit in their struggle for power. There is a need to construct a common identity, a pan-Ethiopian identity. We must find symbols that are representative enough to build a common future based on a democratic culture. We know that identities can be constructed or invented (Ranger, 1996; Hobsbawm and Ranger, 1983). According to Sorenson (1993:5):

> The Horn of Africa is the site for a clash of nationalist struggles that offer competing narratives of the past and of contemporary forms of identity, imagining Ethiopia in sharply contrasting ways. Greater Ethiopian nationalism has created for itself a genealogy that stretches into the biblical past, and suggests a virtually primordial and essential identity shared by all those who are within the current boundaries of the Ethiopian state, regardless of their particular ethnic affiliation.

Being Ethiopian is not an identity that only the Amhara carry. It is an identity shared by many Ethiopians, despite language differences. Hence, one can argue that it is an identity which is a synthesis of many cultures. Moreover, if we take the constructionist view "that ethnicity is perpetually defined and redefined by social actors in the course of interaction, and that membership of ethnic groups, their boundaries, and the cultural stuff upon which they draw, are all, to some considerable extent, variable" (Jenkins 1997:142), then it would be very difficult to take ethnicity as an end in itself and organize society accordingly. There is a need to look for something that transcends group and ethnic identities and is more enduring. This is where the argument for nation-building by the state makes sense. "Whereas earlier it was considered self-evident that 'a nation is a community which normally tends to produce a state of its own'", as Max Weber put it (1947:176), experience in Africa supports Ernest Baker's dictum that "it is states that create nations" (Markakis, 1987:272). That is to say, nations and nationalism are superior forms of sociopolitical organization to ethnicity, and the building of nations is a higher project and demands the full support of the state.

For a state to do this, it has to be above ethnic politics. On these grounds, there is a lot to be desired from the Ethiopian state at present, since it has taken the initiative in promoting ethnicity among the people. It is wrong for the state to allow itself to become a testing ground for social experimentation. This is a mistake of the past and it must not be allowed to continue. The experience of the military regime could serve as a lesson. In a public speech about one month before he fled the country, Mengistu Haile Mariam reflected, "In our desire to teach equality and democracy during the period of the revolution, we may have gone beyond proportion in dealing with the question of nationalities and languages in Ethiopia. As a result, we could have misled and misguided the people" (*Addis Zemen*, April 1991).

Conclusion

The common objective is to build a society based on mutual respect and equality, a society that is responsive to the interests of all. It is essential to redress the social, economic, political and cultural imbalances inherited from the past. The role of the state in this regard is quite significant. "The state here is viewed as an actor, that although obviously influenced by the society surrounding it, also shapes social and political processes. There is a recognized need to improve conceptualisation of the structures and capacities of states ... and to explore in many settings how states affect societies through their interventions—or abstentions—and through their relationships with social groups" (Evans, 1985:vi). To work for a pan-Ethiopian identity is to work for higher ideals, with due recognition of the rights of ethnic groups.

For those individuals and groups who feel strongly about their ethnic identities, the state must create conditions for them to develop these identities. They must be allowed to be what they want to be. At the same time, the state must create conditions where, these groups can, gradually and of their own free will, come to share values, symbols, political, economic and social objectives that are commonly agreed upon and developed through a national (pan-Ethiopian) consensus. For those individuals and groups who do not feel strongly about ethnic identities, and are ready and willing to adopt a pan-Ethiopian identity with the common values, symbols, political, economic and social objectives commonly agreed upon, the state must allow and encourage them to do so. It is for the attainment of these higher ideals that the author has argued against the promotion of the Amhara ethnicity that is now in the making with the active support of the state.

Bibliography

Addis Zemen. (Ethiopian Calendar Miazia 12, 1983/April 1991, Tir 1986/January 1994), Addis Ababa, Ethiopia.

Andargachew Tsigie, 1993, *YeAmhara Hizb: Keyet Wedet (The Amharas: From Where to Where)*. Addis Ababa: Bole Printing Press.

Bahru Zewde, 1991, *A History of Modern Ethiopia 1855–1974*. London: James Currey.

Baxter, P.T.W. and H. Blackhurst, 1978, "Vercingetorix in Ethiopia: Some Problems Arising from Levine's Inclusion of the Oromo in his Delineation of Ethiopia as a Culture Area", *Abbay* 9.

Clapham, C., 1988, *Transformation and Continuity in Revolutionary Ethiopia*. Cambridge: Cambridge University Press.

Desta Teklewold, 1970, *The New Amharic Dictionary*. Addis Ababa: Artistic Printing Press.

Evans, P., D. Rueschemeyer and T. Skocpol (eds.), 1985, *Bringing the State Back In*. Cambridge: Cambridge University Press.

Getachew Haile, 1992, "Amhara Speakers and the Question of Nationalities", *Ethiopian Review*, May, 2, 5.

Gorgendiere, L. et al. (eds.), 1996, *Ethnicity in Africa: Roots, Meanings and Implications*. Edinburgh: Centre of African Studies, University of Edinburgh.

Hobsbawm, E. and T. Ranger (eds.), 1983, *The Invention of Tradition*. Cambridge: Cambridge University Press.

Hutchinson, J. and A.D. Smith (eds.), 1996, *Ethnicity*. Oxford: Oxford University Press.

Institute for the Study of Ethiopian Nationalities, 1985, *Achir Ye-etiopia Behereseboch Maweqiya* (Brief Introduction to the nationalities of Ethiopia). Addis Ababa.

Jenkins, R., 1997, *Rethinking Ethnicity: Arguments and Explorations*. London: Sage Publications.

Kessate Berhan Tessema, 1959, *Amharic Dictionary*. Addis Ababa: Artistic Printing Press.

Kidane Wold Kifle 1956, *The New Book of Grammar, Verbs and Dictionary*. Addis Ababa: Artistic Printing Press.

Levine, D., 1974, *Greater Ethiopia*. Chicago: University of Chicago Press.

—1992, "Meles Zenawi and the Politics of Ethnicity", *Ethiopia Review*, September.

Ludolf, H., 1982, *New History of Ethiopia*. London: SASOR.

Markakis, J. 1987, *National and Class Struggles in the Horn of Africa*. Cambridge: Cambridge University Press.

—1996, "The Political Challenge of Ethnicity", in L. Gorgendiere et al. (eds.), *Ethnicity in Africa: Roots, Meanings and Implications*. Edinburgh: Centre of African Studies, University of Edinburgh.

Mesfin Araya, 1991, "The Politics of Ethnicity in Ethiopia", *Imbylta*, 2, 1.

Ranger, T., 1996, "The Nature of Ethnicity: Lessons from Africa". Unpublished manuscript.

Sorenson, J., 1993, *Imagining Ethiopia: Struggles for History and Identity in the Horn of Africa*. New Brunswick: Rutgers University Press.

Takkele Taddese, 1994, "Do the Amharas Exist as a Distinct Ethnic Group?", in H. G. Marcus (ed.), *New Trends in Ethiopian Studies. Proceedings of the Twelfth International Conference of Ethiopian Studies*, II. New Jersey: Red Sea Press.

Triulzi, A., 1983, "Competing Views of National Identity in Ethiopia", in I.M. Lewis (ed.), *Nationalism and Self Determination in the Horn of Africa*. London: Ithaca Press.

Vaughan, S., 1996, "Ethnicity and the Prospects for Democratisation in Ethiopia", in L. Gorgendiere et al. (ed.), *Ethnicity in Africa: Roots, Meanings and Implications*. Edinburgh: Centre of African Studies, University of Edinburgh.

Weber, Max, 1947, *The Theory of Social and Economic Organization*. Glencoe: Free Press.

The Politics of Identity—The Case of the Gurage in Ethiopia

John Markakis

Introduction

In the ongoing debate on ethnicity, a consensus has emerged on two of its key features. One concerns the formation of ethnic identities, and the other the functions ethnicity performs in the contemporary setting. It is generally agreed that ethnic identities are social constructs defined by the historical conditions in which they emerge; "the ever-changing product of social and historical dynamics" (Atkinson, forthcoming). What we see today is not the atavistic remnants of an earlier age, but fairly recent creations shaped by social and political change.

The historical point of reference for contemporary ethnicity in Africa is the colonial period, a watershed in the modern history of the continent, when its peoples were obliged to react and adapt to radically changed circumstances. The forging of new ethnic identities and the dissolving of old ones, as well as change in the functions ethnicity was required to perform— that is, the purposes for which identity was asserted—were part of this reaction, as Africans adapted to the exigencies of the colonial situation.

This is not to say that identities of precolonial vintage did not survive, nor that new identities were woven of entirely new cloth. It is simply to say that ethnic identities, like all social constructs, are subject to change, and so are the functions ethnicity performs. For Africans who found themselves in the emerging urban sector during the colonial era, for example, ethnicity acquired new contours as well as functions. The "invention of tribes" during that period was not simply the result of administrative expediency on the part of alien rulers, but also the African response to change in the socio-economic and political environment.

Though colonialism may be the historical point of reference, nearly half a century of independence has also left its mark on ethnicity, as Africans were obliged once again to respond to changing conditions. A striking aspect of this response has been the politicization of identity, that is, the use of it for purposes of political mobilization. Certainly, this is not a novelty. Ethnicity has always been one of the factors determining political choice in Africa and elsewhere in the world. In recent years, however, ethnicity appears to have become the only factor that determines political choice in many African societies afflicted with poverty, social tension and political insecurity.

The case study of the Gurage in Ethiopia presented here illustrates some of the points made above. The intention is not to reinforce a line of analysis—constructivist or instrumentalist—with documentary proof, but simply to suggest how it can be applied to shed more light on a social phenomenon about which "there is too much knowledge and not enough understanding" (Horowitz, 1985:xi).

Traditional society

The Gurage occupy a compact territory on the central Ethiopian plateau. Major rivers form its boundaries: the Omo in the west, the Gibe in the south, the Awash in the northeast and the Wabe in the northwest. Lesser rivers criss-cross the territory. Being shallow, these are not used for transportation, and did not facilitate interaction between the various parts of Gurageland. Instead, rivers often serve as boundaries between districts inhabited by the various groups into which the Gurage are divided. Gurageland has many mountains, including the majestic Mount Gurage which reaches over 12,000 feet. These peaks also serve as boundaries in intra-Gurage spatial and social divisions. Like most of the plateau, Gurageland is deeply dissected and includes land at widely differing elevations under widely differing climatic conditions.

The Gurage share a material culture whose foundation is the cultivation of *enset* (false banana), which is the staple foodstuff of many ethnic groups in southwest Ethiopia. *Enset* cultivation is land-intensive and does not require fallowing: therefore, it is able to support higher population densities than other crops in the highlands. Although its calorific value is low, *enset* has a high agronomic yield and can support perhaps twice as many people per hectare as cereals. The Gurage region has one of the highest population densities in Ethiopia. *Enset* production determines not only the Gurage diet, but also the work calendar and division of labour, as well as the spatial pattern of Gurage settlements. Its by-products are used for hut construction, fuel, fodder, the production of utensils, medicine and detergent. *Enset* cultivation requires fertilizer: therefore, it is combined with animal rearing. *Enset* gardens are attached to the large, tall conical huts that are the artistically distinctive houses of the Gurage (Lebel, 1969). Tending them does not involve the time- and energy-consuming travel associated with other food production systems on the highlands.

Gurage households are grouped together in compact villages which are the matrix of socioeconomic organization and political authority. Gurage social structure is based on patrilineal descent groups, which range in depth and size from the extended family, to subclan and clan, and villages are collections of related patrilocal households. Territory is identified with clan, but not all who live in the same clan district belong to the same clan. Traditionally, marriage took place between neighbouring villages, although the Gurage also intermarried extensively with neighbouring Oromo, Amhara, Sidama and Hadiya groups. Gurage political organization was highly segmented. Corporateness was a feature of local descent groups which were quite autonomous, while authority was exercised at the village level by a council of household heads.

The Gurage are distinguished by their Semitic speech, in the midst of Cushitic speaking peoples (Sidama, Oromo). However, Gurage is not a language but a linguistic family. Leslaw (1992) assumes that there was a proto-Gurage language from where these clusters and dialects originated, but the nature of subsequent differentiation is not clear. Shack (1966) sees the influence of Sidama, while Leslaw (1992) finds connections with Harrar and Gafat. According to Leslaw (1992:298), linguistically speaking, Gurage "is the most intriguing region of Ethiopia", meaning it is the most complex. Those who have studied it identify three geographically distinct linguistic clusters situated east, west and north, comprising a total of at least twelve dialects, several of them mutually unintelligible.

The Gurage share a traditional religion whose deities have followers and ritual leaders throughout Gurageland. Three major cults—*Wak* (Warrior God) for men, *Damwamwit* (Goddess) for women, and *Bwaja* (Thunder God) for both sexes—are organized on a territorial basis, and have a hierarchical structure beginning at the subclan level and culminating at a paramount figure who resides at a fixed place where annual pan-Gurage festivals take place. The centralized and hierarchical form of the traditional Gurage religious system contrasts sharply with the highly segmented and acephalous traditional authority system described below.

Islam and Christianity made deep incursions in Gurageland. Christianity came from Abyssinia centuries ago, and Islam was established long before the Abyssinian conquest of Gurageland last century. They came from different directions, and Islam became predominant in eastern Gurageland while Christianity was entrenched in the north. While some groups are almost exclusively attached to one or the other of these faiths, Muslims and Christians can be found in almost all districts and clans. There is also a sprinkling of Catholics and Protestants, products of recent European missionary activity.

Traditional political authority among the Gurage reflected genealogical segmentation, with clans and subclans functioning quite autonomously and lacking an established hierarchy. Clan leaders for administration and war were assisted by councils of elders. Collective decisionmaking occurred at the level of those who were involved, whether descent group, village, sub-clan or clan. Nothing resembling political integration or authority emerged beyond the clan, and the Gurage have no tradition of political unity. On the contrary, oral tradition is a tale of violent strife between and within clans. Such strife reached a high point in mid-nineteenth century, when Gurageland was devastated by a series of violent clashes among clans vying for hegemony. Shortage of land may have been the cause of it. A foreign traveller described the region at the time as being in a state of anarchy (Harris, 1844, vol. 3:313).

Identity

The pattern of social organization sketched above is quite complex, but not unusual in precolonial Africa. It comprises an intricate network of relation-ships among groups based on genealogy and territoriality, which may or may not share the conventional attributes of ethnicity, such as language or religion. In this social pattern, identity is contextual, multidimensional and fluid. The assertion of a person's identity is intended to give meaning to an encounter with others. Meaning refers to the purpose for which identity is formulated in a given context. Its formulation depends on which attributes —genealogical, geographical, cultural, historical—are given priority in con-structing meaning, and this will depend on who the others are: that is, what is the relationship between oneself and them. Depending on the context, identity may be based on any of the attributes mentioned above.

Context is what one author terms the "political ecology" of ethnicity (Abbink, 1991:1), and understanding it is essential to our understanding of identity. The factors that pertain to it can be studied objectively. Un-doubtedly, subjective factors pertaining to social psychology also play a role, and there are analytical approaches that focus exclusively on these (Moyni-han, 1993). Two problems confront these approaches. First, by the very na-ture of their subject, any assessment of its weight in the calculus of identity formation is itself impressionistic, not to say subjective. Second, there is a tendency to isolate the phenomenon from the situation that gives birth to it: "By isolating 'ethnicity' as a focus of research, one easily loses everything else from sight" (Eriksen, forthcoming).

Among the western Gurage, the clan (bet) provides the main basis of identity. Earlier, there were five clans in this area known collectively as amist bet (five clans), to which two more were added recently and are now known as sabat bet (seven clans). The sabat bet represent the western linguistic clus-ter, with at least seven mutually intelligible dialects, one for each bet. These clans were in the thick of the internecine struggle of the mid-nineteenth century, at the end of which they decided to establish a common political institution to preserve the peace among them. The Yajoka is an assembly of *sabat bet* clan chiefs and notables, whose function is to make laws, adjudicate cases, and resolve interclan disputes. This was as far and as high as political organization reached among the Gurage.

Territoriality is more important for social and political organization among the Soddo in the north, whose region is divided into *ager* (clusters of hamlets) that provide the foundation of local identity formation. There is no counterpart of the *Yajoka* among the Soddo. However, when it is required, an all-Soddo assembly attended by elders representing their districts, performs the same function. The Soddo speak a language unintelligible to other Gurage. The solidly Christian Soddo are also known as *Kistani* (Christians), and their tradition traces their origin in the Tigray region of Abyssinia in the north. In their case, religion provides a prominent dimension to their identity, albeit not a dominant one. There is considerable admixture in that region with Oromo who arrived there long ago, and the name Soddo is itself Oromo. Although quite assimilated by the *Kistani*, the Oromo element was preserved in the identity of exogamous clans and was asserted in appropriate situations.

By contrast, religion is the cornerstone of identity among the Silte-speakers in the east. They comprise the third cluster of the Gurage linguistic family, representing five dialects, all quite different from the Soddo and *sabat bet* tongues. The solidly Muslim Silte-speakers place their origin in the east, whence Islam came. Tradition has it that they are related to the Hadiya, a non-Gurage group, and in fact they are called *Yeren* Hadiya (Upper Hadiya) by the *sabat bet*. Traditionally, Silte-speakers identified themselves simply as "Muslims", and if asked what language they spoke, were likely to answer "Islamic". On the other hand, they were likely to identify all Christians as "Amhara", the dominant Abyssinian group. Indeed, within Gurageland, no people identified themselves as Gurage, because that identity had no meaning in that context.

Conquest and transformation

The pattern sketched above is a long way from the familiar image of the ethnic group as perceived by the Western anthropological imagination—with clear-cut boundaries, cultural uniformity and political solidarity. Nevertheless, in the first half of this century, the Gurage came to be thus perceived by others, and were themselves inclined to share this perception. How this came about is not different in essence from what happened elsewhere in Africa at the same time. Two sets of factors were involved. One was conquest and subjugation by an alien power, and the need of the conquerors for clear and expedient principles to guide the administration of their subjects. Another was the necessity of subject peoples to adjust to the loss of independence and to the socioeconomic exigencies this entailed.

The Gurage were conquered by fellow Africans, yet the "tribalization" process was essentially the same as elsewhere in Africa during the colonial period. Gurageland lay in the path of the Abyssinian expansion southwards, launched by Emperor Menelik when he was still only a provincial ruler of Shoa, just north of Gurageland. The Gurage fought with spears against the rifles of the Abyssinians and lost. The first Shoan thrust in 1875 was fiercely resisted and failed to subdue them. It took ten years of war and negotiations to bring all but one Gurage group to heel. The last battle was fought in 1886 on the Wabe River between the Shoans and the Chaha, one of the *sabat bet* clans. The Chaha were punished severely for resisting, many were sold into slavery, and their district became crown land. According to the quasi-feudal *Gabbar* system that applied throughout the conquered territories, a large part of the best land was appropriated by the state and was distributed to Abyssinians and their allies, who now became landlords and rulers of the region. The Gurage who lived on appropriated land were reduced to quasi-serfdom, obliged to share the produce of their labour with the landlord and to provide him with sundry other goods and services.

Abyssinian rule brought most of the Gurage groups into one administrative unit. Gurageland became an *awraja* (district) of Shoa province, extending from the Omo River in the west to Lake Zway in the east, and the Awash River in the north to the Kambata region in the south. Gurage *awraja* was subdivided into five *wereda* (subdistricts). *Wereda* boundaries were arbitrarily drawn, and did not separate communities along clan, linguistic, or religious lines. The congregation of most Gurage into a single administrative unit was the first stroke in the process of fashioning a single Gurage ethnic identity.

The Gurage were among the first to be drawn into Addis Ababa, the newly founded and fast growing capital of Ethiopia. One reason for this was geographical proximity. The northern border of Gurage *awraja* was no more than fifty kilometres from Addis Ababa. The main reason was economic need. The fragile rural economy was upset by the *Gabbar* system and the exactions of the Abyssinian rulers. Although normally the peasants were not evicted from the land, they had to share its produce and their labour with the landlords. Initially, the tribute (*gibr*) due to the landlord was paid in prepared *enset* food (*wusa*). Because *enset* did not appeal to the northerners, a grain tithe was imposed on the peasants, who also had to provide the landlord with butter, honey, wood, fodder and corvee labour. The grain tithe was paid in *teff*—the staple Abyssinian foodcrop—barley, peas and wheat. Since none of these was produced by the Gurage, they had to be bought. Later on, the tithe was made payable in money only. It was the need for money that sent Gurage men into migrant labour in Addis Ababa, and the *fanonet*, as the practice became known, became an integral part of the local economy and Gurage way of life. *Enset* cultivation is seasonal and does not require year-round labour. Moreover, among the Gurage it is the women who convert the uprooted plant into food, a complex and time-consuming process. It was possible, therefore, for Gurage men to spend part of the year away from home and still maintain *enset* production. Even when they settled permanently in town, the Gurage did not loosen their ties with the homeland. They retained property in their villages, and those who could afford it maintained a second home and family there.

In Addis Ababa, the Gurage initially engaged in manual labour, and their willingness to perform despised work earned them the contempt of the haughty Abyssinians. The social stigma attached to the migrant labourers came to apply to all Gurage who, as far as outsiders were concerned, comprised a homogeneous ethnic unit. From manual labour, the migrant Gurage progressed to petty trade, and in time came to dominate the retail trade and service sectors in Addis Ababa and other towns of central and southern Ethiopia. They ran retail shops, bakeries, teahouses, restaurants, bars and inns. Later, they branched into trade in imported goods, accumulated capital and became a major force in the economy. Shedding the social stigma attached to their forefathers, the Gurage came to be respected for their diligence, sobriety and business acumen.

The migrant community excelled in fostering economic cooperation and social solidarity among its members. New migrants normally found employment with ethnic kinsmen, and Gurage merchants supported each other in many ways. The provision of credit, for instance, was a communal affair. The Gurage founded the revolving credit scheme known as *Iqub*, in which a number of people contribute a fixed sum periodically, with the whole going to each in turn. They also pioneered the formation of informal cooperative associations, like burial societies, and acquired a reputation for ethnic solidarity which reinforced the impression abroad that they constituted a homogeneous, tightly knit ethnic group. So little was known of their background, that the first survey of Ethiopia to be published referred to them as "mainly a pastoral class" (Luther, 1958:25).

This reputation was enhanced by the activities of the Gurage self-help associations. The Gurage Roads Construction Association (*Ye Gurage Menged Sera Derigit*) was founded in 1961 in Addis Ababa, and its president was the first Gurage to reach the rank of general in the Ethiopian army. Funds were raised among the migrant community in the capital and in the countryside, and a road building programme was launched. This was the first successful endeavour of its kind in Ethiopia, and greatly reinforced the image of Gurage entrepreneurship and ethnic solidarity.

Around the same time, this image was further bolstered by the work of an American anthropologist, published under the title *The Gurage: People of the Ensete Culture* (Shack, 1966). The title was a misnomer, because the study concerned only the *sabat bet* of western Gurageland. As a cultural anthropologist, Shack laid heavy emphasis on the integrating force of shared cultural factors, and believed these bound all the people of Gurageland and distinguished them from neighbouring groups. "Apart from the varied forms of language and religion, there exists a common set of artefacts, a common technology and mode of production, a common design in house building and patterns of settlement, and a common form of economic and social organization" (p. 37). "Gurage culture is essentially uniform", Shack declared, and distinguished the Gurage from other *enset* cultivating groups in the region. He even detected distinct physical attributes, reporting that the Gurage are considered to be "the handsomest of Ethiopian peoples" (p. 7). Being the first work on the Gurage in print, Shack's book put a scientific gloss on the outsiders' perception of the Gurage as a solid ethnic entity.

It did not suit the Gurage themselves to challenge this perception. On the contrary, it was in the migrants' interest to expand the social circle upon which they could rely for support in the alien urban sector. To insist upon the many divisions and distinctions that divided the Gurage in their homeland would have narrowed that circle and resulted in hardship, especially in the early stages when the size of the migrant community was small. Gurage informal associations at the time ignored clan, territorial, linguistic and religious distinctions in recruiting membership. Shack observed that "many of these associations have expanded their membership so as to include all Gurage, although clan and other lineage distinctions are still important" (1968:110). Another scholar noted: "The Gurage have also pointed the way to using the *mahebar* [informal association] in a way that transcends the narrow tribal or territorial passions which it has thus far tended to canalize" (Levine, 1965:279).

In dealing with the imperial authorities too, it was advantageous to assert the image of a large, unified ethnic group, especially on the part of those who emerged as spokesmen of the migrant community. Petitions to the emperor were made in the name of the Gurage people, and this was the name chosen for the first road building association. It was a time when identity contours were broadened to encompass a pan-Gurage universe. The urban migrants accepted an ethnic identity, i.e., Gurage, which had no currency in their homeland. Its function, obviously, was to ease the economic adaptation these people were obliged to make under Ethiopian rule. This fact did not escape Shack, who noted that "... in both rural and urban areas Gurage relationships based on kinship and clanship have an economic co-efficient" (1968:110).

The emerging Gurage identity appeared to transcend the cleavages of traditional society, but it did not diminish them. Strong dissent was registered against Shack's generalizations only a few years after its publication. It came from the first Gurage anthropologist, who happened to belong to the Soddo group in the northern part of Gurageland. According to Fekadu Gedamu "many of the generalizations and conclusions [Shack's] do not apply to the Soddos" (1972:3). Fekadu rejected Shack's depiction of the Gurage as a culturally homogeneous and socially integrated ethnic group.

"The Gurage-speaking peoples do not form one society or even a sub-society", Fekadu wrote (p. 3), pointing out that the Soddo did not understand *sabat bet* languages, so their difference on that score was not merely dialectal. The basis of Soddo social organization is territory, he added, while that of the *sabat bet* is clan. Furthermore, while the Soddo are all Christians, there are more pagans and Muslims among the *sabat bet* than Christians. Finally, Fekadu pointed to a strong link between Soddo and Oromo through intermarriage. Fekadu concluded that the Soddo constitute a distinct ethnic group. His rebuttal appeared in a doctoral dissertation whose subject was the Gurage self-help associations. It was not published and was little noticed.

Fekadu's critique of Shack hinted at the strained relationship that had developed between the Soddo and the *sabat bet*. Being closer to the capital, the Soddo were the first to engage in migrant labour and to enter trade in Addis Ababa. Numerically smaller than the *sabat bet*, they grew resentful because the first road building association came to be dominated by the latter, and was allegedly focusing its activities on the western part of the Gurage region, the *sabat bet* homeland. This led to the founding of a second association, the Alemgana-Wolamo Road Construction Association, headed by a police general and dominated by Soddo people. It aimed to link the northern end of Gurageland with the Hadiya and Kambata regions to the south.

Under the guise of national integration, the imperial regime promoted an unabashed policy of assimilation into the culture of the ruling Abyssinian group, the Amhara. Amharigna was the official language of the state, and all other ethnic languages were banned from education, print, broadcast and public occasions. Monophysite Christianity was the official state religion, while Islam was ignored and Muslims played no role in public life. Mention of ethnic divisions in the imperial realm was severely frowned upon, and research into the history and culture of societies other than Abyssinian was strongly discouraged. The Gurage were considered amenable to assimilation, partly because a good many of them were adherents of monophysite Christianity, and partly because, lacking a common language of their own, they quickly adopted Amharigna as their lingua franca. The Muslims among them found it politic not to highlight differences of faith, and not a few young Muslims took Christian names in order to ease their entry into the state education system. The overall effect was to enhance commonality among Gurage of all groups, at the expense of particularity. As Shack noted, "under pax Aethiopica pan-Gurage has taken new forms in tribal solidarity" (1966:39).

By the end of the imperial era, the image of a compact Gurage identity had taken firm hold, as far as outsiders were concerned. "It is sometimes surprising to outsiders", remarked someone who had a closer look, "to observe the highly complex political and social structure that has emerged in

Gurageland ... It contrasts strongly with the once firmly held static images associated with its inhabitants" (Lebel, 1974:106).

Revolution

The collapse of the imperial regime in 1974 ushered in a period of political instability, economic dislocation and social unrest in Ethiopia that has still not ended. A key feature of this period is the rise of ethnicity to preeminence in public life. The escalation of the Eritrean revolution and the resurgence of Somali irredentism were followed by the appearance of dissident movements among the Tigray, Oromo, Afar and Sidama, who took up arms in the name of ethnic liberation. The flimsy facade of Ethiopian nationalism behind which Amhara rule was concealed fell apart, and the integrity of the imperial state was threatened. Keenly aware of this threat, the military regime that seized power denounced the cultural chauvinism of its imperial predecessor and proclaimed the equality of all ethnic groups. The Christian church lost its official status and state subsidies, while Islam gained recognition and public observance of its major holidays. The ban on the use of ethnic languages was lifted, although Amharigna retained its official status. Indigenous languages appeared in print and broadcast, and the first tentative attempts to study the history and culture of subordinate groups were made. Ethnic cultural associations proliferated. The celebration of cultural diversity was officially encouraged, and a season of cultural festivities, featuring mostly songs and dances, followed.

As soon as it came to power, the regime launched a massive campaign in the countryside to bring the revolutionary gospel—which included radical land reform—to the peasantry that made up nearly 90 per cent of the population. For this purpose, it enlisted the student population who, along with their teachers, were despatched to the rural areas for two years. An adult literacy programme was part of the campaign, and it was decided to employ vernaculars where Amharigna was not familiar, using the Geez alphabet of the Abyssinian languages. Consultations were held in the ministry of education with educated members of various ethnic groups, and fifteen vernaculars were chosen. There were several Gurage involved in these deliberations, including staff members of Haile Selassie University. They were not keen to replace Amharigna with any of the Gurage languages, there being many of them, and no demand for any one to be used for this purpose. Their recommendation was to use Silte in eastern Gurageland and Amharigna elsewhere. The use of Silte was justified on the grounds that the eastern region was least exposed to the Amhara language and culture, and the use of Amharigna for teaching literacy there was tantamount to using a foreign language. No Silte-speaker was involved in this recommendation: one was engaged subsequently to help prepare teaching material in that language. It was seemingly an innocuous choice that was to bear political fruit two decades later. In the 1980s, the regime undertook a second mass literacy campaign which claimed impressive results. Again, Silte was the only Gurage language used.

Although the military regime promoted ethnic cultural emancipation, it made no political concessions. Instead, it proceeded to centralize state power even more, and increasingly relied on force to implement policy. As a result, it fomented resistance throughout the country and was soon engulfed in multiple violent conflicts. Under pressure from the Soviet Union, its main ally abroad, and in order to entertain expectations it had raised at home, it was obliged to produce a politico-ideological facade. Not surprizingly, it chose the Soviet model. Its Programme of the National Democratic Revolution (1976) recognized the right of nationalities to self-determination, and promised to put this principle into practice in the constitution. For this purpose, it established an Institute for the Study of Ethiopian Nationalities, to which a number of university teachers and civil servants were assigned and were ordered to prepare a draft constitution.

The Department of Cultures and Languages in the Institute of Nationalities was given the task of identifying and cataloguing the country's rich ethnic heritage. Information was gathered from many sources, including field trips, and an inventory was prepared listing eighty-nine groups. Language was the main criterion used and, on that basis, over thirty entries appeared under the code number 43 assigned to Gurage-speakers. This involved considerable duplication, because some groups were listed more than once under different names—for example, Soddo and Kistani—while the *sabat bet* clans and some Silte groups were listed individually. In 1984, the first attempt was made to take a population census in Ethiopia. The results, albeit partial, provided the first glimpse of the country's ethnic composition. The census put the total Gurage-speaking population at 1.85 million (less than 5 per cent of the total), half-a-million of which resided in towns outside Gurageland. Soon afterwards, the constitution of the Peoples Democratic Republic of Ethiopia was adopted. It sought to mollify the rebellious groups—Eritreans, Tigray, Afar, Somali—through an offer of regional autonomy, and redesigned the administrative map for the rest of Ethiopia, allegedly in order to satisfy criteria for development. Nothing came of the scheme, and conflict intensified, causing the collapse of the regime in 1991.

The Gurage remained politically quiescent throughout this tumultuous period, save for the participation of some youth in the radical student movement that opposed the regime in its early years. As befitted their geographic position and economic situation, the Gurage were attached to the centre of the Ethiopian state and cooperated with its rulers. Few of them attained high state office, and those who did manifested no political ambition. Furthermore, as a rule Gurage merchants and intellectuals were strong supporters of Ethiopian unity and mistrusted the motives of the belligerent ethnic liberation movements. They took care to avoid political entanglement of any sort, and the Gurage self-help associations escaped the fate that befell an Oromo association in the 1960s, when it became politically suspect and was brutally suppressed (Baker, 1992).

Although some Gurage lost property as a result of the sweeping nationalization carried out by the military regime, the merchants were among the beneficiaries of that policy. This cleared the country of a large and diverse expatriate sector that had dominated trade and closed the door to foreign investment. It opened new fields for indigenous entrepreneurs, and the Gurage merchants prospered. In time, they came to be recognized as a major economic force and won commensurate respect. The land reform of 1975, which dispossessed the landlords and divided the land equally among the peasants under usufruct rights, had no appreciable impact in Gurageland, where landholdings were minimal. Having maintained close ties with their rural homes, the migrants retained rights to land under the reform. When the regime relaxed its hold on the economy in the late 1980s, some of the capital was invested in Gurageland, where commercial crops like vegetables, grain, coffee, *chat* (a mild stimulant) and eucalyptus trees proved profitable.

The Gurage were affected by the atmosphere of ethnic cultural emancipation that pervaded Ethiopia under the military regime (1974–91). In 1988, the *sabat bet* controlled road building association decided to expand its scope to include development in general, and renamed itself the Gurage Peoples Self-Help and Development Association. An effort was made to include all Gurage, and some seventeen distinct groups were represented. At the end of the decade, a task force was formed to organize research into the culture of the Gurage. It began with an inquiry to determine which groups belonged to the Gurage. Charts were drawn and displayed in public places, inviting comment from the people. The Soddo soon followed suit, turning the rival road building association into the Soddo Economic and Cultural Development Association.

The focus on culture was bound to have a dissolving effect on the Gurage identity, given the diversity that prevailed in that realm. The natural tendency was esoteric, with each group focusing on its own specific cultural endowment, rather than on the Gurage universe. Inevitably, elements that distinguished one group from others gained emphasis. Research, such as it was, had to involve rural elements for whom the pan-Gurage identity had little meaning. This gave parochialism additional emphasis. By this time, the urban Gurage community had grown large and economically strong, and the need for coalescence was no longer imperative. With nearly 200,000 people in Addis Ababa, and as many dispersed in other towns, the informal associations had become parochial, recruiting more narrowly on the basis of clan and territory.

In a dramatically changed Ethiopian context, an unambiguous ethnic identity had become something of a cultural asset, and there was a felt need to unearth cultural roots. Wealthy merchants were willing to finance studies and approached educated members of their groups. One such effort was made by the Azernet Berbere association in Addis Ababa, whose members came from a Silte-speaking area of that name. They approached two compatriots at the university who, some years later, produced a book on the history and culture of that group (Abraham and Habtamu, 1994). By that time, the situation had changed dramatically once more, and the appearance of this book was perceived as a political statement.

Empowering ethnicity

The collapse of military rule in 1991, and the advent to power of a regime controlled by the movement representing the Tigray ethnic group, resulted in a dramatic transformation of political life in Ethiopia. Overnight, ethnicity became a legitimate and preferred principle of political organization, and provided the foundation for a reconstructed Ethiopian state. Ethnic groups throughout the country responded to the new regime's invitation to form political organizations to represent them, and soon there was a plethora of such parties, some of them bearing names most Ethiopians had never heard before.

The process of empowering ethnicity began with a conference in Addis Ababa in July 1991. Existing ethnic organizations which, until then, were waging war with the Ethiopian state, were invited to take part, and all ethnic groups were invited to participate through their political organizations. The only condition was the prior submission to the government of a programme and rules for the organization.

Among those who responded were the leaders of the *sabat bet*-dominated self-help and development association, who called a meeting in Addis Ababa for this purpose. Nearly all the seventeen groups, including the Soddo, were represented. After some discussion, it was decided to accept the regime's invitation, and three prominent members were chosen to draft the programme and rules of the Gurage Peoples Democratic Front (GPDF). These were submitted to the organizers of the conference, who allocated two seats out of a total of eighty-seven to the Gurage "nationality" (the preferred designation in Ethiopia since 1974). The two men who were chosen to attend the July c onference both belonged to the *sabat bet*, a fact that did not sit well with the Soddo. The conference established a Council of Representatives as part of the transitional government, with the Gurage allotted two seats there also. In order to give all Gurage sections equal opportunity, a complex procedure was followed to select the two representatives for the council. Each of the three main Gurage sections (east, west, north) first chose three candidates, ranked in order of preference. All groups then voted together to choose three out of the nine, and a final collective vote chose two out of the three, one *sabat bet,* the other Soddo. By way of compensation later, a Silte-speaker was named acting chairman of the GPDF.

After this initial show of ethnic political solidarity, a process of fragmentation commenced which split the Gurage along lines few had anticipated. The first split occurred when the ruling coalition, the Ethiopian Peoples Revolutionary Democratic Front (EPRDF), began sponsoring ethnic affiliates in nearly every part of Ethiopia, in order to acquire a countrywide political base. Its affiliate in Gurageland was called the Gurage Peoples Revolutionary Democratic Movement (GPRDM). In the years that followed, this party had the full support of the regime and the resources of the state at its disposal, with which it intimidated and overwhelmed the opposition, making a clean sweep of all electoral contests held during 1992–95. The GDPF's aspirations to forge a solid political front for the Gurage were frustrated from the start, and this party made little effort to establish itself in the countryside.

The reform of the state administrative structure to represent ethnic divisions had the effect of blurring the Gurage ethnic image. Initially, Gurageland became a zone (subdivision) within Region Seven, along with the adjacent zones of Kambata and Hadiya. Subsequently, five regions in the south were merged into one. Gurageland (1994 pop=1.55 million) became one of nine zones in the Southern Nations, Nationalities and Peoples Region (1994 pop=10.3 million). Constitutionally, zones enjoy a fair degree of autonomy within a region, yet the ethnic profile they represent is politically diminished compared to what it would be if the ethnic unit was both administratively distinct and politically autonomous. The main reason for the merger of the five southern regions was the fear that divided they would be overshadowed by their giant neighbour, the Oromo region, the largest in the country in size, population and resources.

Indeed, the Oromo factor had caused the first crack to appear in the image of the Gurage identity. This occurred in the northern section, where Soddo Gurage are mixed with Oromo. Groups of Oromo origin are found in twenty of the twenty-four Soddo *agers* (clusters of hamlets), and are the majority in three of them. Though predominantly Christian and largely integrated into Gurage society, they retained a distinct identity as exogamous descent groups and were known as Soddo Jida. In the urban migrant setting, they had accepted the Gurage identity in preference to the even less esteemed Galla, as the Oromo were known in imperial Ethiopia. This preference changed with the dramatic political changes introduced in Ethiopia in 1991, when the Oromo emerged as potentially the largest and most powerful ethnic group, championed by a militant movement, the Oromo Liberation Front (OLF). The OLF was only one of several Oromo political organizations, all of which demanded the inclusion of all Oromo peoples within the borders of Oromia region, and vigorously contested cases where ethnic identities were confused, such as in the Soddo region of northern Gurage-land.

Members of the Soddo Jida group in Addis Ababa, led by a retired army officer, began agitating for the inclusion of their home district in Oromia region, on the grounds that its inhabitants were not Gurage but Oromo. Apparently, one consideration was the commercial advantages of belonging to the largest and wealthiest region, which included the national capital. They approached the OLF and were advised to form a political organization of their own, which they named Soddo Jida Democratic Action. The OLF held rallies in Soddo on their behalf, urging people to reclaim their Oromo identity and culture. When the delineation of ethnic regions got under way, the Soddo Jida demanded the entire Soddo district be incorporated into the Oromia region, and were supported by the OLF, the Oromo Peoples Democratic Organization (OPDO), an ethnic affiliate of the ruling EPRDF, and the Islamic Front for the Liberation of Oromo (IFLO). They were opposed by the other Gurage political organizations, and a commission was set up by the central government to adjudicate. It polled the peasant associations in the contested area, and more than a dozen chose Oromia. The experience embittered the Soddo Gurage, who now formed their own political party named the Soddo Gordena Democratic Action.

Another schism involved the Silte-speakers in the eastern section of Gurageland. They share linguistic and religious attributes, but these had never been asserted as the basis of a distinct ethnic identity. Indeed, the name Silte first came into use in the 1970s in the literacy campaign and was borrowed from the linguists. The Silte districts had participated in both road building associations, and one of the presidents of the Alemgana-Wolamo Road Construction Association was a Silte-speaker. The main road this association constructed passed through their homeland. In 1991, the Silte were represented in the meeting that chose Gurage representatives to the transitional government.

Nevertheless, certain differences had distanced the Silte from other Gurage groups. Inhabiting the south-central area of Gurageland, the Silte are furthest away from Addis Ababa and were among the last to engage in migrant labour. As a result, they remained manual labourers until the 1950s, and were late in entering trade, specializing in tea-houses and bakeries where profits are modest. Being pious Muslims, they resisted acculturation and refrained from sending their children to state schools, thus falling behind other Gurage groups in this respect. There were no Silte-speakers among the prominent Gurage personalities, and the Silte region generally was considered less developed and its inhabitants backward.

The assertion of a Silte ethnic identity coincides with the politicization of ethnicity in the process of reconstructing the Ethiopian polity in the early 1990s. It was in an atmosphere of ethnic ferment and political anticipation that a group of young, moderately educated men in Addis Ababa began to promote a distinct Silte ethnic identity and political claims. They had come together earlier under the aegis of the Azernet Berbere association, which had a youth branch and a football club. They were encouraged and financed by a wealthy merchant in Addis Ababa, who had once represented the Silte in the road building association. By his own admission (to the author) he had never heard the name Silte used in an ethnic context earlier and did not apply it to himself. They formed a political organization called the Silte Gogot Democratic Party. In the Silte language and tradition, *gogot* is a mass meeting held to resolve communal differences and signifies unity. The party was recognized by the regime and was able to campaign for the separation of Silte-speaking districts from the rest of the Gurage. The separatists maintained the Silte are a distinct "nationality" and are entitled to have their own political representation and separate administration. They claimed the Silte (1994, pop=542,000) were dominated by the *sabat bet* (1994, pop=700,000), who monopolized the development resources made available to the zone. An autonomous Silte district, they argued, would be able to claim its fair share from the regional and central governments. Moreover, Wolkite, the capital of the *sabat bet* district, was too far from the Silte area and it would be better if the latter had its own distinct capital. Later, the youthful radicals of this party split from their wealthy patron, who lost little time in setting up another separatist organization named the Silte Peoples Democratic Unity Party.

There was no consensus on this issue among Silte-speakers. The Gurage link was upheld by a second group, led by another wealthy merchant who, in fact, hailed from the same village as the leader of the separatists. These two had a history of rivalry for local preeminence. The anti-separatists founded the Silte Gurage Peoples Democratic Movement. The battle of rival identities was fought initially within the Azernet Berbere association to which both the protagonists belonged. Initially, the battle was focused on the study that had been sponsored by the association some years earlier. The separatists wanted the study to focus on the Silte as a whole, and for the book to bear that name in its title. Their opponents wanted it confined to the history and culture of the Azernet Berbere alone. When the book finally appeared in 1994 (Abraham and Habtamu), it proved a disappointment to the separatists, because it dealt only with the Azernet Berbere. Worse yet, following the linguists, it placed the Silte in the eastern Gurage cluster.

The separatists were also opposed by the Gurage Peoples Revolutionary Democratic Movement, which monopolized the zonal administration with the support of the central government. To confuse matters even more, the head of this party and the chairman of the zonal administration were both Silte. What the rural people thought of all this is difficult to discern. The separatists made no gains in the elections, but attributed this to fraud and intimidation by the GPRDM. Nonetheless, their efforts were not entirely in vain. Their agitation put separatism on the political agenda, and several meetings were held in Addis Ababa and other towns, as well as in the Gurage zone, to debate it. Academics and elders were invited to present their views. The separatists applied for recognition to the House of the Federation, the upper chamber of the Ethiopian parliament, where nationalities are represented. There followed a complex procedure to select representatives for the various Silte communities, who gathered in the small town of Butajira in August 1997. The rival political parties were there to present their views, and regional and zonal officials attended. A resolution passed at the end of the meeting went against the separatists, and the head of the regional government, no doubt prematurely, declared the matter closed.

Another group that asserted its own identity at this time were the Kebena, a minuscule group (1994, pop=28,000) inhabiting the northwestern fringe of Gurageland. They call themselves and their language Womba, and are thought to be related to the Hadiya, Kambata, Tambaro and Alaba groups in the south. They are separated from these groups by Gurage speakers—*sabat bet* and Soddo—and are to a large extent assimilated by them. The Kebena are multilingual, speaking one or more Gurage languages as well as their own, they intermarry with the Gurage, and were accepted as part of the Gurage world, though only their nearest neighbours were aware of their existence. Most of the Kebena are Muslim, and they have a history of enmity with their Soddo Kistani neighbours going back to the Abyssinian conquest. As a result, they were not invited to join the Alemgana-Wolamo Road Construction Association. They were invited to participate in the 1991 meeting which founded the Gurage Peoples Democratic Front. With the new ethnic self-government scheme in preparation, some educated Kebena voiced doubt whether their tiny and largely unknown group would gain any benefit from an autonomous local administration that was bound to be dominated by the *sabat bet*. When they communicated these doubts to the local EPRDF cadres, they were advised to form their own ethnic political organization. Thus was conceived the Kebena Nationality Democratic Organization, whose emblem is the Islamic half-moon. Two local school-teachers were at the helm of the organization, and they strove to promote a Kebena political consciousness among their kinsmen.

The latest assertion of a distinct identity came from the Wollene, a small group in northern Gurageland, neighbours of the Kebena and the *sabat bet*. Linguistically, they belong to the eastern Gurage cluster and are Muslim: consequently they were consigned to the Silte congregation. Initially they were members of the road building association controlled by the *sabat bet*, but grew resentful and later withdrew, because they felt their own district was neglected in the road building programme. In the mid-1990s, a Wollene Peoples Democratic Party made its appearance. Like all the others, it was organized by petit bourgeois elements in Addis Ababa and financed by wealthy merchants. Its goal was to reject the Silte identity loosely applied to the eastern cluster in favour of a distinct Wollene identity, and to claim autonomous political recognition and administrative representation.

Conclusion

This case study lacks the scope required for conclusions to be drawn about the nature of ethnicity. However, it does provide the material upon which some pertinent observations can be based. To begin with, it illustrates the alloyed, multifaceted and unbounded nature of identity in the traditional setting, a far cry from the notion of the "tribe", the figment of the anthropological imagination. It is clear that different components of identity acquire prominence in different contexts. These could be genealogy, religion, language, territory, history, etc. In the case of the Gurage, there is no correlation between any of them, so neither singly nor in combination could they serve to anchor an identity for the Gurage as an "ethnic" group. Nor was there a need for such an identity before this century, since there was scant interaction among wholly unrelated peoples.

A Gurage identity appeared when the need for it arose. It was wrought in an entirely new setting outside Gurageland, as a response to the socio-economic and political exigencies that confronted the migrants in the urban sector. This was a new identity, but it was not wholly invented. It was a new pattern woven with old threads. It had a specific function: that is, to provide a viable basis for cooperation and solidarity among the migrants who found themselves bereft of economic, social and political resources in an alien world. The centralized and authoritarian ethos of the imperial state facilitated the process of identity formation by collecting into one administrative unit named Gurage all the groups which, thereafter, were designated by the same name. Used in all official transactions and references to these groups, the name gained widespread currency outside Gurageland as an "ethnic" label. The people concerned did nothing to modify the perception outsiders had of them, for they, themselves, pursued cooperation and solidarity on an all-Gurage level. Every collective endeavour undertaken aspired to be all-inclusive, though it seldom succeeded. Finally, came the Western anthropologist to lend scientific support to the process of identity creation.

The demise of the imperial regime was followed by a veritable social revolution in Ethiopia. It swept away the antique, quasi-feudal Abyssinian social structure and emancipated the peasantry in the conquered regions from the serf-like conditions imposed by the conquerors. Unable to consider political solutions, the military regime chose to see the crisis of the Ethiopian state as a cultural issue, and proposed to deal with it by proclaiming cultural emancipation. Its actions in this field, albeit futile for its purpose, had the consequence of making ethnicity a cultural value to be exploited. In order to claim equality for one's own culture, one had to exhibit its wealth. Enthusiasm for cultural study led to introspection, which acted as a solvent for the newly minted Gurage identity. The fact that rapid growth of the migrant community in numbers and wealth had greatly diminished the need for cooperation and solidarity on an all-Gurage level, obviously had something to do with this dissolution. A mutual reinforcement of external and internal factors is detected in this phase of identity formation too.

In the latest phase that began in 1991, the dramatic transformation of the political landscape turned ethnicity into a political asset. Formally, the initiative came from the new regime, itself a coalition of ethnic movements and apparently determined to re-fashion the political system in its own image. In fact, the regime had little choice in the matter, because ethnicity had already become highly politicized, given the powerful presence of the ethnic liberation movements that had played a key role in the collapse of the regime. Ethnicity is a political asset because it provides access to resources. Given the reorganization of the state on a decentralized basis with auto-nomous ethnic units as its constituent parts, it is highly preferable to be re-cognized as a distinct ethnic entity with a measure of autonomy in one's own administrative district, and thus be able to claim a commensurate share of state resources, than to be swamped politically and ignored within a large district dominated by larger ethnic groups. This is the main motive of most ethnic political organizations that have emerged since 1991. The value of ethnicity attracted numerous ethnic entrepreneurs eager to turn it into polit-ical capital. They came from the same merchant sector that previously had stayed clear of political involvement, but who now took up the task of weaving identities. Obviously, these are not fashioned of entirely new cloth. Africa's cultural heritage offers an immense wealth of material to chose from. Even within the same village, as in the Silte case, enough sustenance can be found to nourish two rival identities.

Bibliography

Abbink, J., 1991, "The Deconstruction of 'Tribe': Ethnicity and Politics in South-western Ethiopia", *Journal of Ethiopian Studies*, 24.

Abraham, Hussein and Habtamu Wondimu, 1994, *The Silte Speaking People of the Azernet Berbere: Society, History and Culture* (in Amharic). Addis Ababa.

Atkinson, R.R., forthcoming, "The (Re)Construction of Ethnicity in Africa: Extending the Chronology, Conceptualization and Discourse", in Paris Yeros (ed.), *Ethnicity and Nationalism in Africa: Constructivist Reflections and Contemporary Politics*. London: Macmillan.

Baker, J., 1992, "The Gurage of Ethiopia: Rural-Urban Interaction and Entre-preneurship", in J. Baker and P.O. Pedersen (eds.) *The Rural-Urban Interface in Africa*. Uppsala: Scandinavian Institute of African Studies.

Central Statistical Office, 1996, *The 1994 Population and Housing Census of Ethiopia. Results for Southern Nations, Nationalities and Peoples Region*, 1, 5.

Eriksen, T. H., forthcoming, "A Non-ethnic State for Africa? A Life-World Approach to the Imagining of Communities", in Paris Yeros (ed.), *Ethnicity and Nationalism in Africa: Constructivist Reflections and Contemporary Politics*. London: Macmillan.

Fekadu, Gedamu, 1972, "Ethnic Associations in Ethiopia and the Maintenance of Urban/Rural Relationships: with special reference to the Algemana-Wallamo Road Construction Association". Unpublished Ph.D. dissertation, University of London.

Harris, W.C., 1844, *The Highlands of Ethiopia*, London: Longman.

Horowitz, D.L., 1985, *Ethnic Groups in Conflict*. Berkeley: University of California Press.

Institute for the Study of Ethiopian Nationalities, 1986, "A Brief Almanac of Ethiopian Nationalities" (in Amharic). Mimeo. Addis Ababa.

Lebel, P., 1969, "On Gurage Architecture", *Journal of Ethiopian Studies*, 7, 1.

—1974, "Oral Tradition and Chronicles on Gurage Immigration", *Journal of Ethiopian Studies*, 12, 2.

Leslaw, W., 1992, *Gurage Studies: Collected Articles*. Wiesbaden: Otto Harrassowitz.

Levine, D.N., 1965, *Wax and Gold: Tradition and Innovation in Ethiopian Culture*. Chicago: University of Chicago Press.

Lewis, H.S., 1993, "Ethnicity in Ethiopia: the View from Below (and from the South, East and West)", in Crawford Young (ed.), *The Rising Tide of Cultural Pluralism: The Nation-State at Bay*. Madison: University of Wisconsin Press.

Luther, E.W., 1958, *Ethiopia Today*. London: Oxford University Press.

Moynihan, D.P., 1993, *Pandaemonium: Ethnicity in International Politics*. Oxford: Oxford University Press.

Shack, W.A., 1966, *The Gurage: A People of the Ensete Culture*. Oxford: Oxford University Press.

—1968, "The Masqal Pole: Religious Conflict and Social Change in Gurageland", *Africa*, 38, 4.

Shack, W.A. and Habte Mariam Marcos, 1974, *Gods and Heroes: Oral Tradition of the Gurage in Ethiopia*. Oxford: Clarendon Press.

Emissaries for Conflict Management among the Zaghawa on the Sudan-Chad Border

Sharif Harir

Introduction

No tribal territory in the drylands of the African Sahel is big enough to sustain the livestock holdings of the tribe many years in a row. There always has been a need to venture out of the core territory of the tribe into territories of other tribes to safeguard the well-being of herds in periods of prolonged droughts, whose cyclical occurrences have been abundantly documented for the drylands of the African Sahel. The historical and current long-range migrations of long-horned Fulani cattle from as far as Nigeria and Senegal across the savannah into the Sudan and Eritrea are a case in point.

Such long-range migrations by pastoralists not only entail the crossing of many state boundaries, but also the intrusion on to the pasture lands and water resources of a multitude of tribal groups, with all the political problems this entails. Security for members of the group and their livestock, negotiating access to water in alien territories, managing new relations of coexistence, finding pastoral niches which are not already occupied by local groups, adjusting to local traditions of management of natural resources, etc., are some among the complex of things migrants need to attend to. Furthermore, dealing with the agents of the political authority in each country a group passes through or stays in, is also an area of management which has to be attended to diligently.

Even within the same country, when pastoral groups have to move out of their territories into other groups' territories, they have to negotiate many things to achieve the move successfully. This is the case with many pastoral groups in the Sudan. The various Baggara groups, e.g., Hawazma, Rezaiqat and Missiriya and other nomads, such as the Rufa'a el Hoi, Kababish, and the northern camel Rezaiqat of Darfur in their migrations from the fringes of the desert in the north to the rich savannah in the south, cover considerable distances and pass through the tribal territories of other groups. Some of these other groups are also pastoral nomads, while others are settled agricul-turalists. In both cases, complex political, administrative and range-man-agement issues arise and have to be negotiated to prevent conflicts or to settle them when they arise.

For those groups who move with their tribal authorities, such as the Rufa'a and a number of Rezaiqat groups, negotiations and the relations re-sulting from them are managed by the two authorities, i.e., that of the mobile group and those of the territories the former group enters. However, for groups whose tribal authority is settled, arrangements about accredited emissaries or roving envoys must be made prior to their entry into another tribe's territory. These are made either on permanent basis through the appointment of a guarantor *(Dhamin)* in market areas, or by the appoint-ment, renewable annually, of an envoy *(Mandoub)* to accompany such mobile groups for each successive season.

The purpose of this chapter is to elucidate the processes related to the management of intertribal group relations that have a direct bearing on dry-land resources management. Intratribal resource management within Dar Zaghawa entails seasonal movements within a defined tribal territory, elab-orate codes of behaviour about how to treat certain areas and their grazing and water resources, rules of resource tenure that follow descent lines and are framed through kinship relations, and local administrative legislation re-lating to tree-cutting and fire-lines which are supposed to protect the range against bushfires. An elaborate and consensually produced corpus of codes for conflict resolution without much interference from district government authorities form part of such management arrangements. Intratribal arrangements take cognizance of the fact that a tribal group consists of sev-eral sections, the building blocks of that society. Such a system exists within a system of administrative and judicial regulation that arises from a process of government that builds from the district to the centre of political power within the nationstate of which the tribal group claims citizenship.

In an intertribal situation, shared culture and common codes of be-haviour are absent and have to be negotiated. Such a situation arises when one tribal group moves temporarily into the territories of another group. Here it is not only the question of general public peace that becomes press-ing, but questions defining resources and access, as well as conflict-settle-ment mechanisms become important, and a commonly acceptable arrange-ment has to be created. This is because the behavioural codes of the groups involved might not be commensurate. Though the host group has sovereignty (theoretically) over the resources in its territory, it cannot practi-cally (legally) exclude the incoming group, because both of them are nationals of the same country. The incoming group has the legal right to be there, and the host group cannot exclude it from its territory. The war be-tween the Fur and the Arabs during 1988–89 illustrates the difficulty of try-ing to exclude an incoming group from Fur territory. Negotiation of a common frame of reference and a joint definition of the situation is the best way to ensure peaceful coexistence. The case of the Zaghawa cited below makes this point very clearly.

The Zaghawa of the Sudan-Chad border

Dar Zaghawa on the Sudan-Chad border is defined geographically by the Wadi Howar basin and the tributaries that run into it. On the Sudan side, the wadis of Hilaliya, Karnoi, Furawaya, Karo and Musbat run northwards into Wadi Howar. On the Chad side, the wadis of Ndjeres, Bahai, Bardaba and Turta-me also run into Wadi Howar. All these wadis run seasonally from July to October, but Wadi Howar retains water in big pools until November in many years. It also provides extensive grazing areas even in the dry season (November–July). The other wadis (tributaries of Wadi Howar) provide permanent water points through wells bored in their beds. Livestock populations are normally spread over a wide area during the rainy season because of the availability of water in various pools, but are concentrated in the dry season because of the limited number of wells. This area is poor savannah in the southern fringes, and semi-arid shrub land in the north. It is hemmed in by the Sahara on three sides, with only the south allowing passage to greener pastures. With the ever-present threat of drought in two out of every four years, there is a constant need to migrate. The distances covered in years of mass exodus are enormous: the Zaghawa travel far into Fur territories around the Jebel Marra massif and beyond into Rezaiqat land. The direction of livestock movement is from south to north and the reverse. The area is camel and sheep country, although some cattle and goats are found in the southern part of it.

The Zaghawa are organized in patrilineal descent groups, the largest of which is called *Ner*, tribe, and the smallest is the *Bea*, lineage. Each group claims ownership of a specific territory with its water, farmland and grazing resources and each has its own separate animal brand. The Zaghawa language has three dialects which correspond to the Bedayat, the Wagi and the Kobe, the three main divisions within the Zaghawa. These divisions also correspond to administrative divisions within Dar Zaghawa. The *Ner* straddle international borders. Thus, in Furawaya area in the Sudan one encounters the Geli Gargi and Kurra Biriyara tribes which one also finds in Ndjeres area in Chad. The fact is that the international border came into existence only in 1924. For the people themselves, Dar Zaghawa remains undivided, and every pastoral family claims resources on both sides of the border.

Every Zaghawa group has first access rights to a certain portion of territory, though in practice it cannot exclude any Zaghawa from it. These are historical claims with certain symbolic value attached to them, but they are seldom activated in daily life. Despite such claims, the Zaghawa groups are

not territorial. Due to intermarriage and constant mobility, all socially defined territories have in fact become multitribal. People are not supposed to
cut trees in the vicinity of villages, camp sites and well sites. They are also
not supposed to graze livestock that does not belong to the village near
village sites. Apart from these restrictions, each Zaghawa family has free
access to the tribal grazing lands.

Managing intratribal conflicts

Each Zaghawa group with a separate animal brand (the signifier of a *Ner*)
claims territorial rights to certain portions of the Zaghawa Dar. While such
claims are recognized traditionally, they are not used to exclude any
Zaghawa group from access to grazing. Farmlands and flood-cultivation
plains are another matter, and they are held for generations within families.
Such claims regulate access to such lands, and set guidelines for resolving
any conflict that might arise. The general rule which lies behind such claims
is the rule of "first occupancy", which carries historical underpinnings. The
claims associated with this rule are substantiated by the existence of objects
sacred to each *Ner*, such as mountains, rocks and trees. These sacral objects
always exist close to wadis that potentially have permanent surface water.
Since permanent water is a critical factor even in years of good grazing, the
water points become points of reference for a tribe's territory. Elaborate
ceremonies are enacted each year at the onset of the long dry season, when
livestock return from wet-season grazing areas.

The onset of drought in the 1970s, accompanied by two decades of
political instability in Chad between 1970 and 1990, resulted in the mass
movement of people and animals. The drought led to the flight of the
Zaghawa population within the Sudan, who moved to the Qoz zone of inner
Darfur: most never returned to Dar Zaghawa. The political instability in
Chad led to the migration of most of the Zaghawa from Chad into the
Sudan, where they remained as reluctant sojourners awaiting a change in
the political climate. This came at the end of 1991, when Idris Deby, a
Zaghawa from Ndjeres, took power in Chad and the political situation in the
Dar Zaghawa region of Chad began to slowly stabilize. By contrast, the situ-
ation for the Sudanese Zaghawa deteriorated at this time, because of
changes in Sudan's national politics, when the National Islamic Front came
to power in a military coup in 1989. Understandably the Chad part of the
Zaghawa range, particularly the Wadi Howar basin, became increasingly
crowded with Zaghawa pastoralists from both sides of the border.

This gave rise to problems of rights of first access. Partly, these problems may have reflected a gradual change of concepts of tenure over a
period of two decades. It also reflected the new political reality of Zaghawa
preeminence in Chad. Minor clashes between herders from Chad and the
Sudan occurred in the pastures of Wadi Howar. Although these were con-

tained, it was becoming clear that Zaghawa herders from Chad had begun to use their Chadian identity to claim rights of first access to grazing areas on the Chadian side of the Wadi Howar basin.

The conflict over resource tenure and access to grazing that resulted from the introduction of an international identity, as opposed to a tribal one, reached its climax with a tragic incident in the winter of 1996–97. This incident reflected new realities and the conflict-resolution process became more complex. The story itself is very simple, but the consequences of it are complex and far-reaching in terms of the management of resources in Dar Zaghawa.

Locality and the state

In a desolate corner of Wadi Howar, Zaghawa camel herders from Chad and the Sudan clashed. The Chadian herders assaulted the Sudanese, claiming they had trespassed across international borders by grazing on the Chadian side of the Wadi Howar depression. When the Sudanese herders reported back to their elders, a party of young Zaghawa who were part of the so-called Popular Defence Forces (PDF) of the Sudanese regime were sent to investigate. Armed with assault rifles issued by the Sudanese Government, the party caught up with the Chadian Zaghawa herders, seized a number of their camels, and returned home. The traditional way of dealing with such a situation would be for the elders of both sides to consult. In this case, however, the young Bedayat sultan, Timan Deby, brother of President Idris Deby of Chad, rashly dispatched an armed group with a machine-gun mounted on a Toyota Land Cruiser to catch the culprits and the camels and bring them to his court in Bahai. When the two armed parties encountered one another, a battle ensued. By the time the machine-guns and AK47 assault rifles fell silent, ten Sudanese Zaghawa and seven Chadian Zaghawa lay dead.

The resulting situation was complex. The participants cut across international and *Ner* tribal identities. Those who died in the clash were mainly from two Zaghawa *Ner*, the Geli Gargi and the Biriyara. Those who were wounded belonged to other Zaghawa *Ner*. The cause of this tragic incident was an issue of principle, i.e., whether one Zaghawa group can exclude another from access to water and pasture on the basis of international boundaries. For most of the Zaghawa, the grazing area that led to the blood-spilling among fellow tribesmen was neither Sudanese nor Chadian, it was in Dar Zaghawa. The key person in this incident was a tribal sultan, who also happened to be the brother of a president whose coming to power was understood to be an all-Zaghawa enterprise, irrespective of national identification.

Conflict management

In the tense aftermath of this incident, a way had to be found to manage the situation in order to avoid all-out tribal warfare, with potential interstate repercussions, since one party was led by the brother of Chad's president and the other comprised Sudanese militiamen. If the chiefs of the Zaghawa in the Sudan responded in kind to Sultan Timan, war was likely. The Wadi Howar range was emptied, as the groups disengaged and regrouped in anticipation of the worst. Normally, intratribal conflicts are dealt with by elders, but, the machine-gun culture had changed all that. Apprised of the incident, the President of Chad in N'djamena, 1,400 km away, immediately dispatched another of his brothers as the head of a delegation to begin a process of containment and reconciliation. Simultaneously, he sent a strongly worded message to Sultan Timan, who dropped out of sight. The fact that Sultan Timan disappeared temporarily was well received by the Zaghawa of the Sudan, as it signified that the president would deal with the problem personally. This rebuff was also a disgrace for Sultan Timan, whose office entitled him to a leading role in the reconciliation process.

Doussa Deby, the presidential emissary, apologized on behalf of the president and distanced himself from the sultan, appealing to blood affinities and the traditions of peace and peaceful resolution of intratribal conflicts among the Zaghawa. For their part, the Sudanese Zaghawa insisted the apology should come from the president personally. Nevertheless, a truce was declared, pending a presidential apology, and the two groups agreed to refrain from hostile action against each other. Finally, the president personally apologized and paid *Diya* (blood money) totalling more that 200,000,000 Central African francs. By so doing, the president "bravely shouldered" the responsibility, as people said, and accepted the public blame for his brother's wrongdoing. This was not seen as a sign of weakness. On the contrary, it was perceived as a sign of strength. The principle at stake, that is access to pasture and water resources within Dar Zaghawa territory irrespective of state borders, was reaffirmed, and the president of Chad became the guarantor. An emissary was designated to accompany the Chadian herders during their Wadi Howar sojourn in order to resolve further problems and prevent aggression.

In the case described above, we see the involvement of a state president in the management of a tribal conflict over resource tenure, the solution of which stipulates that tribal tradition overrides international law concerning state borders. This, of course, is an exceptional situation, because the ruling African elite have shown very little interest in pastoralists. As M. Horowitz (quoted in Timberlake, 1985:78) notes, "with the exception of Mauritania and Somalia, the ruling elite in African states are drawn from non-pastoral groups which also view pastoralism with ambivalence at best and often with outright hostility". In this case, the president has a pastoral background and retains strong ties with the ethnic group which, in fact, helped him to win power. As the guarantor of the peace agreement reached in this instance, he appointed an emissary to accompany the Chadian Zaghawa to prevent the repetition of similar incidents. The idea of an emissary accompanying mobile pastoral groups and acting as an intermediary between the host population and incoming groups is not new among the Zaghawa. This episode revived an old idea which was practised in the management of Zaghawa relations with groups such as the Fur, the Masaleet and Rezaiqat Arabs whose lands have been reception areas for Zaghawa herds in years of mass exodus due to drought.

Long-distance migration and expansion of environmental space

The Zaghawa of the Wadi Howar basin count time in terms of years of good rain, which are few, and rainless years when mass exodus is necessary. Thus *Bare Bere* (when people have to go to Wadi Bare in Dar Masaleet), *Joul Bere* (when they went to Fur country), *Ershiqat Bere* (when they went to Dar Rezaiqat) are some of the key dates one hears about. Temporary exodus from Wadi Howar is an essential aspect of herd management. Major migrations tantamount to mass exodus occur in two out of every four years. In fact, Dar Zaghawa seems to confirm the assumption that in the drylands of Africa no single tribal range is big enough to provide security against drought. The need to encroach on other groups' territories is constant, and has to be managed carefully.

When it comes to the Zaghawa, British colonial records dating from 1917, when Darfur was annexed, give a clear picture of how this management occurred. The four main Zaghawa chiefs (the Sultan of Dar Kobe, the Shertai of Dar Galla, the Melik of Dar Tuer and that of Dar Artaj) collectively supported an emissary to accompany the main body of the tribe entering another territory. Known as *Mandoub,* this emissary carried papers stamped by the Zaghawa chiefs and addressed to the chiefs of territories through which the Zaghawa passed. After the British reorganized native administration in Dar Zaghawa in 1951, each Zaghawa chief could appoint as many emissaries as required, depending on the scope of the Zaghawa exodus. These emissaries had to be approved by the district commissioner, who also gave them letters for his counterparts in the districts they were to visit.

The emissaries presented their credentials to the local authorities in the reception areas and mediated in any conflicts between the Zaghawa and the host communities, in conformity with the legal and customary codes applicable in the area of reception. They also gave assistance to the local authorities, producing men wanted for offences committed there, and ensuring the meeting of liabilities arising therefrom. A major responsibility of an emissary was to transmit information concerning resource use in the area of reception. This might relate to tree felling, trespass on farmland, grazing in the vicinity of villages, etc. Any damage resulting from misuse by an unknown culprit was collectively borne, and the emissary had to see to the discharge of the collective responsibility. This was the practice revived in the settlement discussed above.

Another envoy who helped with issues related to the management of peace and intertribal relations, was the guarantor *(Dhamin)*, who was accredited to a market area to guarantee the identity of Zaghawa livestock sellers. He was approved by the local Zaghawa authority, as well as the local government authority in the market area, to seal transactions between Zaghawa livestock sellers and purchasers. His main roles were to guarantee the identity of the seller and to undertake to trace this person in case the animal sold was disputed by a third party at a later date. He received a commission on sales and entertained Zaghawa livestock sellers in his house.

Conclusion

In the arid lands of the Sahelian Sudan, one encounters two types of pastoral movements in response to the constraints imposed by an environment characterized by scarce resources: a predictable seasonal movement within one's own territory, responding to the seasonal shortages of water and pastures; and long-range migrations that take herds and people to the territories of other groups. The first type of seasonal migration occurs most years among the Hadendowa (Beja) of eastern Sudan, the Shukriya of Butana, and the Kababish of northern Kordofan, among others. The second type of migration is practised by the Rufa'a el Hoi, who follow the Blue Nile into Khor Yabus in the Ingessena area, the various Baggara groups, who move from the lower fringes of the semi-arid lands to the southern riches of the savannah, and the Zaghawa, who move from the Wadi Howar basin down to the Fur and Masaleet territories.

In the first type of movement, the management of scarce resources is governed by the repertoire of custom and tradition that regulates tenure and access to resources within the "we" group. While these codes do not eliminate the occurrence of conflict within the "we" group, the resolution of such conflicts follows a traditional path illuminated by custom and historical precedent. Where such a precedent is lacking due to the atypical nature of the conflict, a tradition is invented on the grounds of common culture and kinship, as shown in the Zaghawa case cited above.

Long-range movement that bring groups together which do not share a common tradition together poses problems of a different nature and order. Common ground has to be created politically. This is not only required to prevent conflict, but also in order to create a common basis for the management of resources in the reception area. Here, emissaries and envoys accredited to the host group play that role. It is in the interests of both groups that resources will be managed in a manner that will not be detrimental to either.

Here *Mandoub* and *Dhamin* play a role in managing conflict relating to resource management.

Bibliography

Harir, Sharif, 1996, "Management of Scarce Resources: Dryland Pastoralism among the Zaghawa of Chad and the Crisis of the Eighties", in A.M. Ahmed and H.A. Abdel Ati (eds.), *Managing Scarcity: Human Adaptation in East African Drylands*. Addis Ababa: Organization for Social Science Research in Eastern and Southern Africa.

Timberlake, L., 1985, *Africa in Crisis*. London: Earthscan.

Dynamics of Ethnicity—A Case Study from the Western Bagamoyo District in Tanzania

Helena Jerman

In Tanzania, the colonial ethnic classification system remained in use officially after the independence up to the 1967 census. Demographical facts showed that the country consisted of some 120 ethnic groups. As this figure, 30 years later, is still cited in national (Tanzanian) and international sources it gives us a good reason to ask: What does this figure tell us? On way to approach this question is claiming that the role of ethnicity in the Tanzanian postcolonial context is different from what it was during the precolonial period and the colonial period.[1] Accordingly, two types of ethnicity can be distinguished analytically: on the one hand ethnicity as an objective phenomenon and, on the other ethnicity based on consciousness. For the precolonial period, ethnicity in Tanzania can be regarded as an objective phenomenon. In this sense, ethnicity implies cultural differentiation. Ethnicity formed an objective characteristic which united a group of people within the framework of a certain social system. An ethnic community was, thus, not necessarily a social unit—due to fusion of several social units, for example, lineages—although it was a result of it. The ethnic consciousness of different units could be weak or strong or even missing altogether, because ethnicity was not socially significant. Ethnicity was thus a cultural rather than a social asset.

Anthropological literature dealing with precolonial Tanzania (and other African countries) offers us evidence that the primary identification for the precolonial community was identification with various social groups, such as age-groups, local groups and religious groups. Thus, for example, age organizations formed important integrating and incorporating institutions across various social units (see, for example, Skinner, 1978:191–92). Marriage

1. This chapter is based on my dissertation *Between Five Lines. The Development of Ethnicity in Tanzania with Special Reference to the Western Bagamoyo District* (Helsinki and Uppsala 1997). *Between Five Lines* began as a part of the *Jipemoyo Project* (1975–1981), a culture research project which applied the Participatory Research Approach. *Jipemoyo* was set up through the cooperation of the Academy of Finland and the Ministry of National Culture and Youth in Tanzania.

also provided a means for the formulation and maintenance of explicit identities by reinforcing group identities on the basis of lineage (Turnbull, 1978:102–4; Goody, 1970:*passim*). In early Arab sources on the coastal zones of Tanzania, ethnonyms are practically absent, with the exception of the Swahili. Yet it is not clear this name has an ethnic meaning (Girenko, 1983:38). As Terence Ranger puts it, "ethnicity was more a matter of role than of origin" (1979:64–66). We can thus state that it was social status based on, for example, age or kinship organization, not ethnic status, that decided the position of an individual in precolonial society and that ethnicity was an aspect of culture (cf. Brass, 1976:226; Girenko, 1983:38). In this objective sense then, ethnicity has always existed.

Certain aspects of the peoples' perception of themselves in relation to one another and the surrounding society during precolonial period can be mentioned. Elders today attach importance to a clan's founding ancestors and consequently to the origins of tribes. The names of these tribes were in most cases not coined by the tribes themselves, but by neighbouring people with whom at some point they came into contact. The name of the Wadoe, for example, stemmed from Walowezi (settlers, intruders), that is, those who have moved from their own place to another and do not go back even to visit—in sum, who have rejected their traditions and customs.[2]

In the late precolonial period and in colonial society, which can be conceptualized as the result of a collision between traditional (in the sense of local African) societal structures and introduced alien ones (Girenko, 1974:59; cf. Afigbo, 1985), a second type of ethnicity prevailed, based on consciousness. This type of ethnicity, which I call subjective ethnicity, implies *ethnic division*. Admittedly, subjective ethnic consciousness occurred among people in the precolonial period, but we assume that ethnicity based on consciousness forms the basis for ethnic processes during independence. As a social phenomenon, ethnicity emerges through interaction between groups in colonial society. The new state system introduced a concept of territoriality which contrasted distinctly with local conceptualizations, in the sense that *political* boundaries acquired great significance. Not only did the imposed boundaries ignore objective cultural boundaries or patterns, they also led to a breakdown of traditional social entities, as well as large networks of social interaction. These were replaced by new ones. Social-stratification systems and ethnicity were altered by the colonial state. In this process, many and various groups based on cultural characteristics were gathered under *one* political system. This meant that within a broader population, the *basic* social unit had to be a *cultural* one (regardless of its social bonds). There are two conditions for an ethnicity based on consciousness, namely, 1) the colonialists' implementation of territorial divisions in order to administer their

---

2. Personal communication F.E. Mukerebe September 1981 and A.O. Anacleti April 1983. Notably, ethnic names in a modern context nominally have a precolonial origin, whatever fundamental change in form and content they have undergone since then.

subjects; and 2) the fact that the created cultural groups ('tribes') had unequal opportunities for social mobility. These factors, naturally, created
"widespread perceptions" of cultural or ethnic stratification (Young,
1982:76–78)

It is possible to recognize two cardinal processes during this period—a
ramifying of relationships on the one hand and a hardening of boundaries
on the other. Thus, parallel to the process of local, regional, social and similar communities (which had been regarded as cultural communities) losing
their distinctiveness under the new conditions, the institutionalization by
the colonial administration of the divide and rule policy gave birth to another process, externally contradictory to the first. This process made people
increasingly aware of the still-existing cultural specifics of their respective
cultures. The cultural attributes of a certain people had to serve as indicators
that the people in question belonged to a specific group, in contrast to another group that did not share these characteristics (Girenko, 1987:133–34).
Hence, cultural distinctions play a functional role only within a common
system of social interaction provided that there are several cultural groups
within that system. As to social stratification, the cultural (ethnic) belonging
was used as a major indicator for defining the position within the colonial
system: the European category was the primary one in the social hierarchy.
It should be stressed that the colonial administration emphasized ethnicity
as the only legitimate base for political authority (Ranger, 1979:82). Thus,
those who in some way formed part of the colonial administration displayed
ethnicity (and used it) in the first place, and caused this phenomenon to
spread to the rest of the population.

As the colonial system raised problems with the prioritization of cultural forms and people were confronted with participation in alien institutions, cultural characteristics gained a social significance. Secondly, when
cultural symbols or characteristics acquire new subjective significance and
consequently are used for the articulation of "we-ness" versus "otherness",
the implication is that ethnicity manifests itself through culture. Ethnicity, as
a form of consciousness that, according to Binsbergen (1985:213), "primarily
[is] a process of self-definition among a set of people perceiving themselves
[for example] as sharing a common history of deprivation" can lead to social
and political mobilization, depending on the situation. Selected cultural
factors are thus used and manipulated in order to strengthen an ethnic
group. Admittedly, subjective ethnicity is theoretically, comparable to
nationalism and nation.

The main cause for distinguishing between two types of ethnicity is
thus based on the argument that, for an understanding of African precolonial, colonial and independent history, it is important to distinguish between
the social and the cultural as relatively independent phenomena which are,
however, inconceivable without each other. In short, in an evolutionary dimension of the societal process, social norms and practice shape culture at

the same time that culture is considered a cause of social action. In sum, our expressed distinction between two types of ethnicity focuses primarily on the presence versus the lack of social significance of ethnicity for its bearers and outsiders.

The precolonial situation: Ethnicity in the town and hinterland of western Bagamoyo district

Although most writers on Bagamoyo claim that it is almost impossible to estimate when the area became populated, it is confirmed that cultivators and fisherfolk certainly lived there before 1750. The earliest evidence of human presence is found in the tombs of the first immigrants, the Muslim Shomwi *madiwani*, two of whose tombs are known to date from 1793 and 1813. These so-called Arabs emerged as a rich ruling class and played an important role in Bagamoyo's economic, religious, social and above all political life during the eighteenth and nineteenth centuries.

Knowledge of the indigenous population who settled in Bagamoyo from its hinterland is scarce. Brown (1970:71–79) notes that Zaramo, Luguru, Kami, Kwere, Doe and Zigua were all represented in Bagamoyo and that their socioeconomic and cultural similarities contributed to the cohesion among them. John Iliffe notes that one-third of the inhabitants were slaves, known as Manyema, originating in the district of the Congo bearing that name. As with most other emigrant "tribes", the Manyema (originally an externally ascribed ethnic identity) consisted of approximately twenty different Bantu-speaking groups. They readily adopted Swahili. The long distance from home, external ascription and differential treatment, resulted in these people being welded into an ethnic group.

The Nyamwezi[3] also stayed in Bagamoyo and its surroundings semi-permanently or even settled there. Because they travelled back and forth between the coast and the interior, the Nyamwezi did not—except those who settled permanently—necessarily attain a group identification in the way the Manyema people did. Unlike the Manyema, the Nyamwezi's different social status prevented them from acquiring the cultural values and traits of the ruling Shirazi.

Power was shared among a) Swahili-speaking *madiwani* of Shomwi or Shirazi origin, b) immigrant Arabs, including the Sayyid's *maliwali*, and c) Asian merchants. Although the nature of Bagamoyo made it an extremely heterogeneous community of ethnic groups, almost every African who settled in the town became a Muslim. According to Nimtz, this was probably because of their desire to assimilate into the community. The undeniably

---

3. The most active traders of the western plateau, the Sumbwa and the Nyamwezi penetrated to the coast around 1800. The term Nyamwezi was given by outsiders and was applied to the areas and to various groups of people who occupied them in the far west interior of Tanganyika. As to the interpretation of the term, there are various etymological variants (see, Abrahams, 1967; and Girenko, 1975).

Islamic disposition of Bagamoyo was present from its very origin (Iliffe, 1979:382; Nimtz, 1973:128–29, 242–243).

Father Cado Picarda noted that the small villages in the hinterland got their names either from the "chief", the *zumbe* or *jumbe* of the village, or from a "chief" in a nearby big village. However, the practice of classifying and designating villages and pointing out "chiefs" seems to reflect the needs and problems of the missionaries rather than of the local inhabitants (Picarda, 1886:235–36, 297). It is interesting to note that this administrative effort of naming and classifying places and people according to personal names later found its parallel in colonial administrative practice. It can, therefore, be stated that much of the 'traditional' correspondence between sites and "chiefs", although nowadays indisputable historical facts, stem from the missionaries' need to map their own respective areas together with cooperative individuals from those areas. In another entry, Picarda actually notes that villages often were named after a tree (1886:235).

Discussions and interviews with some *wazee* [4] of the village of Miono reveal the importance of *isi* (indicating a certain geographical entity in Zigua and in Kwere; in Swahili *nchi*) for people's ethnic identification outside the coastal settlements. It is evident that *isi* formed the most important geographical entity in precolonial times in the western Bagamoyo district. *Isi* were a network of land related through the Zigua. They divided the area according to particular events and deeds and served also as a principle of social organization. Arguably, the importance of *isi* or *nchi* in the local context of today is almost decisive for a person's ethnic consciousness.

There were few important variations as to the system of authority in the hinterland settlements. In Ukwere and Uzaramo, for example, ruling heads of all families seem to have been originally equal and independent (Brain, 1962:231; Swantz, Ll, 1966:18). Although the villages were politically independent in relation to nearby towns they recognized the towns' commercial and cultural leadership. The *diwani* or *jumbe* (different names were used in different places) ruled the coastal towns. They also led or administered their wards, together with their subordinate men. The *jumbe's* task was above all to settle disputes. One village could have several *majumbe*, each of whom had defined territorial jurisdiction within the village (see Iliffe, 1979:36–38, 43; Nicholls, 1971:31, 38–41). It was in the interests of the *majumbe* to live at peace with their neighbours in the hinterland, because their economic prosperity depended to a high degree on their function as middlemen. They dealt in goods brought by people from the hinterland and interior. So, for instance, consultation, with the hinterland people took place when a new *jumbe* was to be appointed in a coastal village (Nicholls, 1971:42).

When Sultan Sayyid Said, Oman's ruler from 1804, moved to Zanzibar in 1840, he first and foremost sought to control East Africa's trade. The

---

4. Elders (sing. *Mzee*).

hinterland of Tanganyika was definitely open for world trade. Thus the sultan greatly extended the island's authority over the mainland coast. The position of the *madiwani* changed in that their appointment normally required the sultan's personal approval. Although the local systems of government were allowed to continue, the inland people could trade with Zanzibar only through coastal middlemen, who demanded substantial fees (Iliffe, 1979:42–43; Nicholls, 1971:314).

Thus the Arab political relationship with the villages usually involved alliances with local leaders to allow for the passage of caravans. If there was no leader, or if the local leader was not willing to cooperate, the Zanzibar authorities established an *akida*. He was a paid official and he was a chosen warleader, responsible for keeping order and controlling public festivities. The *akida* was in turn subordinated to the *liwali* of a coastal town (Iliffe, 1972:180). When the missionaries arrived on the mainland seeking land they caused the first serious strains in the alliance between Arab and local leaders (Brown, 1970:72).

German colonial rule—a division of the territory and its people

The German administrative structure and the geographical division of the protectorate into districts, the boundaries of which ignored previous networks of social interaction, had long-term repercussions for ethnicity. The German strategy was to maintaining order in the districts: the military administrators had to protect them from incursions by other tribes (Admiralty, UTAf 1977/25.2–6). This new concept of territoriality contrasted sharply with local ideas. The population was classified according to a detailed system that was laid out in a handbook on how to collect information about natives.

The resistance against the German encroachment involved many sectors of the heterogeneous coastal society (Iliffe, 1979:93) and included both people from different cultural backgrounds from the caravan trade and about two-thirds of the *madiwani* of the coastal settlements. The Germans incorrectly called this resistance The Arab Revolt, a rebellion of slave traders frightened of losing their economic position (see Müller, 1959:370, 393). Glassman suggests that deep social tensions lay at the root of the social rebellion. These had been growing over the previous two decades in the coastal towns opposite Zanzibar. The diminished authority of the *majumbe* can be cited as one of many reasons for the growing conflict (Glassman, 1988:483).

The ethnic dimension of colonial warfare

Colonial warfare in precolonial Tanzania has been dealt with by several researchers. Helge Kjekshus (1977), for instance, points to, besides economic aspects, the conventionally termed tribe-nation axis of the colonial wars. His map of military operations (in a total of eighty-four locations) covers the period from 1888 to the Maji Maji uprising in 1905.

Kjekshus takes up the question of "intertribal cooperation" in connection with his analysis of colonial warfare, his point of departure being the common observation of "the lack of unity among the African peoples". At the same time, he questions whether "ethnic cooperation" during the period has been paid enough attention by researchers. Leaning on Rochus Schmidt's description of the surrender of Bwana Heri, the rebel leader, he notes that the number of tribes that were cooperating was overwhelming and that Bwana Heri expanded his intertribal contacts while the fighting was going on (Kjekshus, 1977:146).

A closer look at the tribes counted in the capture of Sadani, for example, Segua, Wadoe, Nguu, Swahili and Wakami (ibid., 188) reveals, however, that at least Segua (Zigua), Nguu and Wakami (Kami) claim the same origin and are the same people, while Wadoe (Doe), if not matrilineal, had much in common with the above mentioned peoples in terms of political systems and material culture. Undeniably the Germans considered the Doe "cunning and secretive". More interesting is that the German records, in point of fact, provide information on cooperation between "tribes": for example, the Doe obtained poison for arms from the Zigua and both groups were influential magicians (UTAf 1977/25.19, 23).

In sum, the people who fought together against the German colonials in the Bagamoyo hinterland had a common social history and were culturally often close to one another. Kjekshus's significant query should, therefore, also be seen against the precolonial background.

Ethnicity and Islam

The Germans took over the precolonial coastal titles of *liwali, akida,* and *jumbe,* but changed the functions of these administrative officers: they were completely responsible to the new rulers. The majority of the appointed *maakida* were literate coastal men and were thus foreigners in the inland districts to which they were posted. The reason for appointing *maakida* was to curb the power of indigenous headmen. Being non-locals, the *maakida* could not establish ties of reciprocity with the people they had to administer. One of their many methods to gain authority was their adherence to Islam. As teachers or as prayer leaders, they obtained local followers, particularly among former slaves or dependants who were looking for new patronage holders (Giblin, 1986:233–75; Iliffe, 1972:180–81; cf., Mrozek-Dumanowska, 1984:23–24). Islam became an alternative to former cultural and political authority and conversion on a large scale occurred during the German period. This was especially notable after the Maji Maji wars and in the Bagamoyo district primarily among the Zigua.

Mosque construction implied ideological as well as political struggles between the *maakida* and the Roman Catholic missionaries. Because the *maakida* had the power to close Christian as well as Koranic classes, the building of government schools, often run by Muslim teachers, was favoured. Changes in local cultural practices were imposed on the people, for example in the observance of food prohibitions (Giblin, 1986:279).

Islam's capability of joining forces with the traditional systems in the coastal hinterland implied that Islam proved in essence to be socially integrating and the cultural adaptations were made within the local social frameworks (see Swantz, 1986:98–102). The German activity to socially disintegrate the population implied that belonging to cultural (ethnic) categories was decisive for people's existence and status. Islam thereby acted as an integrating factor in the development of ethnicity and caused loyalty between people torn by disruptive forces.

British colonialism

The British capture of Bagamoyo took place in August 1916 with the routing of the German forces. Men in the district were forced to join the British Army. People born at the turn of the century could still remember this in the late 1970s. An elderly man in Miono related the episode in the following way:

> Well, war began. The English fought against the Germans. This was, you see, a colony of the Germans ... We saw that the Germans made our forefathers carry loads. They went there to prevent the English from crossing the border. Whipping them, they forced [the forefathers] to carry ammunition boxes on their heads. They were in big trouble. We saw how our forefathers were being punished. It did not take long before we saw the Germans flee. The English chased them ... The Germans moved away ... then the English began to rule the colony. (Donner, 1998)

Britain took over the German system of provinces and districts which they modified several times before 1961. From 1920 to 1961 the number of districts was increased from twenty-two to fifty-seven. The British considered "tribes" as natural groupings of people sharing a certain number of distinguishing characteristics, territory, history, language and customs. The Bagamoyo district was accordingly sliced into tribal divisions: the tribal division Ukwere belonged to the Kwere while Uzigua belonged to the Zigua. The aim was to unite, as far as possible, separated entities of tribes (whatever that might mean) under one chief and to place the tribal entity so formed within one administrative district. Created ethnic groups were not necessarily socially homogeneous units, since fission and fusion of groups of people had always taken place in the territory.

People's trading and social networks were narrowed as they were clustered together in tribes. Suffice it to say that many of the conditions which prevailed under German rule were not improved during the British colonial period. People were, for example, oppressed by tax and labour demands. As with German rule, the principles of precolonial famine-prevention were violated during the British period. People sold their crops in order to pay taxes. The most severe famine of this century in the Bagamoyo district was in 1932–34 and is still remembered among people who survived it. An old man born in the village of Kwadirima during this Bushi famine said that food at that time was called *mdudu* after the roots of a tree that people ate. (UTAf 1977/22.39; cf., Giblin, 1986:493).

The colonial regime and traditional social institutions

The procedure of divide and rule closely followed the system which had been in force for about twenty years in Nigeria. This pattern of governing colonies has been associated with Sir Donald Cameron, governor of Tanganyika from 1925 to 1931. Cameron ordered district officers to establish "chiefs" and to form "tribes". This was opposed by the Secretary for Native Affairs, Charles Dundas who, due to his long experience in East Africa, recognized the tribal complexity that was the result of, for example, numerous migrations. Dundas called for the development of village and regional policies rather than the scientifically advocated creation of "tribes" (Graham, 1976:5).

The British fear of growing nationalism among Africans was genuine. It was considered that the German use of *maakida* accelerated the disintegration of tribal custom and that tribal organization had been seriously weakened by the African uprisings and wars against colonial rule. The British system aimed at "making the fullest use of the traditional institutions of rule existing in African society" (Hailey, vol. I, 1950:212–213). Cameron assumed that "restored chiefs" would, in contrast to "alien" *maakida*, gain support among local people and thus improve, for example, tax collection (Giblin, 1986:405). There is, however, an important point to remember: the system of artificially created chiefdoms had a history which went back as far as the German period and was entirely subordinated to the socioeconomic system of the colonial power. Social development of traditional society now took place within the system of native administration. The ethnographic materials collected in this period by colonial officers more often than not describe pseudo-traditional societies (Girenko, 1974:59–60). The records also include falsifications of customs and traditions, due to certain resistance of the Africans towards the colonialists (Anacleti, 1978:27–28). This means that the 'true' indigenous alternatives to the *akida* system in the Bagamoyo district, imposed in the German period, were not critically questioned by the British.

It is evident, writes Girenko, that the native authorities were to be "isolated" from the traditional societies (these were to serve the interests of the colonialists). The strategy arose from the conflict of interest between colonial administration and local communities. This difference of interest between the native administration and the colonized society, "despite the formal preservation of tradition", is thus one of the main characteristics of the native authorities: "one part of the 'native' society was exploited by means of the other" (Girenko, 1974:60–61). This proved to be especially the case in the Eastern Province (which included the Bagamoyo district), where the indigenous representatives of the native authorities changed from year to year throughout the first twenty years of British rule. The native authorities—under the supervision of government administrative officers—controlled, for example, a number of social and economic matters in the tribal areas. There were violations of social everyday culture in the Bagamoyo district. The limit on brideprice was one example, as the prohibition on marriage of "immature" girls (see Hailey, vol. I, 1951:219).

Although the colonial rulers admitted that there were no striking differences in tribal custom and that most of the inhabitants in Bagamoyo district spoke Swahili (Hailey, vol. I., 1951:219 and 313), they also wrote innumerable notes in the district and provincial books speculating on ethnonyms and ethnic identification. Eastern Province was in this context a veritable problem for the system. We can well imagine a district commissioner sitting in front of his desk, biting his pencil and tearing his hair in order to make the facts fit the theory. In a certain division, there should be a common culture for a group of people described in ethnic terms, which had to correspond to a social entity. The existence of "proven" ethnic groups thus formed the basis of what were considered basic social entities within a broader population. As a matter of fact district officers in the 1930s took their anthropological investigations to heart. British professional anthropologists called for serious research using the functional method instead of so-called contemporary domestic anthropology (Austen, 1967:603). In the case of the Bagamoyo district, ethnographic notes supplied by missionaries of the Holy Ghost Fathers were also used for analyzing native culture (UTAf 1977/11.94).

Borders and tribes

The classification and reorganization of cultures was realized in ethnic maps, which even included newly created ethnic categories. The groups which were established by the colonial administration were easily conceived as analogous to precolonial social communities and formations. Ethnic consciousness arose, based on these situations.

When the commissioners marked out tribal units in the Bagamoyo district, this resulted in disputes over villages. Such disputes took place between, for instance, the Doe Native Administration and the Shirazi headman of the people in Winde (BDB II, /21/, 1926). This meant that once a boundary was drawn, it was inevitable that some of the people found themselves on the wrong side of the border. Many people, therefore, may have been forced to change ethnic identity, sometimes several times, depending on how the borders were altered. The change in ethnic identities was one problem, but a more complex problem for people was choosing an explicit ethnonym. The dilemma is verbalized by a man from Bagamoyo district who remembers having changed his ethnic label at least three times: "In the last census [1967] I was counted Kwere ... under different times I have been counted differently. I lived under Luguru and Zaramo. If you study them closely you will see that they are the same people" (personal information provided to author, 1989). When I asked him the conventional question of what he thought himself to be in ethnic terms, he said, "This is an other problem, because [the] Luguru, Zaramo and Kwere are the same people." An excerpt from the Bagamoyo district book, captures the confused nature of the contradictory classifications, and the inevitability of their failure:

> It is not easy to describe the Wazigua as a whole owing to the fact that they appear never to have been united under one paramount chief. One important distinction is at once noticeable, i.e., the Wasigua living in Bagamoyo District and the Wasigua living outside it. Of the former the name Wasigua implied a somewhat artificial unity ... It is thus seen, that the Wasigua of Bagamoyo District are composed of at least 4 tribes: Wazigua, Wadoe, Wakwere and Waru/n/guru. (BDB, II, /35/; cf., UTAf 1977/11.1–2)

This statement actually makes our point particularly strongly—differentiation between the social and cultural as relatively independent phenomena. Thus in the endeavour to identify 'tribes' in the Bagamoyo district, differences between "tribes" were found to be small or altogether nonexistent. On the other hand, it was puzzling to the British commissioners to find out that many 'tribes' were far less culturally homogeneous than they had previously thought. The above thus contains the very essence of our main argument on the phenomenon of ethnicity: ethnic groups are not socially homogeneous units, due to splitting and assimilation processes in different political societies. Indeed, splitting creates an ethnic group comprising different social communities.

Tribalism

The division of people into tribes was not restricted to economic or political matters. Cultural forms, for example music, served to manifest the tribal divisions. The Tanganyika Broadcasting Company (founded in 1951) transmitted traditional *ngoma* music as tribal music (Donner, 1986).

Leaders of tribal associations and unions manipulated culture to gain political power for themselves or for their communities. As a full-scale social phenomenon, tribalism spread to other sectors of society. Tribalism was in its essence incompatible with tradition and culture. Ethnicity manifested itself, however, through culture: language, customs and origin were used to articulate contrasting "tribal" identities. In Bagamoyo district, the emblems of office were the symbols of the headmen of the different local clans. Certain clan symbols became symbols for whole "tribes" to clearly mark out native authorities of different tribal areas (see, e.g., UTA 1976/55). This is an example of how cultural forms were given new content under native administration.

The idea of reviving tribal institutions was difficult to adapt in Bagamoyo district, where no corresponding political organization had existed. It was impossible to find tribal histories and tribal customs, because in practice these did not exist. This implied contradictions. Appointed native authorities invented tribal history and used it in their competition for political posts at the local level over different areas (BDB, I, /68–69/, II, /138/). It was possible to manipulate ethnicity.

The emotional appeal was the real power of this subjective ethnicity, based on consciousness. Paraphrasing Ernest Gellner, this means that ethnicity in the colonial society bred ethnic groups, and not vice versa. To quote Gellner, "Admittedly, nationalism uses the pre-existing, historically inherited proliferation of cultures or cultural wealth, though it uses them selectively, and it most often transforms them radically" (Gellner, 1988:55).

Arguably, a 'tribe' would perceive other 'tribes' in its contest for political power or economic benefit. However, at the same time, 'tribes' failed to recognize social processes analogous to those of the colonial state. Forms of culture, that is tribes, were clearly perceptible, whereas the content of culture, that is the societal process or colonialism, was not. When one recalls the tendency of people to unite against colonial rule prior to the establishment of indirect rule, it is easy to agree with Giblin when he writes about the politics of this period. According to him, politics had "abandoned [the] wider perspectives" that had been emerging in the decade before indirect rule (Giblin, 1986:414).

Islam—an integrating force

Although new relations of interdependence suffered under the native authority system, Islam continued to be an integrating force, not only in the sphere of religion, but also in the field of education. It is true that by the end of the 1930s native education remained largely in the hands of the Holy Ghost Mission in the Ukwere, Udoe and the Uzigua areas. However, Native Authority Schools, founded by Muslim *majumbe*, became very popular. The existence of these schools depended on local initiatives. They did not demand proselytization. (ARPC 1944:27–28; ARPC 1945:29). Education in these schools was generally conducted on tribal lines (ARPC 1939:24).

It is noteworthy that the exchange of people and goods between the hinterland and the coast had a long history. As a consequence Islamic elements had come to the hinterland through kin relationships and had adjusted to local culture. Furthermore, in the late precolonial period, Muslim and indigenous leaders occasionally united in resisting external pressure. During the German colonization, Islamic influences became increasingly prominent in Bagamoyo district and cultural forms of Islam were expressed in local societies. After Maji Maji, a majority of the leaders of the Muslim brotherhoods—the key political institutions in the Muslim community— were Africans. The *tariqa* leaders gained many adherents when Bagamoyo became a major centre of Islam in East Africa.

It was in the interest of Muslims who had gained power to compete for office as native authorities. These *majumbe* strengthened their authority through Islam and created networks of patronage. They were urged by the government to start native authority schools, a task that they fulfilled far beyond expectations. This was a way of fostering the coming generation.

In this way, Islam consolidated its position in the political sphere, ob-structing ethnicity. The Bagamoyo branch of the African Association, the forerunner of the Tanganyika African National Union (TANU) that was founded in 1954 to achieve independence, became very strongly associated with the Qadiriyya brotherhood. This was also evident during the national-ist struggle in Bagamoyo district when Islam performed its political function through the *tariqa* (see Nimtz, 1980:55–70).

Independent Tanzania—national identity reflected in history

Ernest Gellner's (1988:1–13) idea that nations are not primordial but histori-cal constructs enables us to assess the historical and cultural context of the phenomenon of ethnicity in Tanzania from independence in 1961 until the early 1980s. Under the colonial administration, the infringement of tradi-tional norms in everyday social culture formed one characteristic feature of cultural change. The positive functions of the ethnic heritage were conse-quently emphasized after Tanzania gained its independence. President Julius Nyerere stressed in his inaugural speech that "the best of the tradi-tions and customs of all our tribes should be sought out and made a part of our culture" (1967:187). The promotion of different aspects of culture during this time can be juxtaposed with the colonial tendency to emphasize "tribal" characteristics. Whereas the latter regime used this policy to divide the pop-ulation, Tanzania's aims were the opposite: to unify the population.

The first years of independence were, as A.O. Anacleti, research direc-tor of the Ministry of National Culture in 1978, notes a time of cultural am-bivalence. It was not until the Arusha Declaration (1967) that "there was a hope at last of making culture the spirit and essence of the nation" (Anacleti, 1978:10, 23–24). Being a historian, Anacleti had the task of using research as an instrument for development. The Arusha Declaration strongly rejects the colonial division of people according to skin colour or national or tribal ori-gin. As an inclusive symbol, the Tanzanian national identity was thus to transcend and subordinate other loyalties, such as tribal, religious and racial ones. Tanzania (like other African states) was an artificial creation of Europeans. Yet, according to Nyerere, after decades of colonialism it was the society that should undertake the nation-building that was first requirement of independence (1967:18). This means, furthermore, that the Tanzanian national identity had to be constructed within a definite social space, and that in creating that national identity the links between the present of a national collectivity and its past were crucial.

Attempts at villagization, that is, to urge people to form village settlements on a cooperative basis, had started prior to the Arusha Declaration. From 1973 until 1976, this process was intensified: people formerly living in scattered settlements were gathered into new or old extended villages. The main aim of villagization was to improve the living conditions of the people by facilitating the provision of such services as health, education and water. Apart from being a huge human undertaking and causing suffering, it also radically affected the ethnic composition of the population. The pastoralists' integration into settled villages, for example, actualized the interdependence between them and the agriculturalists.

The foundations of the Tanzanian nation-building project rested very much on a redefinition of the country's cultural heritage. Nyerere described the traditional African family, in the sense of villages of extended families, as cradles of freedom, equality and unity. Three vital principles which governed traditional life welded the family into a social unit. These factors, based on certain practices and attitudes were 1) an attitude of mutual respect and obligation which linked the members together, an attitude which might be described as love; 2) common property; and 3) an obligation to work (Nyerere, 1967:8–9 and 1968:337–39). The *ujamaa* village was, however, not to be understood as the revival of old traditional settlements. Rather, learning from earlier failures, the nation had to use the traditional system and was to be rebuilt upon the three fundamental principles which permeated the customs, manners and education of the people (Nyerere, 1968:337–40). *Ujamaa* and unity as an idea were depicted on postcards and on skilfully carved pieces of wooden art. Thus, large areas of life among the people were directly related to the so-called national culture.

Culture was not to be a matter of mere academic interest in Tanzania. Culture was analyzed for practical and political purposes. The Ministry of National Culture adopted a broad view of culture. Anacleti's plea that "there is nothing which most of our people know better than their culture" (1985:20) expresses well the view that development has to start from people's evaluation of their own situation and that separation between so-called spiritual culture and its societal and material base cannot come into the question (Swantz, 1979:15).

Admittedly, nationalism as well as ethnicity are powerful symbols and unifying factors which can conceal different social realities. It is without doubt in the interest of policymakers to create a sense of continuity with a supposed past. However, while agreeing that the past can be read in several ways, Smith, for instance, strongly emphasizes that a particular community has its own past—"not any past"—with its unique events and people. According to him, inventions may, as it were, be assessed as a modern re-combination of a community's elements. The important issue in this process is, however, "to ensure their lasting success and popular acceptance" (Smith, 1991:358–59).

Apart from Ranger's important remark that the notion of invention "makes little allowance for process" (1993:80), Anacleti's argument that shared knowledge and experience were gained through the interaction of people even before the colonial period, is relevant here. According to him, the spread of this common experience to many parts of Tanzania should be considered fundamental to the development of a common culture (1985:4-5). Furthermore, a condition of national identity and its continuity is that it exists as a cultural practice in people's life, a life they share from day to day.

In this way, Tanzanian identity is, as a *process*, juxtaposed with Tanzanian history. The concept of historical consciousness has been developed by several Tanzanian historians, such as Kimambo, Temu, Katoke and Gwassa. Moreover, Katoke and Lucas give a prominent place to historical conscious-ness in their elaboration of a culture shared by Tanzanians (1975:8–27). This aspect of Tanzanian history emphasizes people's responses and initiatives over centuries in bringing about change in Tanzania. The attempts of Tan-zanians as social actors to influence and control the course of their history is seen as a result of a Tanzanian identity. The idea of nationalism based on a shared history and culture, equality and a common destiny enables us to look at nationalism as a cultural process and/or cultural phenomenon.

During the independence struggle, tribalism was counteracted through the activities of the African Association and TANU. The Arusha Declaration, with its appeal for a common Tanzanian national identity, reflects a recog-nition by the new political leadership that tribalism could not be erased overnight. The implications of the colonial manipulation of ethnicity were still evident. In Zanzibar, for instance, President Karume forbade a number of ethnonyms used by the British. According to Karume, all people in Zanzibar were *wana wa Afro-Shirazi*. The question is whether a socialist pol-icy can erase ethnic contradictions—an issue which came to the fore in European socialist countries after nearly a century of socialist rule.

Evaluation analysis of ethnicity and Tanzanian identity

Most of the societies occupying a continuous geographical area in the Baga-moyo district are predominantly matrilineal and have many other social fea-tures in common. The Zigua, Kwere, Zaramo and Luguru living in the re-search area have similar languages, material culture and environmental conditions. Also, their traditional political and kinship systems as well as terminological, religious and cosmological systems are related (Beidelman, 1967). Two stories from the oral tradition indicate that some of the Kwere people, for example, are from Uzigua, where they had first settled. According to a third story, the Kwere originate in Luguru (Muro, 1979:15-17). There are also small but important colonies of non-matrilineal peoples, for example the Doe, who have migrated into the area. They are culturally quite close to their matrilineal neighbours. The Doe are patrilineal, as are the Parakuyo, who are pastoralists and constitute the 'ethnic minority' in the area.

Using a method of evaluation analysis juxtaposing villagers' own evaluations and my analytical interpretations with ethnicity and Tanzanian identity as promoted by national policy, I examine how phenomena associated with ethnic groups and the nation were conceptualized and used in the postcolonial society.

Interviews with villagers, mainly *wazee*, on the general topic of *mila na desturi* (customs and traditions) naturally led to reflections on *kabila*, a word which had come into widespread use with the colonial division of people. The concept of *kabila* (tribe) was used for administrative purposes and became especially relevant on the coast among the Swahili-speaking people. Ethnic classification of people became deeply rooted in cultural and socioeconomic institutions.

One possible analysis of apparently clashing meanings of *kabila* is to juxtapose a general meaning of *kabila* with meanings given to a specific *kabila*. These folk evaluations can lead us to the essence of ethnicity and its possibly shared cultural forms.[5]

It is worth mentioning that one ethnic classification was in use as late as the early 1980s: forms for school or work required information on one's *kabila*. During this time, in a general sense, *kabila* meant a group of people who reside in a common area, share the same culture (traditions and customs) and language and have the same kind of social organization.

Such a definition was based on a consensus of its use among officials and can be equated with general definitions of ethnic group which can be found in anthropological dictionaries. These definitions combine both social and cultural criteria in distinguishing one group from another in a society, and thus meet the criteria that were required to delineate a "tribe" in the colonial framework. A closer analysis of the main elements commonly listed for *kabila*, i.e., common area, language, culture, folkways etc., suggests the essence of one's ethnic identity. The use of the concept of *kabila* and the meanings given to it by different administrations in different periods, meanings which seem to have been commonly rooted in the minds of people, give an additional dimension to the folk meaning of *kabila*.

---

5. For an extensive discussion and analysis of villagers' ways of perceiving and expressing ethnicity in the western Bagamoyo district see Jerman, 1997:272-318.

Following the official abolition of the term *kabila*, the concept *jamii* (society) was introduced for official dealings (e.g., official reports) with ethnic groups. Although *jamii*, as a term comes close to ethnic group or 'tribe', emphasizing a sharing of a common language, common values and culture, it differs from *kabila* on an emotional level. Whereas the existence of several *makabila* denotes potential conflict between them if they came together, a group of several *jamii* connotes at least a sense of unity between them. The difference in connotations has an historical dimension: *kabila* implies tribal division and *jamii* emphasizes national unity. *Jamii* also denotes a process towards unity.

It can, of course, be argued that the meaning given to *jamii*, despite its emphasis on a process, simply replaces that of *kabila*. From a political perspective this is true. Yet, *jamii* introduces a sociological presentation of the Tanzanian population as opposed to the anthropological term *makabila*. The unification of the *jamii* thus required, according to an informant, three key factors—a common language, political mobilization and a common political party "capable of maintaining the unity of different *jamii*" and an economic policy aiming at reducing social and regional inequalities. This suggests that from an ethnic perspective, the "unification of different *jamii*" implies above all a common Tanzanian culture and identity.

Integration of a national culture

When chiefdoms were officially abolished in 1962, this signified the end of the chiefs' administrative and judicial powers. The administration was reorganized and new symbols emphasizing national integration were created and distributed in order to forge a common Tanzanian culture. This unifying process was supposed to take place on a wider scale than local ('tribal') institutions. African values were emphasized to the extent that the integration of culture transcended even national boundaries. From the very start, Pan-Africanist ideology had viewed Africa as a whole both historically and culturally. Shortly after Nyerere became president of the Republic of Tanzania he wrote that "African nationalism is meaningless, is anachronistic, and is dangerous, if it is not at the same time Pan-Africanism" (1967:196). He considered Tanzania's goal for Africa to be a United States of Africa (ibid.:189). New holidays celebrating the history of the republic offered a renovated set of national values which could be shared by everyone: Zanzibar Revolutionary Day (12 January), Union Day (26 April), Saba Saba Day (7 July) i.e., the seventh day of the seventh month, the very day when TANU was established in 1954 and Tanzanian Independence and Republic Day (9 December).

Khangas and *kitenges* (wrap-around cloth, worn by women) were sometimes decorated with national symbols and slogans to strengthen the unity of the people. Besides, a *khanga* with the text "Black beauty—black fashion" reminded its wearer of a common black popular culture shared by Africans as well as Afro-Americans. This culture traced its roots back to the black political organizations (e.g. Black Panthers) in the United States that emphasized cultural nationalism in the 1960s and 1970s (Duffield, 1984:105–106). In this way, political considerations penetrated local culture.

However, the uneven socioeconomic development of the country during the colonial period had clear repercussions on ethnicity once Tanzania gained its independence. There were problems with the civil service apparatus, e.g., the relocation of often unwilling former leaders from their home regions to other places in the country. There was also a thorny connection between ethnicity and the allocation of financial resources. People had the impression that these were primarily allocated to areas which had been socioeconomically developed during the colonial era.

Two examples of the connection between ethnicity and employment programmes will suffice. In July 1977, the workers of the Tanganyika Packers factory threatened to go on strike due to preferential treatment of a certain "tribe" (Haya) by some senior managers. Also, unofficial investigations (1976–77) into the teachers training college in Chang'ombe and the University of Dar es Salaam revealed that one-quarter of the pupils in the Chang'ombe college were Haya while one-quarter of the students at the university were either Haya or Chagga (UTAf 1977/22.48). This had to do with the educational pattern in the country: the Haya and Chagga come from areas with a better educational infrastructure because of mission work. The ensuing letters to the editors of two newspapers (*Daily News* and *Uhuru*) on the matter of *ukabila* (tribalism) were highly illuminating.

Developing Swahili as a national language "which best expresses the Tanzanian cultural reality in spirit and personality" (Katoke and Lucas, 1975:21) is a measure specifically aimed at developing a national culture. In this process, incompatible languages and special forms of culture are inevitably left out of the new national unit. Put in other terms, the idea of the Tanzanian identity contains some ambiguous and contradictory elements. Roughly speaking, the strategy was to develop "Tanzanian-ness" side by side with the Swahili language. A Tanzanian identity was constructed out of different 'tribal' cultures. 'Tribal thinking' was striking in the administrators' attitudes.

To underpin my suggestion that attempts at creating a common Tanzanian culture have affected ethnicity in the western Bagamoyo district, I outline some observations on ethnicity in this particular context. Admittedly, people who did not belong to dominant tribes in a specific area of a *jumbe*, were called *wageni* (strangers), or outsiders during the colonial period. A similar 'classification' of people reappeared in new form with the restructuring of villages in the 1970s. The objective effect of the villagization experiment was thus a separation of cultivators and pastoralists. This had disastrous consequences for the Parakuyo (see Mustafa, 1986:66–122). The Parakuyo were henceforward considered *wageni* in the Bagamoyo district.

In addition, *makabila* ('tribes') were no longer administrative entities for the local leaders—the village was now considered the basic unit. Accordingly, ethnonyms were officially not to be used, since they lacked relevance in a society whose aim was cultural integration. In the special case of Bagamoyo district, rural Tanzanians were consequently referred to as either *wafugaji* (pastoralists) or *wakulima* (cultivators). In everyday speech, however, it was common to use ethnonyms in general, and particularly with respect to ethnic minorities. The Parakuyo who were called Kwavi,[6] and the Makonde (another ethnic minority in the area which had come as refugees from Mozambique) were referred to by tribe. Kinship relations still played a role in social organization at the local level and led to conflicting leadership roles (Swantz, 1980:15–16). Old administrative practices were deeply rooted in everyday life, notwithstanding new structures. Important matters were always discussed and dealt with at traditional meetings attended by people who shared a specific ethnic tradition. On the other hand, on the village level in the district, the explanation for a specific feature of *ngoma*[7] was commonly expressed in this way, "it has to do with our *jadi* (tradition)". Hence one did not talk about *kabila*, but tradition. Moreover, the villagers in the research area preferred to talk about the history of a particular area than about the history of a particular ethnic group.

The language spoken at home depended on the parents' cultural heritage. In cases where the parents were of different ethnic origin, the ethnic identity of their children was solved, for example, in the following way: the children of a Doe wife and a Zigua husband got their ethnic identities by turn through puberty rites. These rites were partly the same and partly different (personal information Donner, 1977). Another informant, whose ethnic affiliation differed from that of her husband, told me that the sex of their children decided which kind of education those children got. In traditional medicine education or in child-rearing practices, for example, a girl goes with her mother, a boy with his father. This means that there were options for ethnic identification, depending on the social situation of the people concerned. Religious identity sometimes competed with ethnic identity, but could also be an alternative to the latter.

The female Islamic puberty rite in Miono constituted an alternative to the traditional puberty rite, *kisazi*. Although almost all Miono inhabitants are Muslim, the majority chose *kisazi* instead of the corresponding Islamic rite. The reason for this was cultural considerations. Furthermore, the Islamic rite

---

6. The Parakuyo are often called Kwavi (a coastal term that they themselves find derogatory) by cultivating people.

7. *Ngoma* is the most vital form of music in Tanzania. The word has many connotations depending on the context in which it is used (e.g. dance, drum, ritual).

is considered to be too ascetic. During the *mwali*[8] rites, Islamic music, *kaswida* and *lika* are played as part of the rites, and tea and sweet small buns made of wheat flour, *maandazi* are served. *Kisazi*, on the other hand, attracts more people because local beer, *pombe*, is served during the feast (Donner, 1978).

The lessons of *ngoma ya selo*, an essential part of the traditional education of Zigua girls in Bagamoyo district and often performed at other rituals related to the lifecycle and weddings, were taught to girls by the *fundi*, and seemed to be strongly anchored in local society. The nightly instruction attracted and involved young and old family members of the *mwali*. Even small girls as young as five often participated together with their older sisters (or where their sisters were ill, instead of them) in the lessons. It is noteworthy that *selo* was taught in many primary schools in the research area, indicating that it was rooted in the wider society as well as in the educational policies of the government. *Ngoma* competitions were another aspect of this policy. In 1978, *ngoma* competitions took place throughout Tanzania. The aim of these competitions was to choose the best dance groups for the first anniversary of the Chama cha Mapinduzi party. According to Donner, local teachers introduced new features in the performances. The pupils were, for example, dressed in uniforms. There was also new metrics in the song texts, uniform movements and rephrasing the texts of political handbooks. The songs were performed in Swahili. This is an expression of how national discipline and mechanical political thinking interact with subtle local patterns.

Multiple interpretations of ethnicity

Arguably, the cultural pluralism of the new Tanzania is a system of perceptually or materially accessible forms of social pluralism. This cultural phenomenon includes forms dating from ancient times to the present. Concepts representing, for instance, old ideological systems considered important by informants for their identity thus suggest the relevance of understanding culture as a cross-section of the societal process. However, the social context for the construction of a national identity was determined by the history of the postcolonial society, which itself resulted from a process of long-standing. It is clear that forms of culture forge the chain of identity, and sharing these forms requires communication. The role and importance of, for example, the Swahili language in Tanzania's history and society is indisputable. Swahili language was widely used in Bagamoyo district even during the late precolonial period. Swahili, the language of administration during the German colonial period and under British native administration, served as a medium of communication in primary school. On the eve of independence, Swahili had benefited from its prominence within a multilingual Tanzania.

---

8. A girl who has begun to menstruate.

My argument regarding the social and the cultural as two relatively in-dependent phenomena allows for distinguishing between objective ethnicity in the precolonial period, on the one hand, and ethnicity based on con-sciousness during the late precolonial and the colonial periods, on the other. Obviously, the latter form of ethnicity was not erased with independence. Hence, I suggest that "Tanzanian-ness" can have different meanings for different parts of the community. Being a Zigua (or a Kwere or a Doe) and a Tanzanian may be perceived and articulated in a number of ways among villagers in the research area. From a historical perspective, I can, in Ranger's words, "trace a constant process of imagining and reimagining" ethnicity. This means that the invention of boundary markers ('tribes') dur-ing colonialism was one factor and the filling of tribal form with imaginative meaning was another. To be more specific, ethnicity "cannot bear a single significance" (Ranger, 1993:89–90, 98, 105). This also implies that the content of tradition given by administrators or researchers has to be distinguished from how people themselves use their tradition, whatever the tradition might be. A 'community' continues and advances spiritually, culturally and biologically, regardless of how it is used (or misused) politically. Moreover, in this process people seem to use different forms in order to preserve their community's continuity. Arguably, these forms are specific aspects of all kinds of social phenomena encompassing people's whole existence.

In a local context, an ethnic identity is fixed in the special relationship between people and their environments and the cultural implications flow-ing from these relationships. Moreover, ethnic-group identification is used as a self-referent. People's perception of the present is a reflection of the colonial practice of dividing people into tribes. Yet villagers in the Bagamoyo district stress commonality—another dimension of ethnic con-sciousness. Moreover, certain aspects of national politics are absorbed by local forms of culture affecting ethnicity in the villages of Bagamoyo district. In this respect Feierman's argument that "the wider world is not external to the local community; it is at the heart of the community's internal processes of differentiation" is relevant (1990:36).

Finally, my suggestion that Islam, during the struggle for indepen-dence, could obstruct ethnicity raises the question of its existence as an alternative source of identification to that of ethnic or national conscious-ness. Considering the ideological basis of Tanzania's national policies, which emphasized social and racial equality rather than religion, tribe and origin, Islam was a hard nut to crack in the nation-building process. Being deeper and bigger than a local "tribe", Islam consolidated its position in the nation-alist struggle. Moreover, we must remember this when we think about more than two "tribes" or tribal associations. Arguably, Islam was used to pro-mote political careers. Thus, we can assume that at the local level, thirty-five years after independence, perceptually accessible forms of culture, condi-tioned as they are by social reality, include this dynamic.

Islamic political activity during the late 1970s and early 1980s was not very conspicuous at the local level in the research area. But, during the 1990s, considering the Islamic headgear adopted by the political leadership, Islamic activity seems to be conspicuous on the national level. Further research on the development of ethnicity to focus on the social significance of this phenomenon would be of benefit.

Bibliogrpahy

Abrahams, R.G., 1967, *The Peoples of Greater Unyamwezi, Tanzania (Nyamwezi, Sukuma, Sumbwa, Kimbu, Konongo)*. London: International African Institute.

Afigbo, A.E., 1985, "The Social Repercussions of Colonial Rule: The New Social Structures", in A. Adu Boahen (ed.), *Africa under Colonial Domination 1880–1935*. London: Heinemann.

Anacleti, Odhiambo A., 1978, "Culture and Revolution", *Mbioni*, Vol. 8, 9.

—1985, "Inter-relationship between Culture and Population in Tanzania". Oxfam. Mimeo.

Austen, Ralph A., 1967, "The Official Mind of Indirect Rule: British Policy in Tanganyika, 1916–1939", in Prosser Gifford and W.M. Roger Louis (eds.), *Britain and Germany in Africa—Imperial Rivalry and Colonial Rule*. New Haven: Yale University Press.

Beidelman, T.O., 1967, *The Matrilineal Peoples of Eastern Tanzania*. London: International African Institute.

van Binsbergen, W., 1985, "From Tribe to Ethnicity in Western Zambia: The Unit of Study as an Ideological Problem", in Wim van Binsbergen and Peter Geschiere (ed.), *Old Modes of Production and Capitalist Encroachment. Anthropological Explorations in Africa*. London: Routledge.

Brain, J.L., 1962, "The Kwere of the Eastern Province", *Tanganyika Notes and Records*, March/September.

Brass, Paul R., 1976, "Ethnicity and Nationality Formation", *Ethnicity*, 3.

Brown, Walter T., 1970, "Bagamoyo: An Historical Introduction", *Tanzania Notes and Records*, 71.

Donner, Philip, 1978, "Ngoma ya Selo from the Bagamoyo District". Dar es Salaam. Mimeo.

—1998, "Uminyonyo". Helsinki. Manuscript.

Duffield, Ian, 1984, "Pan-Africanism since 1940", in Michael Crowder (ed.), *The Cambridge History of Africa*, Vol. 8. Cambridge: Cambridge University Press.

Feierman, Steven, 1990, *Peasant Intellectuals. Anthropology and History in Tanzania*. Madison: University of Wisconsin Press.

Gellner, Ernest, 1988 (1983), *Nations and Nationalism*. Oxford: Blackwell.

Giblin, James L., 1986, "Famine, Authority and the Impact of Foreign Capital in Handeni District, Tanzania, 1840–1940". Ph.D. thesis. University of Wisconsin, Madison.

Girenko, N.M., 1974, "Kolonyal'nyi režim i traditsionnye sotsial'nye instituty (na primere Tanzanii)", *Sovetskaîa Etnografiîa*, 1.

—1975, *Traditsionnaîa sotsial'naîa organizatsiîa Nyamwezi (Osnovnye tendentsii razvitiîa v dokolonial' nyi period*. Dissertatsiîa na sosykanie uchenoi stepeni kandidata istoricheskikh nauk. Institut Etnografii im. Miklukho-Maklaîîa, Leningrad.

—1983 "Dinamika kul'turnykh izmenenii i Vostochnaja Afrika XIX-XX gg", *Afrikanski Sbornik: Istorîa, Etnografiîa*. Pod redaktsii D.A. Ol'derogge. Moskva: Nauka.

—1987, "Vzaimodeistvie kul'tury i obshchestva v leninskoi dialektike", *Leninism i problemy etnografii*. Pod redaktsii Iû. V. Bromleîa i R.F. Itsa.

Glassman, Jonathan, 1988, "Social Rebellion and Swahili Culture: The Response to German Conquest of the Northern Mrima, 1888–1890". Ph.D. thesis. University of Wisconsin, Madison.

Goody, Jack, 1970, "Marriage Policy and Incorporation in Northern Ghana", in Ronald Cohen and John Middleton (eds.), *From Tribe to Nation in Africa*. Scranton: Chandler.

Graham, J.D., 1976, "Indirect Rule: The Establishment of 'Chiefs' and 'Tribes' in Cameron's Tanganyika", *Tanzania Notes and Records*, 77–78.

Hailey, W.M., 1950, *Native Administration in the British African Territories, Part I, East Africa: Uganda, Kenya, Tanganyika*. London: His Majesty's Stationery Office.

—1951, *Native Administration in the British African Territories, Part IV, A General Survey of the System of Native Administration*. London: His Majesty's Stationery Office.

Iliffe, John, 1972, *Tanganyika under German Rule 1905–1912*. Nairobi: East African Publishing House.

—1979, *A Modern History of Tanganyika*. Cambridge: Cambridge University Press.

Jerman, Helena, 1997, *Between Five Lines. The Development of Ethnicity in Tanzania with Special Reference to the Western Bagamoyo District*. Jipemoyo. Development and Culture Research 8/1997; TAFAS, 38. Helsinki: The Finnish Anthropological Society and Uppsala: The Nordic Africa Institute.

Katoke, Israel K. and Stephen A. Lucas, 1975, "Cultural Development as a Factor in Social Change". Dar es Salaam. Mimeo.

Kjekshus, Helge, 1977, *Economy Control and Economic Development in East African History. The Case of Tanganyika 1850–1950*. London: Heinemann.

Mrozek-Dumanowska, Anna, 1984, *Social Functions of Black Islam*. Warsaw: Poligrafus.

Muro, Asseny, 1979, "The Study of Women's Position in Peasant Production and their Education and Training. A Case Study of Diozile I Village in Bagamoyo District". M.A. thesis, University of Dar es Salaam.

Mustafa, Kemal, 1986, "Participatory Research and the 'Pastoralist Question' in Tanzania: A Critique of the Jipemoyo Project Experience in Bagamoyo District. Ph.D. thesis, University of Dar es Salaam.

Müller, Fritz Ferdinand, 1959, *Deutschland-Zanzibar-Ostafrika. Geschichte einer deutschen kolonialoberung 1884–1890*. Berlin: Rütten & Loening.

Nicholls, Christine S., 1971, *The Swahili Coast. Politics, Diplomacy and Trade on the East African Littoral 1798–1856*. London: Allen.

Nimtz, August H. Jr., 1973, "The Role of the Muslim Sufi Order in Political Change: An Overview and Micro-Analysis from Tanzania". Ph.D. thesis, Indiana University.

—1980, *Islam and Politics in East Africa. The Sufi Order in Tanzania*. Minneapolis: University of Minnesota Press.

Nyerere, Julius K., 1967, *Freedom and Unity/Uhuru na Umoja*. London: Oxford University Press.

—1968, *Freedom and Socialism/Uhuru na Ujamaa*. London: Oxford University Press.

Picarda, Cado, 1886, *Les Missions Catholiques*, Tome 18. Lyon.

Ranger, Terence, 1979, "European Attitudes and Africa Realities: The Rise and Fall of the Matola Chiefs of South-East Tanzania", *Journal of African History*, 20, 1.

—1993, "The Invention of Tradition Revisited", in Terence Ranger and Olufemi Vaughan (eds.), *Legitimacy and the State in Twentieth-Century Africa. Essays in Honour of A.H.M. Kirk-Greene*. London: Macmillan Press in association with St. Antony's College, Oxford.

Skinner, Elliott P., 1978, "Voluntary Associations and Ethnic Competition in Ougadougou", in Brian M. du Toit (ed.), *Ethnicity in Modern Africa*. Boulder: Westview Press.

Smith, Anthony D., 1991, "The Nation: Invented, Imagined, Reconstructed?", *Millenium*, 20, 3.

Swantz, Lloyd, 1966, *The Zaramo of Tanzania. An Ethnographic Study*. Syracuse University.

Swantz, Marja-Liisa, 1979, *Culture and Social Change in the Restructuring of Tanzanian Rural Areas. Bagamoyo Research Project 'Jipemoyo'*. Final Report. Helsinki: Jipemoyo Project Archives.

—1980, "Western Bagamoyo as an Area for Cultural Research", in Philip Donner (ed.), *Jipemoyo. Development and Culture Research*, 3. Helsinki: Transactions of the Finnish Anthropological Society, 9.

—1986, *Ritual and Symbol in Transitional Zaramo Society with Special Reference to Women*. Uppsala: Scandinavian Institute of African Studies.

Turnbull, Colin M., 1978, "Society and Sociality: An Expanding Universe", in Brian M. du Toit (ed.), *Ethnicity in Modern Africa*. Boulder: Westview Press.

Young, Crawford, 1982, "Patterns of Social Conflict: State, Class and Ethnicity", *Daedalus*, 3, 2.

District and Provincial Books:

Bagamoyo District Book Volume I. Tanzania National Archives, Dar es Salaam. (Microfilm Reel 13) (The "new" Bagamoyo District Book, I).

Morogoro (Eastern Province) Provincial Book Volume II—Bagamoyo and Ulanga District Books (The "old" Bagamoyo District Book, II).

Tanganyika Territory. Annual Reports of the Provincial Commissioners, 1939, 1944, 1945. Eastern Province.

Jipemoyo Project Archives :

Fieldnotes: UTAf 1977/11 HJ; UTAf 1977/22 HJ; UTAf 1977/25 HJ; .

Tape recordings: 1976/55–56.

Oral Information (Not Anonymous):

A.O. Anacleti, P. Donner, F.E. Mukerebe

Other Sources:

Donner, Philip, 1986, *Utamaduni wa Mtanzania, Tansanialaisen kulttuuri*, in *Miten luodaan Kansallinen musiikki*, part V. Radio programme, Finnish Broadcasting Company, 8 January.

Ethnopolitics and the State—Lessons from Uganda

E.F. Byarugaba

Uganda is a country richly endowed with divse cultures, languages, values and norms. It has many ethnic groups which include the Acholi, Langi, Baganda, Banyankole, Basoga, Batoro, Banyoro, Bagisu, Bakiga, Iteso, Karimojong and Madi. They are subsumed into larger categories in anthropological literature as Bantu, Nilotic, Nilo-Hamitic and Sudanic people. Numerically, the two main clusters are Bantu and Nilotic, situated in the southern and northern parts of Uganda respectively.

This chapter examines ethnic pressures on the state, taking Uganda as a case study. Specifically, it explores how ethnicity has impacted on Ugandan politics. Besides examining ethnic contradictions, it will also show how ethnicity generates strong and persistent ethnopolitical divisions, often leading to civil strife and military coups.

In Africa, the state is often a major actor in ethnic politics, and it is the principal instrument for personal advancement and aggrandizement. It is important to note that the bureaucracy not only formulates economic policy but is the main beneficiary of it. Therefore, at the heart of ethnic struggles is the desire for power, because in developing countries political power leads to economic power.

Although the map of Uganda shows a neatly divided country with clearly marked boundaries and territory, it conveys a misleading image of people's ethnic identities. Apart from dividing ethnic tribes at the borders (Samia in Kenya and Uganda, Lugbara in Uganda and Zaire, Banyarwanda in Uganda and Rwanda), tribes were arbitrarily divided by district boundaries for ease of administration. For instance, to reward the Baganda collaborators, parts of Bunyoro were excised and given to Buganda by the British. Although the first independence government tried to return Buyaga and Bugangaizi counties to Bunyoro, this problem has never been solved. Buhekura, Buruli, Bulemezi and part of Singo, which were part of Bunyoro, and Mawogola and Kabula, which were part of Ankole, remain part of

Buganda. This unresolved problem reemerges every time there is a change of regime, in the hope that the new government will solve it.

The facilitators of ethnocentrism were the colonial masters. They wanted each tribe to remain, as far as possible, separate from the others for ease of administration. Using the same policy, they recruited the army from people who were regarded as martial. Hence the army of the time was recruited among the Nubians—Langi, Acholi, Mahdi and Kakwa—all from the northern part of Uganda. This situation persisted until 1986, when the National Resistance Army (NRA) took power. In the same way, politics in the previous ten years were dominated by Bantu groups. This includes Baganda, Banyankole, Batoro, Basoga and Banyoro. The NRA itself was predominantly composed of those groups.

The counties demarcated by the colonial administrators still hold today, and the tribes still regard themselves as unique entities, although they accept rule from the centre. Successive governments have tried to create new, economically and politically viable districts, without interfering visibly with the internal politics of the groups. With the exception of West Nile Bugisu, Bukedi, Toro and Kigezi, where the ethnic units were not considered viable, native authorities or districts still coincide with ethnic boundaries.

Another important pillar in the entrenchment of parochial sentiments based on ethnicity was indirect rule. This system of administration lasted until the 1940s, when Creech-Jones, the colonial secretary, in 1947 announced a new policy aimed at converting the system of indirect rule into a democratic, efficient, and modern system of local governance. Some scholars (Rupesinghe, 1989) argue that this led to the enactment of the *Local Government Ordinance* in 1949, which gave legal and corporate powers and responsibilities to the district councils, and introduced the elective principle within local administrations. It should be pointed out, however, that the ordinance did not apply to Buganda. Administrative districts (including kingdoms) generally coincided with tribal demography, and the effect of the 1949 ordinance was to institutionalize ethnically based local government.

Within the domain of native administration, Buganda was governed by the Uganda agreement of 1900. The issue is whether the agreement gave Buganda a privileged position in Uganda. Baganda and non-Baganda believed it to be so, and the British encouraged this belief. This constitutional divide proved a source of conflict in postcolonial Uganda.

During colonial times, ethnic groups were often "manufactured". In regard to several of the inter lacustrine kingdoms, British rule did sustain and strengthen the cohesiveness of these states. Even more so, the colonial administration grouped together various clan units whose linguistic or other affiliations, facilitated the development and assertion of common political orientations, notwithstanding internal factionalism. None of these measures could fully reflect the subtle shades of ethnic differentiation, either within or across groups. The effect, therefore, if not the intent, seems to have been a freezing and formalization of ethnic differentiation at certain levels.

Ethnic conflicts, class conflicts, occupational conflicts, and regional antagonisms are part of a multidimensional and complex reality. All forms of identity exist, ranging from class, ethnicity, religion, tribe, occupation to region and language groups. Ethnicity is a dynamic concept which may have an ethnic character as well as a class character, and class and ethnic conflicts may be waged simultaneously. It is for this reason, therefore, that some have defined ethnic conflicts as protracted social conflicts, characterized by such enduring features as economic and technological underdevelopment and unintegrated political systems.

Furthermore, postindependence regimes in the developing world, including Uganda, have taken advantage of the weakness and fragility of political structures to "ethnicize" the state. It is for this reason that ethnicity became increasingly useful for political legitimization and domination. Consequently, anti-imperialist or anticolonialist ideologies were replaced by hegemonic ethnic assertions, thereby providing the ideological impetus towards authoritarian rule. What finally evolved was a state formation strongly bound by patron-client loyalties, with some groups excluded and others included.

Ethnicity and democratization

There are many reasons why democratization can fail. Some of these are the resistance of the entrenched civilian or army elite, the weakness of civil society, and ineptly designed political institutions. In Africa, Eastern Europe, Asia and the former Soviet Union, a major reason for the failure of democratization is ethnic conflict. Democratization is about inclusion and exclusion, about access to power, about the privileges that go with inclusion and the penalties that accompany exclusion. In severely divided societies, ethnic identity provides clear lines to determine who will be included and who will be excluded. In ethnic politics, therefore, inclusion may affect the distribution of important material and social goods, including the prestige of ethnic groups and the identification of the state as belonging to one group rather than to others. Ethnically divided societies thus possess a special version of the usual democratic problem of assuring decent treatment for the opposition. An ethnically differentiated opposition can easily be depicted as consisting of particularly dangerously enemies, enemies who do not accept the current identity of the state and who are plotting to break the state or to steal it for their own group (Plattner, 1993:19). Uganda is among the most severely divided societies. The problem of ethnic rivalries began way back during the precolonial era, when Buganda and Bunyoro were the chief protagonists. Their differences were exacerbated by colonialism, and for this reason some scholars have argued that national unity was undermined when the British colonialists played on the differences between Buganda and Bunyoro.

The shadow of ethnicity has darkened the country's independent political life to the present time. This is not to say that there were no successes in postcolonial Uganda. One explosive political problem the government handled constitutionally was the long-standing dispute between the Bunyoro and Buganda kingdoms over the "lost counties" issue. The so-called "lost counties" were tracts of land that belonged to Bunyoro before the onset of colonialism, but which were given to Buganda for assisting the British to defeat Bunyoro. After successfully dodging responsibility for settling the problem they had created, the British left it to the government of newly independent Uganda to settle the issue through a referendum in the disputed counties two years after independence. The referendum was held in 1964, two of the counties under dispute were returned to Bunyoro and the dispute was solved, at least for the time being. This democratic solution, however, which ought to have solved the problem, provoked more antagonism between Buganda and Bunyoro. The Baganda were not content with the way the dispute was handled by the government of Milton Obote, although this was done strictly in accordance with the law. Throughout 1963, the kabaka (king of Buganda) and his government undertook a massive exercise of settling "dependable" Baganda from other parts of Buganda in the disputed counties in the hope that these people would vote in support of Buganda's claim to the counties. This was blocked by the central government, which decreed that only persons on the electoral register of 1962 could vote in the counties concerned. This foiled the Baganda immigrants and the kabaka's hopes of retaining the counties. It is this event, more than anything else, that caused serious strains between Buganda and the central government and eventually led to the break up of this political alliance.

The influence of ethnicity in Ugandan politics can further be seen in the general elections of 1961 and 1962. The 1962 elections were boycotted by the Kyaka Yekka (KY), the kabaka's political arm, which urged its members to ignore the event. Scholars have interpreted this move as an attempt to secede from the country, which, of course, did not augur well for national unity and state consolidation. As a result of the boycott, the Democratic Party (DP) won a majority of the seats in the election, and Benedict Kiwanuka was appointed chief minister. The 1962 independence elections were also held against the background of Buganda's demand for a special position, and this was encouraged by the British. The British position was spelt out clearly in the Muster report, which recognized that Buganda was in a different position from other districts and kingdoms. The report argued that, for years, Buganda had enjoyed considerable autonomy, which made it difficult for the Baganda to agreed to have it taken away. Given this support, the kabaka and his government refused to send representatives to the London constitutional conference, and demanded powers over courts of law, police, and security in Buganda, and indirect elections to the national assembly. Conceding the last demand, the ruling Uganda Peoples Congress (UPC) allowed the Lukiiko, the Baganda assembly, to elect twenty-one of its members to sit in the national assembly. This was a betrayal of the UPC manifesto, which promised not to uphold undemocratic procedures. In effect, the Lukiiko and the kabaka disfranchised the Baganda people by not allowing them to vote in the 1961 elections, and by allowing indirect elections which swept to power the UPC-KY alliance in 1962. This was not an encouragement to democratization, and it is right to conclude that the Muster report recommendations were a prelude to the disruption of Ugandan unity.

The 1966 crisis was a culmination of three political developments. The first was the break up of the ruling UPC-KY alliance, which led to the estrangement of the kabaka's government from the central government. The second was the leadership struggle within the UPC, which resulted in the arrest and detention of some of Obote's ministers. The third was the suspension of the Independence Constitution and the dismissal of the kabaka from his post of president and head of state. All this led to the breakdown of relations between Buganda and the central government. From the time when the central government set itself on a collision course with Buganda by ordering a referendum in the disputed counties, Obote and the UPC had clearly anticipated an eventual breakup of the alliance with the KY. Accordingly, Obote proceeded to make his party less dependent on KY support in parliament. Through the effective use of patronage, many DP and KY members of parliament renounced allegiance to their own parties and joined the UPC. By 1964, when the "lost counties" referendum was held, the UPC had gained an absolute majority in parliament. When the alliance was finally dissolved, Obote's government was not particularly bothered. As a matter of fact, it was Obote himself who took the initiative in terminating the alliance by removing KY ministers from office in August 1964. However, the termination of the UPC-KY coalition, and the weakening of the DP parliamentary opposition, precipitated major problems for the central government which culminated in a major crisis.

Nevertheless, it was the contradictions and leadership struggles within the UPC itself that were to trigger the crisis of February–May 1966. From its very formulation in 1960 as a splinter group of the radical Uganda National Congress, the UPC comprised two factional tendencies, one progressive and socialist-inclined and the other conservative and pro-capitalist. These factions came into open conflict for the control of the party during the annual delegates conference that was held in Gulu in 1964. In the election for the key position of secretary-general of the party, the radical socialist John Kakonge lost to Grace Ibingira. Ibingira aspired to the leadership of the party itself and ultimately of the government, thereby antagonizing Obote. In the shadow of the struggle for political power was the ethnic factor, as well as the north-south divide. Kirunda (1995) has argued that Obote and his closest aides and supporters were from the north, a fact resented as "northern domination" by many southern people. In addition, the sidelining of Buganda after the breakup of the UPC-KY coalition, meant that the southern Bantu majority was denied the opportunity to play an effective role in national politics.

Following a secret deal with the kabaka, Ibingira sought to reverse the situation by bidding for national leadership within the ruling party. Accordingly, he put together "a Bantu formation" within the UPC and proceeded to undermine the position of Obote with the aim of ousting him as party president and, eventually, as prime minister. On 22 February 1966, contrary to the provisions of the Constitution, Obote assumed full powers and ordered the arrest and detention of five ministers of his government, including Grace Ibingira. All belonged to the Bantu ethnic group. It is worth noting here the ethnic dimensions the crisis had taken. All those arrested and detained were southern Bantu politicians, the so-called "Bantu formation". There followed another political coup by Obote. The suspension of the constitution effectively removed the kabaka of Buganda, Sir Edward Mutesa, from the office of president and head of state, a position he had occupied since 1963 under the terms of UPC-KY alliance. Obote then proceeded quickly to consolidate his power. On 15 April 1966, he introduced in the national assembly a new constitution and had it adopted without debate. This became the 1966 Interim Republican Constitution, which made him president and head of state.

Having inflicted preemptive strikes on the forces of the opposition, Obote prepared to deal with the aftermath of his action. Indeed, compared with what was to follow, the crisis had just begun. Obote's singlehanded dismissal of the kabaka from the position of head of state, and the removal of another traditional ethnic leader, the kyabazinga of Busoga as vice-president, was not only humiliating to both leaders personally, but also constituted a dangerous political development that had to be resisted. The Interim Constitution left Buganda and the kabaka grossly weakened. This is why Buganda decided to resist the central government, and went on the political offensive against Obote. The retaliation of Buganda came after numerous warnings, culminating in May 1996, with a call to central government to remove its seat of government from Buganda soil. The central government interpreted this as an act of rebellion by Buganda, with secessionist overtones. The ordering of the Ugandan government out of Buganda implied that Buganda was no longer part of it. Obote moved quickly again with what had by now become his familiar style.

Barely two days after the Lukiiko resolution, Obote ordered an armed attack on the kabaka's palace at Mengo on the pretext of looking for arms planned for use in the rebellion. The results were disastrous. After a spirited battle, the kabaka's palace guard capitulated and Sir Edward Mutesa fled into exile. An important point to note is that the defeat and dismemberment of the Buganda kingdom marked the end of the conflict between the traditional and modern elites in Ugandan politics. The remaining traditional rulers in other kingdoms were too weak and too timid to confront the central government, which emerged from the crisis with unassailable power and authority. Hardly before a year had elapsed, Obote moved to consolidate his power and rule the country on his own terms. He did this by promulgating the 1968 Constitution which abolished kingdoms and heads of districts, and made Uganda a republic with one central government. He argued that ethnicity and tribalism promoted rebellion and had to be fought. He created new districts independent of ethnicity.

Ethnicity, the army and politics

In the colonial era, the army had been recruited from tribes in the north, while the people of the south were mainly in the civil service. At independence, there was a need to Africanize the services, both civil and military, and the problem was how this could be done. This was especially difficult in the case of the army. The commander in chief of the Ugandan army was the kabaka of Buganda who was also the president of Uganda. Figures available from 1963 show that 50 per cent of the army was drawn from Acholi, and most of the remainder from West Nile. It has been argued that in the power struggle between the president and the prime minister, Obote could invoke regional sentiments to mobilize the military in his favour. Mutesa had no such potential ethnic power base within the army (Omara-Otunnu, 1987:53). If Africanization was to be put into practice, the command structure would inevitably become dominated by men from northern Uganda. In the light of these circumstances, it was politically expedient for Mutesa to retain British officers in the top ranks of the Uganda army.

The army mutinies in East Africa in 1964 showed how far ethnicity had penetrated Ugandan politics. Omara-Otunnu (1987) has argued that the variations in response to the mutinies between the three countries can be attributed to the degree to which the ruling party was entrenched in the country, and to the ethnic factor in the army. The position of the UPC in Uganda was precarious, and its hold on government was based on a coalition. In the army, the majority of troops came from the north, the prime minister's own ethnic base. These two factors combined to make it imprudent for Obote to take harsh measures in reaction to the mutiny. Ethnopolitical considerations prevented him from disciplining the army, and finally led to the promotion of characters like Idi Amin, who overthrew Obote in 1971. Obote promoted and appointed Amin to head the army on ethnic grounds. With the demise of the UPC-KY alliance, the UPC finally allied itself with the army in the period 1966–71.

Before the 1971 coup, the conflict that developed between Obote and Amin saw both of them resort to manipulation of ethnic and regional variables to win support in the armed forces. Whereas Obote's support in the army was diffused and not confined to any particular sector, Amin found a stronghold in the military police, a force created in the aftermath of the 1966 crisis and then under the command of Amin's allies. It has been argued that Amin's coup in 1971 was carried out to save his skin. It was a matter of who would strike first, Obote or the army commander. Hence, it could be said to have been precipitated by personal factors. However, the ethnic and regional imbalance among the troops was maintained after 1971. There was open discrimination against officers from regions other than the north, both in promotions and dismissals. During Amin's time, promotions were specifically from West Nile. During Obote's time, this process was repeated in the civil service. Both in the military and the civil service, Obote's administration interpreted political allegiance in ethnic terms. Ethnicity during Amin's time reached a peak when thousands of Acholi and Langi soldiers were massacred for refusing to accept the change of leadership in the army and for being closely related to Obote. These two groups were widely perceived as the main beneficiaries of Obote's administration, and the majority of people from other ethnic groups tended to be indifferent to the massacres that were taking place. This continued virtually the whole period Amin was in power. When complaints were raised about this apparent discrimination, his commanders assumed names that hid their ethnic origin.

Another lesson from Uganda is provided by the events that followed the fall of Amin in 1979. A two-year interim administration under the Uganda National Liberation Front (UNLF) was set up. Thereafter, Milton Obote and his UPC party came to power for the second time, following the disputed general elections of 1980. Once again, Obote established a government propped up by the dominance of Langi and Acholi in the Uganda National Liberation Army (UNLA). It was in response to these developments, and particularly to the widespread belief that the 1980 elections were rigged in favour of the UPC, that Museveni organized a resistance movement, the National Resistance Army (NRA), which came to be dominated by southern Bantu, most notably Banyankole and Baganda. The coup against Obote in 1985 shows that ethnic alliances cannot always be relied upon. In July 1985, Acholi officers under the leadership of General Tito Okello, UNLA commander, broke ranks with their traditional Langi allies and overthrew Obote's government in a military coup. Obote, who had been a master at playing ethnic and other factions against each other, now found his schemes had boomeranged.

Conclusion

The problems of Uganda over the years are closely associated with ethnic politics. Indeed, ethnic conflicts and their attendant problems constitute the hallmark of the country's postindependence history. Certainly, the events leading to the abolition of kingdoms, the problems within command structures in the army in almost all regions, the disputed 1980 elections and the consequent civil war of 1981–86, the insurrections in the north and northeast of 1987–92, are all major landmarks in the country's history which were directly linked to the central problem of ethnicity. From this analysis, therefore, the central problem in Ugandan politics is inherent in the multiethnic structure of society, the rivalry among the dominant groups, the exacerbation of differences between ethnic groups by British colonialists and the structures of power that depend on the military for their strength. For democracy to be consolidated in Uganda, inclusive political institutions representing all ethnic groups, must be built. Inclusiveness would make such institutions neutral arbitrators in national crises involving various ethnic groups.

Bibliography

Brass, Paul, 1996, *Ethnicity and Nationalism; Theory and Comparison*. New Delhi: Sage Publications.

Doornbos, Martin, 1996, *Not all King's Men: Inequality as a Political Instrument in Ankole, Uganda*. Paris: Mounton Publishers.

Gidden, Anthony, 1996, *Politics and Sociology in the Thought of Max Weber*. London: Macmillan.

Government of Bunyoro-Kitara, 1988, "Petition of Bunyoro-Kitara to Her Majesty the Queen", in H.B. Hansen and M. Twaddle (eds.), *Uganda Now: Between Decay and Development*. London: James Currey.

Gurr, Ted Robert and Harff Barbara, 1994, *Ethnic Conflict in World Politics*. Boulder: Westview Press.

Horowitz, Donald, 1985, *Ethnic groups in Conflict*. Berkeley: University of California Press.

Kirunda, A.M., 1995, *The Crisis of Confidence*. Kampala: Fountain Publishers.

Mulira, Peter, 1994, "Federalism is not Secession", *New Vision*, 20 June.

Nisambi, A., 1994, "Federalism Facilitates Unity", *New Vision*, 28 June.

Ntale, A., 1961, "Conspiracy to Destroy Buganda", *Uganda Argus*, 21 September.

Omara-Otunnu, Amii, 1987, *Politics and the Military in Uganda 1890–1985*. London: Macmillan.

Plattner, Marc F. et al. (ed.), 1993, "The Challenge of Ethnic Conflict", *Journal of Democracy*, 4/4.

Rupesinghe, Kumar (ed.), 1989, *Conflict Resolution in Uganda*. London: International Peace Research Institute in association with James Currey.

Seymour, Jennifer, 1988, *How Can Africa Survive?* New York: Harper and Row.

Shaw, Timothy, 1979, *The Politics of Africa: Dependence and Development*. London: Longman.

Sill, David (ed.), 1968, *International Encyclopaedia of Social Sciences*, 17. New York: Macmillan.

—(ed.), 1972, *International Encyclopaedia of Social Sciences*, vol. 5 and 6. London: Macmillan.

Uganda Argus, 1961, "Lukiiko to Nominate 24 Members of the Legislative Council UPC", 20 September.

—1966, "Premier Suspends Constitution", 25 February.

Uganda Government, 1962, *Uganda (Independence) Order in Council*.

—1995, *The Constitution of the Republic of Uganda*.

Widmalm, Sten, 1993, "Explaining Ethnic Conflicts", Department of Government, Uppsala University.

Neutralizing Ethnicity in Uganda

Frank Emmanuel Muhereza and Peter Omurangi Otim

Introduction

The National Resistance Movement (NRM) has ruled longer than any previous regime in Uganda. This is not a coincidence, but it is due to the manner in which the NRM built its social base in the struggle to gain power, and later organized the state to exercise power. Central among all these factors has been the way in which the broad question of national security and national unity have been handled.

Ethnicity has permeated every aspect of Uganda's political life. The colonial state used ethnicity to gain control over its subjects in the colonies. Through the creation of ethnically bounded institutions of control, it defined the parameters of both the native authority and local state apparatus. This system was inherited by postcolonial governments. In Uganda's post-independence era, ethnicity was to become a very important tool for those in power, as well as the main weakness of regimes that failed to transcend the limitations of ethnicized politics. This chapter examines the background to ethnicity in Ugandan politics, and examines President Museveni's NRM in its struggles to rid politics of ethnicity and sectarianism.

Ethnicity and ethnic groups in Uganda

Ethnic groups in Uganda are synonymous with "tribes" or "nationalities", although the concept of ethnicity is not contingent on the existence of "ethnic groups", since it also refers to religion and other form of association. Mafeje (1995) has argued that the concept of ethnicity is generally used in Africa to acknowledge the existence of particular identities deriving from common linguistic and cultural origins. It is relative, and has been used as a metaphor for a variety of things which could be understood differently.

The main ethnic divides that are discernible through the various uses of the term are national, regional, tribal and religious. Thus, ethnicity is used to describe the mainly Nilotic speaking people of the north ("northerners") vis-à-vis the mainly Bantu speaking people in the south ("southerners"), as if the country is ethnically divided into two halves. In this case, ethnicity is regionalized. Among the Nilotics and Nilo-Hamites, reference is sometimes made to "tribal" or "nationality" affinities, such as the West Nilers (Alur, Madi and Lugbara), the northern Luo (Acholi and Langi), southern Luo (Japadhola), the Nilo-Hamites (Karimojong and Iteso). The people from western Uganda have on several occasion been described as "westerners" or *"basheshe"*. Others have described them as *"Banyarwanda" (nyarus* in derogatory terms).

Ethnic identity is often used in specific circumstances to make a case for a particular claim. For example, the Acholi sometimes pit themselves against the Langi, although they seem to belong to the same ethnic group. The Baganda have attempted many times to assert an independent cultural identity as opposed to other nationalities in Uganda.

Ethnicity and politics in Uganda—a background

The role that ethnicity has played in the politics of Africa in general and Uganda in particular has been the cause of major weaknesses in anticolonial struggles and struggles against oppression. Mamdani (1997) has pointed out that anticolonial struggles were mobilized using ethnic paradigms, but that this very premise became the cause of their demise. Ethnicity reproduced itself in the struggle against the colonial state, as well as in subsequent struggles, and every protest movement was shaped by the very structure of power against which it rebelled. Colonial and postcolonial structures of control based on ethnicity imploded.

No statesman understood better than Museveni how ethnicity broke up an otherwise strong political force. In his recently published book *Sowing the Mustard Seed,* Museveni (1997:90) describes how the person from whom he learnt guerrilla tactics viewed tribalism: "Samora Machel described tribalism in Africa as the 'Commander-in-Chief' of enemy forces, meaning that it was the greatest single tool by which ignorant opportunists destroy the unity and strength of un-politicised groups". Museveni (1997:90) adds that during the initial years of the struggle against dictatorship, he had proof of this very fact: "As soon as one gathers a group of more than ten from different tribes, the opportunists will seek to discover who are the 'majority' among the group. Then someone will claim that, as he is from the largest tribe, he should be the section leader".

Having understood that the regimes he was up against held on to power by appealing to ethnic paradigms, Museveni sought to build a social base by appealing against the politics of ethnicity and sectarianism.

Museveni (1997:187) attributes Uganda's problems to sectarianism and socioeconomic underdevelopment. Preindustrial societies like Uganda's tend to be vertically polarized on the basis of ethnicity. In his opinion, the strongest blow to sectarianism is monetization of the whole economy, some-thing which would undermine the subsistence existence of most Africans. The commodity relationship between one area and another would, in time, undermine sectarianism. He goes on to argue that sectarianism and ethnicity are short-term problems, caused by the leaders' failure to identify the real interests of the people.

Unlike his predecessors, Museveni is also aware that ethnicity is not only bad politics, but is also a weak ideology for organizing society, pre-cisely because ethnicity reproduces profound dilemmas within society. Therefore, the NRM in its 10-point programme set out to introduce a fun-damental change in the structures and exercise of state power. Its pro-gramme stated: "... post-independent governments of Africa and Uganda in particular, espoused wrong politics, e.g. sectarianism, a repressive style in dealing with the masses, and a conspiratorial approach in dealing with polit-ical colleagues and opponents" (NRM Secretariat, 1986).

One of the main objectives of the NRM administration is the consolida-tion of national unity. It is argued that the lack of national unity enabled for-eign powers to colonize Africa, and perpetuated colonialism for much longer than would otherwise have been the case.

> Sectarianism enabled dictators and idiots to emerge, take power illegally and perpetuate their stay in power with much greater ease. Obote has been thriv-ing on divisions as did Amin. The politics of Uganda at Independence was unabashedly sectarian: the Democratic Party (DP) for Catholics, the Uganda People's Congress (UPC) for Protestants outside Buganda, and Kabaka Yekka (YK) (King Only) for Protestants in Buganda. In the army, opportunistic fac-tions emerged according to the opportunistic politics and manipulations of the day: Bantu versus Nilots in 1966 (where Bantu included the Iteso who do not speak a Bantu language, and where the Nilotics included the West Nilers most of whom do not speak the Nilotic language). In 1970, the West Nilers versus the Acholi and Langi; then as Amin's rule progressed, Moslems versus Christians; after the downfall of Amin, the re-introduction of DP and UPC having undergone some fresh permutations of sectarianism; and Obote, fol-lowing the elections, trying to erect a new alliance of Acholi, Langi and Iteso against the "enemies"—principally Baganda and Banyankole. (NRM Secretariat, 1986)

Institutional structures to "neutralize" ethnicity

On assuming power in 1986, Museveni's NRM administration set out im-mediately to establish structures designed to curtail the influence of ethnic-ity in the exercise of state power. These included establishing popular democracy at the grassroots level, where people were organized in resis-tance councils. Transparency in elections was ensured by having voters line up behind their candidates of choice. To ensure the population is not manipulated, the NRM embarked on a conscious campaign to educate the public through political education courses, dubbed "Chaka Mchaka". A national school for political education was started in Kyankwanzi, where leading civil servants and public figures were taken for political education and basic military science training. The courses proved so popular that they had to be offered at sub-county level throughout the country.

A legal approach has also been adopted to deal with ethnic issues. The *Penal Code Act* of 1988 (section 42A, part 1) states that a person who prints, publishes, makes or utters any statement or commits an act which is likely to:

a) degrade, revile or expose to hatred or contempt; or

b) create alienation or despondency of; or

c) give rise to discontent or disaffection among; or

d) promote, in any other way, feelings of ill will or hostility among or against, any group on account of religion, tribe, ethnic or regional origin, commits an offence, and shall be liable on conviction to imprisonment for a term not exceeding five years.

The NRM was aware that the people of Uganda belong, first and foremost, to tribes or nationalities, and the resulting differences cannot be legislated away in order to achieve national unity. However, the existence of this law would act as a deterrent to activities likely to promote "sectarianism" in all its various manifestations.

Nevertheless, ethnic sentiments are still very much alive in Uganda today, despite all the good intentions of the NRM. The examples below illustrate how the NRM has administration has grappled with the contestation of political power in a highly ethnicized domain.

Restoration of traditional rulers

One of the most contentious issues which confronted the NRM on its coming to power in 1986 was the status of the traditional kingdoms. There was a very strong lobby for the restoration of the Buganda monarchy to its pre-1966 status, when it held executive powers. The Baganda are one of the major ethnic groups in Uganda. Allegedly, the Baganda were demanding what Museveni had promised them in return for their support during the guerrilla war. When the constitution-making process was initiated in 1988, the status of the traditional rulers was one of the key issues in the debate. The other key issue was the unbanning of party political activities. According to a survey of organized groups carried out in Buganda (Oloka-Onyango and Tindifa, 1995), there was an overwhelming demand for the restoration of traditional rulers and for freedom of association. The NRM regarded both as inimical to the interests of the state. It introduced a system its critics have described as a de facto one party state, although the NRM insists it is an all-embracing political movement of people with different political convictions. While the unbanning of party political activities was seen as a direct challenge to this movement system, the restoration of powers of traditional rulers was a direct challenge to the authority of the central government, the cause of the 1966 crisis which led to abolition of the traditional kingdoms in Uganda in the first place.

The NRM chose to advocate the lesser of two evils—the restoration of traditional rulers, but as figureheads—and used this to deflect the demand for the restoration of political parties. In 1995, it was decided in the Army council that the Buganda kingdom must be revived. This took place in July 1995. The revival of the traditional kingdom in Buganda has kept many strong traditionalists debating the role of the king, what the king should be or not be, and away from party political activity. This is one reason why, despite donor pressures for the restoration of a multiparty system in Uganda, there has been no strong demand for it from the local population, especially in the rural areas.

It is argued that the restoration of the Baganda monarchy preempted the constitutional debate on whether or not Uganda should have traditional rulers. At about the same time, in 1995, in an attempt to prevent the emergence of a strong traditional rulers, the government passed the Decentralization Statute. This transferred the effective powers of the executive from the central government to the districts and their subdivisions. In Buganda, this limited the extent to which the newly created kingdom could challenge the central government for executive power, because such power was devolved to lower councils. Attempts to create a Buganda charter that would, in effect, define and delimit the powers of the districts in Buganda with the kingdom of Buganda have been rejected. The people in the districts argued that they cannot surrender powers which the central government has given them to a regional body, the kingdom.

Creation of new districts—the case of Nakasongola

In May 1996, the government created six new districts. Most of these were carved out of existing districts in order to improve service delivery. They included Busia, Sembabule, Bugiri, Bukholi, Koboko and Nakasongola. Two districts, Sembabule and Nakasongola were carved out of Buganda. Nakasongola, carved out of Luwero district in Buganda, is mainly inhabited by the Baruli people, a small ethnic group. The Baruli believe they are different from the Baganda. Historically, Nakasongola was part of Bunyoro but became part of Buganda in 1898 after the defeat of Bunyoro. It is one of the lost counties. The Baruli people in Nakasongola allege they were marginalized in Luwero district, and demanded a district of their own. During the 1995 presidential campaign, Museveni launched his election campaign in Luwero, where he had waged six years of guerrilla war. At Nakasongola, his rally was attended by only a handful of people, and the word was that the Baruli people had boycotted the rally. Afterwards, a minister of state was appointed from Nakasongola, a precedent for the Baruli people. A few months later, they were accorded district status, something that further limited the extent to which the Buganda monarchy can form a united front against the central government. It is very unlikely that new districts in Buganda (cf. Nakasongola and Sembabule) would agree to join the Buganda charter, that makes them surrender some of their executive powers to the Mengo Government of the Kingdom of Buganda.

Nakasongola, previously as part of another district in Buganda, would have very limited influence on the monarchical tendencies in greater Buganda. As a district entity its demans are easier to assent. The same is largely true of the Sembabule district in south Buganda inhabited predominantly by cattle keeping tribes from Ankole.

This was an ethnic gamble which has paid off for Museveni's NRM in Buganda. In areas where the political capital to be gained out of restoration of traditional rulers is at the minimum, such as, in Ankole, the NRM government has strongly resisted the restoration of the monarchy. The traditional rulers have been restored in two other areas: Bunyoro and Toro.

Political appointments

A cabinet reshuffle is a moment of great political anxiety in Ugandan society. Attention is focused on what the president is seen to be doing for a particular region, in return for its support in the liberation war of the 1980s or its support for President Museveni during the 1996 general election. This is gauged by how many "sons and daughters of the soil" the president appoints to ministerial positions. The last cabinet reshuffle, following Museveni's election victory in May 1996, showed that the ethnic factor is far more prominent than it was thought to be. Districts sent delegations of elders and prominent politicians to the president to demand their share of cabinet posts. An analysis of cabinet appointments shows that out of twenty-one cabinet posts, twelve went to Protestants, five to Catholics, and four to Muslims. Catholics were embittered by their small share. The western region was well represented with ten posts, including the presidency and ministry of defence; Buganda with six, including the premiership and ministry of finance; the east had three posts and the north two. Only two women were appointed. Overall, fifty-one ministers (cabinet and state) were appointed: eighteen from the west; fourteen from Buganda; while the north (Acholi and Lango) "took the crumbs". Of the thirty-one major nationalities in Uganda, including Asians, only nine were represented in the cabinet, some with more than three portfolios (*Monitor*, 8–10 July 1996).

Public reaction to the appointments had a tribal tone and flavour. Areas like Karamoja, Sebei, Acholi, Nebbi and Teso complained of having been given "only ministers of state", who do not sit in cabinet unless the substan-

tive ministers are absent. Districts like Kibaale, Masindi and Hoima complained of not having fair representation in Resident District Commissioner
(RDC) appointments. Even some NRM insiders made public statements
with strong ethnic undertones. The current premier, Kintu Musoke, told a
public rally that his appointment was a reward by Museveni to the people of
Buganda for their overwhelming support in the presidential elections
(*Monitor*, 26–31 July 1996). The ethnic factor pervades the appointment process at all levels. The support a candidate has for his/her appointment from
his/her ethnic group has a significant impact on his/her chances of being
appointed to cabinet.

Westerners are alleged to have benefited more than other Ugandans in
appointments and promotions in some of the leading parastatals. At the
now privatized Uganda Commercial Bank (UCB), it was once reported that
of forty-five top positions, people from western Uganda held twenty-eight,
and of eleven promotions to senior manager, eight were westerners (*New
Vision*, 4 March 1994). Nevertheless, some westerners complain that they are
victims of intraethnic discrimination, because most jobs have gone to only a
few areas of the western region. One writer complained in the press that it
was "very difficult, if not impossible, for a Munyankole/Mukiga to pass the
interview for any advertised job in a parastatal where, on the principle of
balanced regional representation, the panel is composed of people from all
corners of Uganda". In an interview for a post at the Uganda Electricity
Board, one person claimed "they openly asked me why I was seeking employment in UEB when it was already full of my tribes-mates" (*Monitor*, 1–3
July 1996).

The NRM and northern insurgency

The northern insurgency is viewed by some commentators as a conflict between regions, specifically north versus south. There are those who believe
the government deliberately dragged its feet over the war, for reasons best
known to the NRM itself (*Monitor*, 15–18 March 1996). Others think the war
was waged by a government intending to exterminate the people of Acholi,
among whom several rebellious movements have appeared in the past.
Among the rebel movements that the NRM has defeated since 1986 include
the Teso rebellion; the Lakwena Holy Spirit movement; the *Cel-i-bong* in
Lango; the Amon Bazira insurgents in Kasese; the West Nile Bank Front of
Juma Oris; and Major Herbert Intongwa's Uganda Democratic Alliance,
Jamil Mukulu's ADF forces in Kasese, and the Buseruka rebels in Hoima
district.

Most Ugandans think arguments that northerners are discriminated
against because their "sons and daughters of the soil" are not in government, or, worse yet, that they are persecuted by the government because

they are northerners hold little truth. An editorial in one of the local dailies states:

> The problem in Uganda has never been that there have been too many politicians from the North, or now from the West, in dominant positions—the question has been how they get there, how they remain in power; and how they behave once in power. It does not really matter if all leaders were from the North or West, as long as they are chosen in free elections by the majority of Ugandans to lead them. And as long as they care for all parts of the country equally when in power. It is an unforgiveable insult, for example, to the Langi, to imagine that their make-up is such that they will prefer an idiot from the North in State House, to a caring and progressive President from the South. (Monitor, 12–15 January 1996)

Insurgency has been dealt with whether by northerners, southerners/ westerners or by people from other regions of the country. The NRM successfully distance rebel movements from winning political support at national level along ethnic lines.

Question of citizenship

A favourite weapon in political contests in Uganda is the claim that an opponent's tribal roots are not Ugandan, implying that he does not qualify for citizenship. Even the president resorts to this in order to "reduce to size" seemingly overbearing cabinet members. It was reported in 1994 that Museveni stated he had assisted the third deputy prime minister, Brigadier Moses Ali, to regularize his citizenship, although it was claimed that he is Ugandan by birth and not Sudanese, as was alleged (*Monitor*, 14–16 February 1996).

Similar allegations were made about Museveni himself during the 1995 presidential elections. A member of the opposition Inter-Party Political Forces (IPF) campaign team alleged that "He [Museveni] came here [to Uganda] at the age of 16 and it is us the [Byanyima family] who brought him up. The cupboard you see there (in her sitting room) was Museveni's library. When you check it you will find his books, a lot on imperialism, with his former name Yoseri Tubuhaburwa" (*Monitor*, 4–6 March; see also *Monitor*, 6–8 march 1996).

The fray was joined by Nsubuga Nsambu who, while addressing students hailing from Buganda at Makerere University, claimed that the majority of the people who had bought land in Buganda were westerners, that they were about to start chasing the Baganda away from their motherland, and he threatened retaliation. "Though we shall not use guns, Buganda is still at war with its fellow Ugandans because they refused to give us (the Baganda) our federal status. We have been friends and we have intermarried. But if they continue to antagonise us, one day, one month we shall smash them. How many *biwumpuwumpu* [bazookas] do we need to smash these castles and houses of theirs" (*Monitor*, 6–8 March 1996).

In the same elections, the Inter-Party Political Forces and the Young Democrats alleged that Museveni had imported millions of Rwandans in order to win the election. The allegation was dismissed by the electoral commission, which found there were only 800,000 new voters. This claim by opposition politicians was also dismissed as unfounded and unfortunate by former presidential aspirant and UPC diehard and supporter of presidential candidate Semogerere, Prof. Adonia Tiberondwa (*Monitor*, 4–6 March 1996). There was no more talk about Rwandan voters. But apparently, the multi-party had hoped to use this Rwandan claim as an attempt to bar Ugandan Banyarwanda from voting, an attempt which the NRM did not take lying down. They insisted that the Uganda Banyarwanda had the right to vote (*Monitor*, 16–19 February 1996).

People of Lango vote against southerners

In Lira and Apac, otherwise called Lango, the home of the twice-deposed former president Milton Obote, it appeared in the run-up to the elections that Museveni was poised to loose the election from the start. The NRM poured in massive amounts of money in support of the NRM campaign team and candidates. The state structures were openly used to campaign for Museveni. In spite of that, presidential-hopeful Semogerere won more votes, and NRM candidates for parliament were miserably trounced. During the Constituent Assembly campaigns in 1994, the people explained their choice axiomatically: "You can play with my stomach—but don't play with my brains". Lameck Lamitkuc-Kuc Aneko, a local musician, captured the mood in Lango in the following song which was very popular in Lango:

> *Adwong DA joo arik yikiwa PIDA ni tin dong pe boo?*
> *Adwong DA yat me ot yat ayam dwong wokki tin dong pe boo?*
> *Adwong wan obuto koyo olok okwalo cuka wa oko. Gi wa romo nwongere!*
>
> DA [District Administrator] where are the people who used to repair our roads?
> DA, where is the medicine?
> DA, cattle rustlers have stolen even our bedsheets. DA can you get them back for us!

The song was used to lure the electorate away from voting for President Museveni apparently on the basis of the underdevelopment of Lango, and the cattle rustling, which affected them for the first time during the era of President Museveni. The state of poverty in Lango was directly associated with Museveni's rule. However, contrary to this opinion, it is also usually argued that northerners are to blame for their backwardness and the underdevelopment of the north: for twenty years they were in power, but they did nothing for their region. Therefore, it is argued that a Northerner "cannot close his eyes to the fact that the many multi-million shilling development projects going on in the north are the fruits of Museveni's initiative" (*Monitor*, 1–3 July 1996).

Ethnicity and the military in Uganda

The colonial army was predominantly recruited from the northern tribes of the Acholi and Langi. This seems to have sown the seeds of regionalizing the army in Uganda. In retrospect, therefore, it should come as no surprise that when Idi Amin assumed power, he had to recruit the army from his own people, the Aringa, Kakwa, Lugbara and Sudanese Nubians. This created a scenario where the majority of the military would always be from the region of the head of state.

There were intense debates over the issue of representation in the army during the constitutional seminars that were conducted throughout the country during the constitutional making process which started in 1988. During one of the these seminars organized for members of the army council, NRA political commissars and legal officers from various units, participants rejected the idea of proportionate ethnic representation in the army for it to be a national army (*New Vision*, 22 January 1991).

Currently, in an attempt to prevent one ethnic group from dominating the military, the government has adopted a quota system where each region is required to send a specific number of recruits to the army. Some regions, like Buganda, have failed to realize their quotas. Appearing on a television and radio interview at the state lodge, Nakasero, in 1994, President Museveni asserted that since the NRM had come to power there had been two national recruitments in which each district had been given a quota (*New Vision*, March 1994).

Despite the criteria used for promoting officers in the army, it was reported in the press that the NRM was becoming an ethnic dictatorship, because of the way in which certain minority ethnic army officers are promoted faster than others:

> Of the 35 army officers promoted and published in the Press, 23 are westerners. All of them speak Runyoro-Rutoro-Runyankole-Rukiga, which was recently named Runyakitara, and live in one area, the west and south-western parts of the country. Of the 23 western officers promoted, 18 are Banyankole. 16 of the Banyankole are Bahiima, who form only 20 percent of all the Banyankole. (*Monitor*, 16–19 August 1996)

This has led to some claims that "power comes from the tribal barrel of gun", since although the NRM war was fought in Buganda with Baganda fighters dominating the army, the most senior army officers are not Baganda but Banyankole (*Monitor*, 30 August–2 September 1996).

The regionalization of Ugandan politics

Similarly, one of the reasons why the debate over Buganda's federal status (FEDERO) failed to sail through the 1994–95 Constituent Assembly was the deliberate move by some Baganda constituent assembly delegates (CADs) to present the debate as a Buganda-versus-the-rest-of-Uganda issue.

The people that can be referred to as typical Baganda are very few in number as intermarriage has been common. Consequently, the political demands of Baganda ethnic groups have not been taken very seriously. After the failure of the Baganda pro-federalist CADs to win federal status for Buganda, the politicians started saying that the NRM had engineered a conspiracy to defeat Buganda's federal demands. The Odoki report indicated that 97 per cent of the people of Buganda and 65 per cent of all the people of Uganda preferred federalism. During the Constituent Assembly, the issue of federalism was discredited when it was presented as if it were a Baganda issue. The ethnicization of the federation issue was its greatest undoing. Some of the leading critics of Buganda federal status were Baganda themselves (such as Bidandi Ssali, Besweri Mulondo and Prof. Apollo Nsibambi—Nsibambi resigned from the Lukiiko because of disagreements over federal issues). The federalists depicted these Baganda CADs as being not true Baganda.

The way ethnicity is used makes it a very weak organizational principle for resisting state kleptocracy. It appears to be used for realizing selfish personal ends. That is why it has been easy for the NRM to neutralize it.

Concluding remarks

In Uganda today, the wheels of fortune still turn in favour of the matchmaker. The return of security of person and property, the macroeconomic stabilization and the economic performance of the country and other achievements including the end of state-inspired violence, have caused many people to give Museveni's administration the credit that it deserves. In spite of this, people who are left out of state power, have resorted to appealing to ethnicity: this is usually alleged as the cause of their downfall or their failure to make the desired ascent up the political ladders. All these cries seem to have played well into the hands of the NRM, so that ethnicity appears to have been neutralized, at least politically and for the time being. Those who have tried to manipulate ethnic tendencies have not received the enthusiastic sympathy they would have received ten years ago.

This does not mean that ethnicity is dead. Once in a while, people appeal to ethnic sentiments. A cabinet minister without portfolio in the office of the president, was forced to resign from his cabinet post in June 1997, following a motion in parliament to censure him for abuse of office, after he was accused of drawing 2,000 litres of fuel from one of Uganda's remaining parastatals, the Uganda Railways Corporation, a year before, allegedly for repairing roads in his home district (*New Vision*, 20 June 1997).

A failed attempt to salvage his image by blocking his censure was made by fellow parliamentarians from within the NRM caucus. After he had been censured, he appealed to his fellow tribespeople in parliament, who convened a meeting to help him save face. He went so far, while addressing a congregation in a mosque, as to say that he was being persecuted because he was a Muslim. It must be remembered, that Muslims had already complained openly that they were underrepresented in the cabinet and it is possible that the former minister was trying to redeem his fortunes by playing the ethnic card.

Museveni went to the bush with twenty-seven combatants. The number eventually grew. Those who went to the bush have formed an "ethnic group" of sorts. They referred themselves as "NRM-CONC", the "we fought" group. The minister who was later censured by parliament and forced to resign, at one time boldly assured critics that "nobody will uproot us from this country and we are not ready to go back to the bush. We were not stupid to go to the bush as some say. We crawled in the bush as if we were not learned people. We had knowledge that is why we are here" (*Monitor*, 29–31 January 1996).

But there are many of those who supported the NRM who felt left out in the cold when the NRM came to power. There have been complaints by peasants from Luwero triangle about unfulfilled promises and from former NRA combatants who had been sidelined. These cut across the narrow ethnic divide as some of Museveni's former close bush "buddies" have been sidelined.

Another minister of state, formerly a chief NRM spy, was accused of involvement in a rent deal between a private firm in which he held shares and a government coporation whereby the government would lose billions of shillings in overpayments was recently censured by Parliament (March 1998). The first to attempts to block the censure motion were mainly pro-NRM members of parliament from southwestern Uganda, the minister's home district. Again, we see how even those within the system, who are supposed to be fighting ethnicity have not managed to escape the entanglements of ethnicity in the form of common tribal membership and common regional origin.

The NRM government's fight against possible sectarianism in its various forms, has been helped by a number of other developments.

a) Parliament has been given full powers to move a vote of censure against any public official who is alleged to have abused his or her office.

b) The inspector general of government (IGG) has also been given the power to order the arrest of and to prosecute public officials found guilty of any crimes.

c) The auditor general can prosecute leading politicians for failing to give proper account of public expenditures. A recent victim of this was none other than the former minister of justice and attorney general, Ekemu (*New Vision*, 18 November 1997). Ekemu, an Itesot, was charged with issuing false documents in an attempt to defraud the state and of diverting money that was meant to restock cattle in his homeland, Teso.

d) The attorney general's office has been strengthened. Recently, a UPDF major general made certain statements during a public inquiry into the Northern Insurgency to the effect that the NRM government, in which the major general was key a player, had failed in its fight against the Kony rebels and should, therefore, resign. The state felt these statements by a high ranking government official were in contempt of the state. Before the army high command could meet to discuss a possible course of action against this officer, a bush-war veteran and former officer in charge of the government's operations against the insurgents in the north, he resigned from the army to preempt any punitive measures. The state refused to accept his resignation. The major general went to the constitutional court, which ruled in his favour. The state appealed against the ruling of the constitutional court to the supreme court, and the supreme court ruled in favour of the state (February 1998).

There are many other examples of President Museveni using an iron hand to deal with his former bush-war cronies and others with whom he now works closely. He forced his own half-brother to resign from the NRA, put him in the reserve force, and only recently put him in charge of the operations in the north. The current third deputy premier, Brigadier Moses Ali, was at one time put in prison on charges of treason, although the state later dropped the charges after he had served the mandatory remand period. Later he was appointed to a senior cabinet post.

If Museveni's NRM government can strengthen the rule of law and resort to the law to deal with its own kind, especially those, who from the NRM's point of view, show recalcitrance, then there is little ground for a person from another tribe, nationality, or who is not close to the NRM, to argue that a similar course of action taken against him or her is motivated by ethnic persecution.

By strengthening the different institutions and structures of governance that serve as checks on the abuse of state powers, President Museveni has largely rid himself of the dilemma of having to deal with recalcitrant 'bush cronies' in the future. He has also rid himself of the dilemma of getting entangled in ethnic politics. At best, the culprits can appeal to the ethnic sentiments of possible sympathisers, whereafter the law must take its course. Similarly, President Museveni does not have to fear the law taking its course. This is the way the NRM has, under the astute guidance of President Museveni, dealt with the question of ethnicity. In other words, President

Museveni has returned the country to the rule of law, and used the law to shield himself and his government from having to exercise the power of the state in a way that is greatly influenced by the perversions of ethnicity.

Bibliography

Hansen, H.B. and M. Twaddle (eds.), 1988, *Uganda Now: Between Decay and Development*. London: James Currey; Athens: Ohio University Press; Nairobi: Heinemann.

Langseth, P., et al. (eds.), 1995, *Uganda: Landmarks in Rebuilding a Nation*. Kampala: Fountain Publishers.

Mafeje, A., 1995, "Demographic and Ethnic Variations: A Source of Instability in Modern African States?" Paper presented at the Conference on Academic Freedom, Social Research and Conflict Resolution in the Countries of the Great Lakes, organized by the Council for the Development of Social Science Research in Africa (CODESRIA), in collaboration with the University of Dar es Salaam, Tanzania and Centre for Basic Research, Kampala. Arusha, 4–7 September.

Mamdani, Mahmood, 1997, *Citizen and Subject: Contemporary Africa and the Legacy of Late Colonialism*. Princeton: Princeton University Press.

Museveni, Y.K. (ed. by E. Kanyogonya and K. Shillington), 1997, *Sowing the Mustard Seed: The Struggle for Freedom and Democracy in Uganda*. London and Basingstoke: Macmillan.

NRM Secretariat, 1986, *The Ten Point Programme of the NRM*. Kampala: NRM Publications and Sapoba Bookshop Press.

Okwundiba, Nnoli, 1989, *Ethnic Conflict in Africa*. Working paper 1/89. Dakar: CODESRIA.

Ololca-Onyango and Sam Tindifa, 1995, *Constitutionalism in Uganda. Report on a survey and workshop of organized groups*. CBL Working Paper No. 10.

Newspapers referred to:

New Vision Newspaper

The Monitor Newspaper

Note on Contributors

Adhana H. Adhana was lecturer at the Department of History, Addis Ababa University. Currently he is Commissioner of Education at Tigray Region, Ethiopia.

Paul T.W. Baxter was senior lecturer at the Department of Social Anthropology, University of Manchester. Recently he co-edited a book on *Being and Becoming Oromo: Historical and Anthropological Enquiries*.

E.F. Byarugaba is associate professor of Political Science, Makerere University, Kampala.

Paulos Chanie is lecturer at the Department of Management and Public Administration, Addis Ababa University.

Martin Doornbos is professor of Political Science at the Institute of Social Studies, The Hague. He has widely researched and written on political transitions in the Horn and Eastern Africa generally. Among his recent publications are *Beyond Conflict in the Horn of Africa* and *State Formation in Europe and India*.

Sharif Harir is a former lecturer at the Department of Sociology and Anthropology, University of Khartoum and a research fellow at the Centre for Development Studies, University of Bergen. Currently he is a member of the High Command of Sudan Federal Alliance, based in Asmara.

Helena Jerman is a researcher at the Institute of Development Studies, University of Helsinki. She has recently published a book entitled *Between Five Lines: The Development of Ethnicity in Tanzania; With Special Reference to the Western Bagamoyo District*.

John Markakis was professor of African History, University of Crete. Currently he is visiting professor at the Institute of Social Studies, The Hague. His recent books include *Resource Conflict in the Horn of Africa*.

Frank E. Muhereza is a research fellow at the Centre of Basic Research, Kampala.

Jay O'Brien is an adjunct professor of Social Anthropology at San Bernardino, University, California. His is the co-editor of the book *Golden Ages, Dark Ages*.

A.B.C. Ocholla-Ayayo is a professor of Social Anthropology. He is the Director of the Population Studies and Research Institute, University of Nairobi. His books include *Lou Ideology*.

Peter O. Otim is a research fellow at the Centre of Basic Research, Kampala.

Eva Poluha is senior lecturer at the Department of Social Anthropology, Stockholm University. She is the author of the book *Central Planning and Local Reality. The Case of a Producers' Cooperative in Ethiopia*.

Ali Said was a researcher at the Ministry of Economic Development Cooperation, Addis Ababa. He has published several papers and chapters on resource competition among Afar pastoralists.

M.A. Mohamed Salih was associate professor of Social Anthropology, University of Khartoum and responsible for the research programme "Human Life in African Arid Lands" at the Scandinavian Institute of African Studies, Uppsala. Presently he is a senior lecturer at the Institute of Social Studies, The Hague. He has recently co-edited a book on *Management of the Crisis in Somalia: Politics of Reconciliation*.

Tegegne Teka was associate professor at the Institute of Development Studies, Addis Ababa University. Currently his is the regional coordinator of the Drylands Research Programme, the Organization for Social Science Research in Eastern and Southern Africa, Addis Ababa. He is the author of a book entitled *International NGOs in Ethiopia: Rhetoric and Practice*.

Index